Civilized Men

A James Towne Tragedy

A Novel By

Ivor Noël Hume

Previous Works by Author

Previous Fiction Includes:

The Charlestowne Scheme
The Truth About Fort Fussocks

Previous Non-Fiction Includes:

The Virginia Adventure
Martin's Hundred
1775 Another Part of the Field
Here Lies Virginia
All The Best Rubbish
In Search of This and That
Something from the Cellar: More of This and That

Dedication

To Oliver L. Perry
Chief Emeritus of the Nansemond Indian Tribe
and champion of truth and justice for the
Indigenous People of America.

**Detail from John Smith's map of Virginia,
first published in 1612.**

1. James Towne.
2. Orapaks, Powhatan's principal village in 1610.
3. Francis West's abandoned fort at The Falls.
4. Werococomoco, Powhatan's principal village until 1609.
5. Location of forts Algernon and Charles, and Kecoughtan Indian village, burned July 9, 1610.
6. The Paspahegh tribe's principal village, destroyed, August 10, 1610.
7. Nansemond tribe's principal village.
8. Appomatoc village burned, autumn 1610.
9. The Warraskoyack's principal villages, burned, 1610.
10. Mattaponi village.

Author's Note

Although a work of fiction, the principal events described as occurring in Virginia in 1610 are all true. While no names have been changed, their motives have in some instances been assumed or reconstructed. Created, also, are the Jefferys brothers and most of the lesser participants, although these, too, are given roles in actual occurrences, horrific though some undoubtedly were.

Prologue

Maggie Beale stood at the door of her house and watched the two men drag her husband's body out onto the frozen ground. His legs stretched white and thin from beneath his soiled shirt. She had stripped him of his shoes, his coat, and his britches. There was no point in burying clothing that could keep her warm — at least warmer. For the past January week, a biting wind had been blowing out of the west down the James River. It raised white clouds of powdery snow from thatched roofs and caused icicles to snap from sagging eaves. England's Virginia colony at James Towne was freezing and dying. Relief was long overdue.

The men pitched the corpse onto their cart where it lay alongside another, both with their legs dangling like broken dolls off its tail. The two-man burial party looked almost as emaciated as their load. Turning to Maggie, one of them lifted her dead husband's shirt tail and with a rasping laugh, asked "Want to take a last look at him, my love? If you should be needin' a bit o' this an' that, you know where to come."

Maggie turned and slammed her door sending a cascade of snow from the roof onto the cart. With one man pushing and the other pulling, they trundled it lurching and creaking across the frozen mud toward the fort gate. No one paid them any attention. As previous tracks through the snow attested, this trek out across Smithfield to the burial ground was too frequent an occurrence to be of interest. The absence of mourners' footprints spoke for itself. Neighbors, relatives, and friends were thinking only of who would be next to ride the cart.

Historians remember this winter of 1609 as the Starving Time, but for Margaret Beale from London's Bermondsey, this was the time and place that God had forsaken. Born on Shrove Tuesday, 1582, she was now twenty-five, but had she owned a mirror she would have known that she looked ten years older. When she was seven her mother put her to work as a kitchen servant to the Prior of Bermondsey, but in reality most of her time was spent scrubbing the tile floors in his church of St. Mary Magdalene. It was there that she met her future husband, Peter, a young stonemason employed to repair the fabric and whose chips and dust had made her work much harder. And she told him so. They were wed when she was fifteen and Peter twenty-two. They had one child, a still-born girl, and Maggie yearned to have another, but not until they were safely settled in Virginia.

Peter had seen Ben Jonson's *Eastward Ho!* when it played at the Blackfriars theater and remembered how eager young emigrants had listened to the tales of Captain Seagull who spoke of savages clad in gold and boys picking rubies and pearls from the seashore. But Peter didn't know the difference between comedy and satire, and so believed every word he heard. Maggie was less easily convinced. Eden, she told him, was not for the likes of them.

"Why, not?" Peter demanded. "We're good, God-fearing people. And if it ain't Eden when we get there, then we'll be the ones to make it so!"

Maggie remembered those words as she stood, back against her door, surveying all that she and Peter had achieved. It wasn't much. The single-room house, with its stick and clay chimney, rough built table and upturned tubs for stools, were all too obviously the work of a stonemason and not a carpenter. Their rope-laced bed frame built from charred wood salvaged from the fort after it burned in the previous year had been their refuge. Now its ragged blankets were soiled by death, and Maggie had neither a cauldron in which to wash them nor water to boil in it.

Across Smithfield at the burial place the colonists knew as "no man's land," the two grave diggers cursed the frozen ground and damned Peter and his companion for putting them to all that trouble.

"Like as not, we'll have arrows comin' at us, afore we're done," muttered one.

"Nah. Them savages won't be out in this weather. Freeze their bloody feet off," replied the other. Grunting and fuming they continued to dig, but gave up after they had gone down little more than two feet. "That's far enough. If some poor bugger wants to dig 'em up and cook 'em, why make it difficult for 'im? That's what I say."

"'Twas only a rumor. I doubt nobody really done that."

His companion pointed with his shovel toward a snow-covered hollow a few yards away. "Who do you suppose done that, then?"

"Wolves, naught but wolves. Or maybe the savages. There's no telling what them bastards 'll get up to."

The grave diggers bundled Peter's corpse into the hole where it lay with one arm twisted under him and the other sticking up, his hand open as though pleading for a more respectful end. They began to shovel the dirt onto him, and then stopped.

"Hey, wait a minute!" said the first man. " If you think I'm going to stay out here and freeze my arse off digging another hole, you can think again. Shove the other one in on top".

And so they did. By nightfall the backfilled grave was white with blown snow; the tracks of the cart had softened into mere shadows; and sitting beside a fire in an abandoned shed the diggers, with a wink and a grin, assured each other that theirs had been a job well done. And nobody would ever be any the wiser.

Alone in her house, Maggie Beale sat beside her own small fire, her husband's coat draped around her shoulders. The fire flickered and smoked, blown by wind that found its way through countless cracks in the clay-coated wattle walls. Melting snowed that dripped down the chimney plopped and hissed in the embers that provided her only light. Her two remaining tallow candles were better saved to eat than to burn. Huddling over the fire, the widow Beale prayed, not for strength or Divine intervention, but that she might quickly die and at last find the Eden that Peter had promised her.

Across the darkened market place, and beyond the church where one of the few surviving rats was seeking sanctuary, light filtered out between the shutters of the governor's house. He still had candles to burn. Interim governor George Percy, gaunt and hollow-eyed behind a bushy beard, sat on the room's only chair at the head of an oak table. On either side, seated on rough-hewn stools, the remaining members of his council listened to Percy's analysis of their plight. The evening meetings were more ritual than substantive. Each day was the same, leavened only by occasional reports of more deaths, and sightings of savages in the vicinity of the palisades. Peter Beale, was on the list as was his companion in death whose name was stated to be Davis Fanshaw.

Percy grimaced. "That brings us down to what, sixty, fifty?" he asked.

"Thereabouts" replied Captain Daniel Tucker. "'Tis hard to tell whose alive and who's as good as dead." Tucker was one of Percy's most reliable aides and had shown great courage in encounters with the Indians. Percy knew he could trust him, which was more than could be said for another at the table. Captain John Martin was one of the seven men appointed to the governing council when the first fleet landed on what would become James Towne Island. He had been a trouble maker ever since.

Said Martin, "I hear tell that more are planning to escape and join the savages."

"Good riddance, then," Percy replied. "Their meal ration will serve the rest a little longer."

"But they will be of the abler sort," Tucker warned. "And we have too few of them already."

Percy shrugged. "At this point we may be better off with sick men loyal than able men treacherous. So let 'em go. And let no man waste powder and shot on them. The savages will kill them soon enough."

George Percy was thirty and a man of some military experience. He had served with the English army in Ireland as well as fighting for the Protestant cause in the Netherlands. His family, however, was tainted by Catholicism. His father, the 8th Earl of Northumberland, had supported Mary Queen of Scots in her attempt to overthrow Elizabeth, and wound up a prisoner in the Tower of London where he was either murdered or committed suicide. Whichever it was, his eldest son, the 9th Earl, had much fence-mending ahead. His younger brother, George, may have had this family history in mind when he elected to sail with the 1607 Virginia expedition. Now, two years later, he was almost certainly regretting that decision.

The leadership had been flawed from the start. The elected president, Edward Maria Wingfield, proved to be an inept administrator whose weakness prompted other councilors to jockey for the job. Distrustful of each others' motives and fearful that some might be closet Papists in league with Spain, looking over one's shoulder became a necessity. One who failed to watch his back was Captain George Kendall who was accused of mutiny and summarily executed. Thus within a year, the seven man council was short a member. Wingfield was deposed in favor of another ineffective individual, John Ratcliffe, who in turn was pushed aside by the most competent and aggressive of the lot, Captain John Smith, whom most respected but few liked. Percy, smarting over having been omitted from the council when it was secretly named in London, had detested Smith and called him "an ambitious unworthy and vainglorious fellow," an opinion shared by another councilor, Captain Gabriel Archer, who actively fostered a faction to be rid of him. When an allegedly accidental ignition of gunpowder sent Smith to what many hoped was his deathbed, the council dismissed him and shipped him home. And so it was that George Percy stepped out of shadows unsullied by the previous infighting. But looking around the table that January night, he wondered how long it might be before a new alliance formed against him.

Archer, though ailing fast, was still there, but his own ambitions were no secret. William Fettiplace had been a loyal follower of John Smith, and though polite and respectful, he surely had to remain resentful. John Martin was a hothead whose beheading of captured Indians had been damagingly undiplomatic and whose judgment was suspect. Others deeper into the shadows beyond the candlelight were men of less prominence, but invited there only because they were of the gentry and still able to function. Social status was still evident from clothing enriched with gold and silver threads, but rips and rough sewn patches rendered doublets and britches fit only for dish rags. Tobacco smoke that rendered those seated at the far end of the table unrecognizable, served the useful function of disguising the odor that accompanied the unwashed leaders of King James's Virginia adventure.

Percy had thought long and hard about its future. If the colony's past history was a measure of what was to come, within a very few weeks there would be none. Letters from London shipped in the previous year had reported the formation of a large supply fleet with the able Sir George Somers as its admiral and an experienced administrator, Sir Thomas Gates, to take charge once it arrived. Six of the ships had come in late in the previous summer, after being battered in a July hurricane. They brought close to 500 more mouths to feed and not enough food to do so. And where were Somers and Gates and their ship *Sea Venture* that was carrying many of the supplies? If no further relief could be expected, Percy reasoned, there would be nothing for them but to pack up and board one of the remaining ships and sail for home. But that would mean surrendering England's foothold in America to the hated Spaniards. How would he, George Percy, be received if he returned to London with such a confession? There would be no knighthood, of that he was sure. Indeed, it might cost him his head -- and drip another dark stain on the family name.

Fearing that sharing his doubts with his fellow councilors and captains would quickly find its way into the mouths and minds of those the gentry called "the other sort," Percy talked, instead, of hope, of a treaty with the savages, and the sun-warmed promise of spring. But alone in the darkness of her little house, Maggie Beale stirred the dying embers and continued to pray that if God was merciful, she would not live to see it.

Chapter One

❦

In England, the morning of February 24, 1610, dawned like every
other in the past several weeks, foggy and bitter cold. The sun
had not been seen since Candlemas. Hoar frost dappled the fields,
and in the woods rooks and jackdaws traded insults in a raucous
cacophony that drowned the crowing of Annie Jefferys' rooster.

"Mornin', Goodwife."

"Good day to ye too, Master George"

"Be you wantin' any eggs this week?"

" No, thank ye kindly. Considering the cold weather, my fowls
am layin' right well."

Annie Jefferys watched her elderly neighbor trudge away down
the lane. "Be sure how you go," she called after him. "They tell me
there still be ice on the bridge."

The Jefferys family had lived at Withyham long before anyone
could remember. According to the word-of-mouth history that had
been handed down through the generations, they had been foresters
back in the twelfth century and had taken their name from their
master John Jefferay of Chiddingly in the neighboring county of Sussex. But that was far too long ago to be sure of. All that Annie really
knew was that she was born at Withyham in 1575 and was wed to
her Will'm when she was scarcely fourteen. Within three years she
bore him two fine sons. "They be the apples in my eyes," she would
proudly say, and none of the women in the village disagreed.

Walking back to her cottage after carefully closing the garden
gate, Annie Jefferys paused as she did every day and asked herself,

"Wouldn't my Will'm have been proud of our boys and the way we've been able to get by?"

Like tenant families across the land, the menfolk knew that they could be called to serve their liege lords in time of war. William Jefferys had been no exception. In 1592 when his master, Lord Delaware, sailed with the Earl of Essex to campaign against the rebellious Irish, William went as an archer as his forebears had before him, and like so many good tenants he never came back. Shot in the back with an Irish arrow said neighbor Tom Saddler, who had been lucky enough to return unharmed. Widowed when she was only seventeen and with her son William only two and John scarcely a year old, Annie's life was back-breakingly hard. She was grateful though that his Lordship had allowed her to keep the tenancy. Many another landowner would not. Year after year she farmed her five acres and never once did she fail to deliver its share of the produce to the manor. By the time her boys were six and eight all three of them worked from dawn to dusk to grow the wheat and tend the livestock. One cow, four hogs, three goats and a fluctuating number of chickens were more than enough to keep every hand fully occupied, though the work was becoming easier as the boys grew older and stronger.

Annie had disciplined her sons just as strictly as her Will'm would have done. And they loved her for it, though the young men were as different as they could be. A foot taller than his brother, Will was already a man. Like a young oak, Annie used to say. Too much of the master's man, some said. Not like young John. "Now he was a real caution," neighbor Sissy Jackson laughed. She was sixteen and smitten by his fair hair and good looks. But John didn't know it, and would have turned bright scarlet if he had.

Now, in February of 1610, Will was nineteen and John seventeen, and Annie could look about her with satisfaction and begin to shed the callouses of a man. Will took care of the field and John tended the livestock. It was an ideal sharing. Plowing and reaping appealed to Will's vigorous nature while John's love of animals made him a good shepherd, or it would have had they any sheep to tend.

But pigs, cows, chickens, all were God's creatures and all worthy of John's caring. And he was learning to read and to write his name.

The Reverend Eustace Laurie, Lord Delaware's chaplain, owned two horses, and knowing John Jefferys' way with animals, when the mare went lame, he had asked him to look after her. In return, Laurie began to give the lad some schooling. Will considered it a waste of time. "Who needs to read the Bible when you can hear it told every Sunday?" he laughed. He added that the Jefferys had done well enough without filling their heads with nonsense. Everything they needed to know had been handed down by word of mouth across the generations. "'Tis the same with songs and stories," Will insisted. "You learn them by heart. What matters is what you know to be so, like when to till and how far ahead you must aim to bring down a bird in flight. You don't find that in no Bible."

He was right, and his mother knew it. But all the same she was proud of John's desire to learn. Who could tell where it might take him? He might even rise to be a shopkeeper or own an inn — though she didn't hold with what went on in taverns. Her only fear was that Chaplain Laurie might lure her boy into the Church and fill his mind with ideas that had aught to do with real life. Nevertheless, Annie considered herself a good Christian and so were her boys. Like everybody else in the village, they followed his Lordship and his people to church of a Sunday and made a point of noticing who was absent – not because Annie was judgmental but because an absence could mean an illness and a neighbor in need of help. She assisted with the harvest festival, and last summer Will had taken his scythe to the churchyard – though only because she made him do so.

That February morning, as the frost-nipped ferns of Bishop's Wood crackled under his feet, Will Jefferys was as happy as any young countryman could hope to be in Queen Elizabeth's England. With the Spanish armada destroyed, fear of invasion had passed, and Will's master, Lord Delaware, showed no inclination for more warring in Ireland or the Netherlands. Will had heard rumors in the village that his Lordship might be going to visit colonists in Virginia, but that would not change things at the manor. His wife, the lady Cecilia, had run the estate during his absences before, and nobody suffered by it. No doubt she would do so again. But there would be one difference. Buckhurst Manor's land and tenants had been watched over by bailiff Bill Barrett. A good man liked by everybody, he had died last Michaelmas and only now had been replaced by a new man whose name, Will thought, was Smothers or maybe Smithers. Nobody knew much about him other than he had previously been bailiff for Sir Philip Sidney at Penshurst. Bill Barrett had been the Delaware's bailiff for nigh on twenty years, and Will would never forget him, not as long as he held Bill's beloved gun. Where the old man had obtained the weapon, Will did not know, but it was the most splendid hunting weapon he had ever seen. Bill had allowed him to handle it, and explained that it had a new kind of firing mechanism called a snaphaunce. He though it was a Dutch word that meant snapping hen, though what in the world chickens had to do with muskets he didn't try to fathom. "It don't matter to me what theys calls it, so long as it draws a good bead," he laughed. Now the gun was Will's. He had traded a winter's firewood and half his mother's next pig for it, and the Widow Barrett was well pleased with the deal. "What would I want with an old gun?" she had asked.

But it wasn't an old gun, and Will was immensely proud of it. A man of standing, even a squire, would be pleased to own such a weapon. Will thought about that as he emerged from the wood and headed across the soon-to-be-plowed field in the direction of Waldgrave Spinney where he knew there was a large rabbit warren. Looking around him over the silent countryside Will again asked himself why a man who owned a snaphaunce couldn't, one day, have lands of his own? Well, why not? Many a yeoman had risen to be knighted and given money and lands for doing something useful for the king. He had heard tell that England's new Scottish king, James I, had given titles to all sorts of people he had met on his way south to be crowned in London. Becoming somebody could happen to anybody if he happened to be in the right place at the right time. So why not me?

Suddenly, with much screeching and flailing of feathers a brace of pheasants rose out of the field ahead of him. Without pausing to think, Will aimed his gun and fired. Before the echo and the blue smoke drifted away, one of the birds lay flapping on the ground. Only then did he give a thought to what he had done. Lord Delaware was a good and generous master, and allowed his tenants to shoot rabbits and even hares anywhere on the estate, but never deer or game birds. For that crime one villager had been hanged, and another whose wife was pregnant, was treated more leniently. Tried and imprisoned in the castle at the county seat of Lewes, he was never seen again. As Jason, the blacksmith, had said, "'Twas a cruel punishment to be sure, but afterwards everyone knowed what's what." His Lordship's fairness extended only to those who lived by his rules. Now Will had broken one of them and the proof of it lay in the open field for all to see.

John heard the shot as he returned to his cottage with an armful of firewood from Copeland Spinney. That'll mean rabbit for supper, he thought. Will and his gun had been a source of amicable brotherly contention ever since he bought it. A stupid modern novelty, John called it. Their father had been a bowman in three campaigns and it was an arrow that finally felled him. The English long bow, John insisted, was the most effective weapon imaginable and it had been for countless generations. "Why do you suppose there's yew trees in every parish churchyard?" he demanded. "Why not chestnuts or poplars?" John knew that his brother knew the answer, but he was going to make his point just the same. "Because, by law, every parish had to supply the king with yew wood to make long bows, that's why!"

"Yes, but nobody cuts it any more. There's no call," Will would counter. But John had not been convinced and swore that he never would. Guns were slow to load; their range was short; they made too much noise. In wet and windy weather they wouldn't fire. They needed powder and shot, both of them expensive, and once fired you couldn't get them back.

All of this was true, and John had often demonstrated that he could shoot a rabbit with his bow and still retrieve his arrow. His mother agreed with him, and would say so — ever mindful that her Will'm had been as fine a marksman as ever drew a bow. Will, however, remained unconvinced.

John was not alone in hearing his brother's gun. A horseman riding down the lane to the Jeffreys' cottage also heard it. But the shot coincided with the horse stumbling and neighing, leaving the rider unsure from which direction and at what distance the sound came. This was just as well. Had Jacob Smithers been sure, he would have been duty bound to track it down, for he was his Lordship's newly appointed bailiff. A freshly nabbed poacher would have meant a groat or two in his pocket and, more important, a good word from his employer. But on this day, February 24, in the sixth year in the reign of his Majesty James I, Jacob Smithers had been given a task even more to his liking, and he intended to make the most of it.

Smithers did not consider himself a fat man, fleshy perhaps, but not obese. In his last position on the Penshurst estate a drunken ostler had called him a filthy lump of lard. It was an insult he would not forget, and when his laborer assistants were done, neither would the ostler. As Lord Delaware's man, Smithers intended to make it clear from the start that he expected to be respected, obeyed, and feared.

Dismounting in front of the cottage, the bailiff took a notebook from his saddlebag before pounding on the door with his ample fist. When it opened he stood intimidatingly grim faced, and making a pretense of consulting his notebook. "And you would be... Ah yes, Goodwife Jefferys?"

"Aye, sir, that I be." Before her words were out, Smithers pushed his way into the room that served the family as kitchen, living room, and for Annie, her bed chamber. Her mongrel hound, Pilot, lying by the fire, sat up and growled. "And who may you be?" Annie demanded. "And what business have you to ...?"

"Your landlord's business, old woman. I am his Lordship's new bailiff."

"Then you are most...welcome." Smithers heard the hesitance in Annie's voice, and read it as fearful subservience. "That Master

Barrett what was bailiff 'afore you, he was a good man. Very fair to us poor tenants he was."

"I'm sure he was," Smithers told her flatly. Then with a thin smile, "And as I mean to be. But its your man I'm wanting."

"And so be I, sir."

"Then?"

"Then, what?" Annie replied.

"You'll not trifle with me, Goodwife Jefferys. Where is your husband?"

"You bein' his Lordship's man, you should know well enough. He be dead with an Irish arrow in his back. That's where he be, God rest his soul."

"I'm right sorry to hear that," Smithers assured her. He did not intend to let her know that he already knew, or that his questioning was designed to test and intimidate her. "Bein' new to his Lordship's service," he went on, "I'm sure I've much to learn — with help from good folks like yourself. You farm this holding on your own then?"

"Aye, just me and my two boys," Annie replied.

"Then you do right well, Goodwife. Indeed, you do. And your boys, how old would they be?"

Annie hesitated, sensing that the bailiff had purpose in the question. "They're just... young lads."

"But old enough to chop wood for your fire?" Smithers asked with a smile marred by several rotten teeth. "Am I right?"

"Aye, sir."

"And push a plow, I'll warrant."

"That too, sir."

Meanwhile, John Jefferys stopped at the garden gate when he saw the bailiff's tethered horse. Not recognizing it, he thought it best to enter the cottage through the lean-to addition behind it. Juggling both wood and axe while lifting the door latch was not easily done, and once inside the room the axe slid off the pile and landed with a thud on the dirt floor. But the dog heard it. "Stay, Pilot!" Annie ordered. Then to Smithers, "Would you take some broth? I have it brewin' Master...?"

"Smithers... Jacob Smithers."

"'Tis a good name. A good Bible name is Jacob."

"About your sons?"

"I don't know what I'd have done without 'em once my Will'm was killed. And that's a fact."

Smithers's nodding grimace was intended to be sympathetic. "No doubt. No doubt," he muttered. "But folks must do the best they can with what they have. There's many a good woman has lost her man in England's cause."

"That I know. And I pities them."

"We live in harsh times, old woman. But like his Lordship says, we're all on this earth to serve. Each in our own way, me, you... your sons, too, when they're old enough. How old did you say they be?"

"They'm just shoots, just young'ns." As she spoke, she could hear John dropping his wood in the back room. Pilot got up and went to the door, his tail vigorously wagging. Smithers followed and jerked it open.

"And who be this, then? Let me guess. You must be one of them young'ns we was just talkin' about. Am I right?"

John stepped over the wood, and with a quizzical look, answered, "I be my mother's son..." Then with a note of defiance in his laugh, he added, "And right proud of it, ain't I, Ma? As proud as can be."

"And she of you, I'm sure of that. A strong young fellow like you, what mother wouldn't be?" Smithers assured him. "And your brother, he's younger than you?"

Sensing trouble, John glanced at his mother for help. But she only shrugged and spread her hands. She had no more idea of where Smithers was heading than did her son.

"Well," John answered. "He'm a mite older than me. But this winter's been hard on all of us, and he's right poorly..."

"But he will recover?"

"In God's good time," Annie hastily answered.

"What is it you want of us?" John asked sharply.

"Mind you words, boy! Don't you know who I am?"

"If I had to guess, I'd say you sound like his Lordship's new bailiff," John told him.

"That I be. And don't you forget it! But what do I want of you? Nothing. No, 'tis what his Lordship wants." Smithers's smile widened into a grin. "And what he wants is you and your brother, and you and your brother he'll have."

"For what purpose?" John demanded.

"To go a venturing, that's what. If you haven't heard, his Lordship's to be the new governor of Virginia, and he needs ten lusty village lads like yourself to attend him. If it weren't that I'm needed here, I'd be beggin' to be one of you. But there 'tis..."

Annie had heard it rumored that Delaware was going away, but she didn't know where. Nor did she have any idea that once again, he'd be taking village men from their homes. Fighting in Ireland and against the Spaniards in Holland had been far enough, but Virginia was so distant as to be beyond her imagination. "This cannot be," she insisted. "How would I live? I need my boys. I have to work this land for his Lordship. We're his tenants and that's his due. And my Will'm paid for it with his life. Delaware can't want this of us... can he?" Her voice trailed away.

"Oh, yes," Smithers assured her. "Yes, he can."

"My dam is right," John insisted. "I can't go. We can't go. 'Tis a tenant's right to appeal, is it not?"

"Aye."

"Then that's what we'll do. We'll go to his Lordship..."

"And much good it'll do you." With a dry laugh Smithers added, "You've got a right young pistol here, old woman, and no mistake."

"You tell him," John persisted. "You tell him that!"

Smithers was enjoying himself. "Oh, I will, and right soon. But now I've got other green wood to chop. So I'll bid ye a good day, Goodwife, and you... young John."

John looked surprised that the bailiff knew his name, but before he could comment, Smithers departed, slamming the door behind him. Earthen dishes rattled on their shelf. Then there was silence as John stood open mouthed, and his mother sank down onto her chair, despair and resignation lining her face.

While Smithers was still returning his notebook to his saddle-bag, Will Jefferys strode down the lane, his gun over his shoulder and his game bag on his belt.

"And who be you, young feller?" Smithers demanded staring at Will over the rump of his saddle. "No, let me guess. You're the poorly one."

"I am?" Will had no idea what the man was talking about, but he didn't like the sound or the look of him.

"Been huntin' have you?"

"Aye."

"A real nice gun you've got there."

"Glad you think so," Will cautiously replied.

"So what did you get?"

"What's that to you?" Will was becoming belligerent.

"Because I'm his Lordship's bailiff, that what."

"Oh, so you're the one."

Smithers chose to ignore the sneer in the young man's voice. "Yes," he replied slowly. "I am the one." Then sharply, "So hand me your bag."

Will smiled, shrugged, and did as he was ordered. Smithers grabbed it across the back of his horse, and quickly untied the draw string. He peered down into the bag and then looked angrily up. "That's it? And you wasted good powder on one scrawny pigeon!"

"What did you expect; a brace of pheasants?" Will's smile further infuriated the bailiff who hastily mounted up, hauling in the reins with such a jerk that the bit tore his horse's mouth. "I've got my eye on you, young feller...as you'll find out soon enough!" With that he rode off at a gallop, disappearing down the lane into the lingering fog.

Will watched Smithers go, then scowling in puzzlement, he opened his front door and went inside to find his mother in tears and his brother distraught. "So what was all that about? A nasty looking toad, that one. What did he want?" As he asked the questions, Will undid the hooks on his leather jerkin and pulled a pheasant from inside his breeches. "You can pluck that brother, but be sure to burn the feathers. We don't want another visit tonight."

John took the bird, but did nothing with it. Instead, while their mother continued to weep, he told all that he knew, ending with, "I told the bastard that I'll not go — and that you'll appeal to his Lordship"

"I will? You said that I will?"

"Of course, you're the oldest. It's up to the head of the..."

"That be so. But there's folks down in the village who'd give their last farthing to be chosen. They say there's gold in the rivers just there for the taking. Enough for everyone who's called."

"They? Who's they?" John retorted. "Old Tom Pritchet, I suppose. He's more full of crap than a bishop's goose."

Will assured him that old Tom hadn't been at the Bell when he heard the news. It came straight from the manor house, and from a very reliable source.

"Like who? His Lordship himself maybe?"

Will kept his temper. Ever since he left the inn, he had been thinking about his options should the call come. And now it seems that it had. But it hadn't occurred to him that John also might be selected. Somebody had to stay. John was right about that, otherwise who would do the work necessary to retain the family's tenancy? John was also right about an appeal and that it should fall to Will as male head of the house to submit it. But being unable to write, he would have to go up to the Manor and make the appeal in person. He had never been inside the place, and, as he would later confess, the prospect of doing so was like standing up in church with his britches down. "Will you pluck the damned bird?" he demanded.

"No," John told him. "Not until you agree that neither of us is going."

"Boys, boys!" Annie cried through here tears. "If his Lordship means to take the both of you, that's an end on it. There's nought more to be said. 'Twas ever so."

Will could not bring himself to admit that he wanted to go, so he made much of his willingness to do all he could to keep his brother at home. If successful he would know that their acres would be safe and his conscience clear.

"How soon?" Annie asked, resignation evident in the words.

Will had no idea, though he doubted that it would be before spring, and he said so.

"I'll need you to kill the hog. I can't do that on me own."

"I know," Will assured her. "There'll be plenty of time for that."

"Don't fret, Ma," John told her. "I'll be stayin'. You'll see."

"So pluck the damn bird, brother. Our Ma can't spit it with the feathers on."

And John did so while Will cleaned his gun. For several minutes neither spoke, though from time to time they glanced at their mother who was staring into the fire. Then John broke the silence. "How far is Virginia? A deal further than Ireland, I suppose?"

"T'other side of the world," Will replied. But having no notion of its size, distance had no dimension. John finished plucking the pheasant, and throughout that afternoon and evening nothing more was said about their landlord's plans. Indeed, there was very little conversation, none of the usual banter between the brothers, and no laughing interjections from their mother. They talked about the frost and hoped that it wouldn't continue, about a neighbor's chicken-stealing nephew, and about the price of bacon. Should they sell half the hog or salt it all? Small talk, carefully avoiding the thought that was foremost in each of their minds. Not until Will was following John up the ladder to their attic beds, did Annie seek his assurance. "You will go to his Lordship on the morrow, wont' you?"

Will smiled and nodded. "Yes," was all he said before reaching the top of the ladder and closing the trapdoor behind him. Below, Annie sighed, and slowly prepared for bed. Her one room home was the anchor of her life; lose it, and she would have nothing. The cottage was newly built when her husband became a tenant while the current earl's father was building his mansion. He had divided Buckhurst Manor into several parcels to be farmed or tended by tenants and had built a similar cottage for each of them. The first thing Will'm had done after he moved in was to construct a box bed in one corner beside the chimney, a cozy place to which he and his young wife could retire. Privacy became more necessary once their children were born, and it was then that Annie hung a woolen curtain that closed the bed off from the rest of the room. The sound of its brass rings sliding along the pole became the alpha and omega of each passing day. On this February evening the clatter of the rings as Annie drew the curtain had a finality about it that left her staring upward into the darkness and wondering what her sons were thinking or hoping. It would not have surprised her to know that one was excited and the other deeply apprehensive.

The cottage attic had been the boys' haven since they were old enough to climb the ladder, but had become noticeably smaller the older they grew. Now, with both brothers of adult stature it had become dangerous to walk about up there without first closing the trapdoor. There was only space for their two cots, the pair of chests in which each kept his clothes, and two barrels, one of meal, and the other of what remained of last year's salted bacon. The chimney stack filled one end of the attic leaving only the other for a small window with horn as its casement panes. None but the wealthy could afford glass, but horn was better than shutters. In the day light came through and when the moon was full it cast a greenish blue light the length of the room. But on this night, there was no moon, nor any sound other than a mouse scratching in the thatched roof.

"You still awake?" John whispered.

"Aye," came the answer.

"It ain't that I'd be afeard of going."

"I know that," Will assured him. "So go to sleep little brother. Go ye to sleep."

The Jefferys' cottage was still dark when the cock began to crow. The morning was dawning no better than it had through most of February, cold and foggy. The last snow had gone, but the ground remained frozen and intractable. It was one of those mornings when lying abed would be an almost irresistible temptation – were it not that there was livestock to be fed and water to be drawn. Annie was already up, and though with only a shawl over her shift and walking barefoot — saving her shoes, she said – she was beginning the day as she did every day, by drawing water from the well. But first she had to jerk the bucket up and down the shaft to break the ice. The bucket had scarcely reached water when she heard a horse neigh and the sound of wheels trundling up the lane. From where she stood she could not see whose cart it was, the hedges on either side of the track being too high. She stopped hauling to stay the creaking of the pulley, and listened. She could hear voices. At this time of the year it was unusual for a carter to have a companion, and if he talked at all it was only to his horse. But here were men's voices, several of them. A moment later she heard someone call, "woe-up!" whereupon the sound of the wheels ceased.

Annie finished hauling her bucket and left it by the well head while she went around to the front of the cottage and peered down the lane. But with no sun breaking through, the night's fog still lay heavy over the ground, and she could see nothing. "Who's there?" she asked, her voice only slightly raised. When no one answered, she waited a few seconds and then went back behind the cottage to collect her pail. Had she stayed she would have seen several silent figures approaching out of the fog.

Annie was back in the cottage through the rear door and calling on her sons to stir their stumps when there came a loud pounding on the front door, so loud that it would have flown open had not the nighttime baton been still in place. She was about to lift it from its hooks when two men burst in through the back door. A snarling Pilot charged at them, but was kicked away.

"Stand aside, old woman!"

Without turning to face the voice, Annie knew that it belonged to Jacob Smithers.

"You know why I'm here, so give me no trouble and I'll do you no harm. It's only them lads I be needin'."

In their attic, Will was dressed and John still in his bed when they heard the commotion and recognized the voice. What they did not know was that Smithers was pointing a pistol at their mother.

"Let's give the bastard something to remember!" Will shouted, as he threw open the trapdoor and began down the ladder. He had only reached the third rung when he found that his rump was about to be impaled on the point of a pike. Jumping quickly sideways off the ladder he grappled with the invader, knocking him down and seizing the weapon.

"How now, master bailiff? Get you out of our...." Will stopped when he saw the pistol in Smithers's hand. "Oh, so that's how it is."

"Indeed, it is. So don't you give us no more trouble."

"Well, let me tell you something, master Smothers or Smitters or whatever your name is, that pistol you're holding ain't even primed."

In the moment that Smithers looked down to check, Will swung the pike shaft and knocked the gun from his hand. But it was to be of no avail. The front door was already open and three cudgel-wielding men were closing on him. John was still struggling into his britches as he came down the ladder only to be grabbed by his feet and pulled to the floor with a thud that knocked the wind out of him. Snarling and baring his teeth, old Pilot alone was still ready to do battle. Smithers retrieved his pistol.

"Not primed, eh?" he said with a laugh. Then he fired. Annie screamed; Will shouted "Bastard!" and Pilot took the bullet in his head.

"Now let's be about our business," said Smithers, thrusting the gun back into his belt. Will was dragged out struggling and cursing; but John, knowing that resistence would lessen his chances of a fair hearing at his appeal, asked only to be allowed to collect his stockings and his shoes. When he left the cottage he was still trying to tuck in his shirt under his unbuckled jerkin. The cart whose wheels his mother had heard was now in the lane in front of the door. Roped together on it were eight young men, one of whom John knew to be the son of another tenant who lived on the other side of the village. He guessed that the rest came from cottages further away.

Will was still calling down the wrath of God on Smithers as he was hand-tied and bundled up onto the cart to fall amongst the other young men, one of whom snarled, "Watch where you're putting your damned feet!" John's hands, too, were roped behind him, but rather than complaining, he asked one of Smithers' men to give him a hand up. Once aboard, the cart's tail was slammed up behind him and the iron linchpins dropped into place.

Smithers untied his horse from the wagon. "That's the lot then, lads. So get you going. Take 'em right through the gate into the courtyard." Then he turned to Annie who was standing silently weeping, her arms crossed over her chest against the cold. "Old woman, you'd best get back inside or you'll catch your death."

But Annie said nothing. She stood watching the cart trundling up the lane, its guards trudging beside and behind it.

"Didn't I see a shawl on your chair?" Smithers asked in a voice that was surprisingly sympathetic. "Let me get it for you." With that he went back into the cottage – but not to Annie's chair. He went straight to the rack over the fireplace where Will kept his musket. Grabbing it down, Smithers stepped back to the door, and only as an afterthought snatched up the shawl. "Here, " he said, tossing it to her. "But this you won't be needin', so I'll look after it until that young poacher of yourn comes home." Then he laid the gun across his saddle bow, mounted, and rode off.

Annie Jefferys drew the shawl over her head and stayed in the lane listening until the last sounds of cart and horse were lost amid the cawing of two crows arguing in a nearby tree. She scarcely noticed that she was still barefoot. All that she could think about was the likelihood that her boys might never come home.

Chapter Two

"**G**ood of him to give us a ride!" Will shouted over the rumble and crunch of the cart's wheels as the little procession wound its way through Buckhurst Park toward Lord Delaware's new but unfinished mansion. Both Jefferys brothers had seen the great brick building before, but only from afar when they had been hunting along the outer fringes of the estate. This morning as the sun crept up over the woods to the east, the brickwork glowed a cherry red, warm and welcoming, at least to those who arrived unfettered.

Sir Thomas West, the 3rd Baron De La Warr, inherited the unfinished mansion from his father who had been building it to replace the old castle that had fallen into disrepair after the previous century's Wars of the Roses. The 2nd Baron had taken his cue from other great men of the Tudor Court and began to build in brick. But unlike his more wealthy friends and kinsmen in neighboring counties, he found the construction bills too many and too big to turn his architect's inspirations into ruddy reality. Instead of building several interior courtyards, Buckhurst Manor stretched in a single, shallow façade limited to a pair of wings flanking the central tower. As in other great Tudor houses, the tower served as a gateway, but all that lay behind it was a menage of nondescript outbuildings.

Expecting a state visit from Queen Elizabeth in 1602, Sir Thomas, the present baron, had gone deeply into debt to tear the offending buildings down and to replace them with a cobblestone courtyard around which he built a great banqueting hall and a set of royal apartments, none of which the queen lived to see. It was into this courtyard that Bailiff Smithers' cart trundled to halt amid clamorous activity, orders being shouted, other wagons being loaded and unloaded, horses neighing and hooves clattering on the cobblestones as their drivers tried to maneuver their vehicles. Several men in Delaware's blue and yellow uniforms were hurrying in and out of the buildings. John could only liken it to market day in Lewes.

Smithers seemed unsure what to do or where to go. Trying to shout his orders louder than anyone else, he told his men to stay with his captives while he "talked personal to his Lordship."

Another of the young men standing in the cart shouted after him, "Bastard! Who do you think we are, leaving us here like gallows meat!"

"Keep on like that, lad, and that's what you'll be," laughed one of the guards as he prodded him with his pike. Will and John managed to sit on the cart's sides, but being across from each other and with standing captives between them, there was no opportunity to talk. But in truth, there was not much to be said. Each sat a prisoner of his own thoughts. John was thinking of escaping. To get one of his companions to work the knots free would have been easy enough. But then what? Where could he run? He wanted to get home to comfort his mother and bury poor old Pilot, but he knew he'd soon be caught. Besides, if he ran, the chances of appealing to his Lordship and being allowed to stay would be nil. The only sensible course was to wait and see what might happen.

Will's thoughts were different – and overridden by his anger at his intent to volunteer being ignored. To do so now with his hands tied robbed him of the dignity of stepping freely forward. As for the odious Smithers, Will had time to consider a dozen ways of cooking his goose, as he watched him talking to a servant at a tower doorway and then disappearing inside.

Smithers was unaware that he had been directed through a servants' entrance, and as he ascended the plain oak staircase to the first floor, he straightened his collar and tugged at his doublet to make sure that he would make his entrance into his Lordship's presence as a man of substance. He was disappointed, therefore, to find himself in an unfurnished section of the house and forced to ask another servant the way to the Long Gallery where the Delaware family was gathered.

True to its name, the gallery stretched the length of the new west wing. Brussels tapestries and family portraits lined one wall interrupted by two large fireplaces. Although the facing wall was made up almost entirely of glass windows, the gallery, nevertheless, remained relatively dark, the brightness of the still hidden morning sun shafting through only two smaller windows beyond the second fireplace. Seated around the first hearth's blazing logs, Smithers found several elaborately dressed women all busily at work on framed needlework. He rightly supposed that the regal looking woman in the high-backed oak chair was his Lordship's lady. Walking purposefully down the gallery toward her, he became wincingly aware of the clatter his hob-nailed boots were making on the wide, uncarpeted boards. One of the women looked up, gave him a disapproving look, and went back to her needlework.

"Ahem," said Smithers. "Would I be addressin' 'er Ladyship? My name is Smithers, Jacob Smithers, I be 'is Lordships..."

Lady Cecilia turned and glared at him. "Who is this fellow?" she asked one of her waiting women. "Find out what he wants. Doesn't he know he's not supposed to be up here? And tell him to take his cap off."

An elderly woman separated herself from her sewing and asked Smithers his business and then directed him to continue down the gallery. As he departed, cap in hand, he clearly heard Lady Delaware declare, "That's a sorry piece of work!" Whether she was referring to him or to a lady-in-waiting's stitching, he couldn't be sure. But being a hollow man beset by private doubts, he suspected the worst. As he passed the second fireplace, Smithers saw a small, ruddy-faced man in a motley uniform of blue, yellow and red, wearing a matching cap with two bells on it that tinkled as he laughed and played with four children. Three of them were girls and the fourth was Delaware's seven-year-old only son. Smithers knew nothing of his master's children, nor did he know the little man to be Tom Dowse, his lordship's family jester.

At the far end of the gallery a small group of men stood talking earnestly together. Smithers recognized Lord Delaware, having been presented to him in the park the day after he had been given the bailiff's job. But he did not know the others.

Delaware was now aged thirty-three. The length of his pale face was accentuated by a short, curly beard that sprouted low on his chin. His nose was long and his mouth thin under a vestigial moustache. The tight line of his lips coupled with his large dark eyes made his a face to remember and a persona not to be crossed. Like his father before him, Delaware had attended Queen's College at Oxford, but left without graduating. Patience was not among his virtues. After a short period campaigning against the Spaniards in the Netherlands, he joined William Devereux, Earl of Essex, to put down rebellion in Ireland. While there he distinguished himself in a battle near Arklow on June 25, 1599, and two weeks afterward was knighted. Three years later, on the death of his father, he succeeded to the title and thus became Sir Thomas West, Lord De La Warr.

Smithers attempted a courtier's elaborate bow; but it was unsuccessful and left him in an awkward, teetering stance as he waited to be recognized.

Delaware was slightly deaf and had not heard his bailiff's clattering approach, and would have continued his conversation had not Chaplain Laurie said something and pointed over Delaware's shoulder.

He looked around open mouthed, staring in wonder at the folded figure. "Huh? What? Who are you? What do you want? Stand up man, you look ridiculous!"

Smithers's jaw tightened, but he managed his best gap-toothed smile. "Smithers m'Lord, your new bailiff."

"Ah, yes, right," Delaware replied. "So what do you want?" In an aside to his steward, Simon Taylor, he added "This feller shouldn't come up here. D'you suppose he knows that?" Taylor was as new to his job as Smithers was to his, having been appointed after Delaware announced that he would be leaving for Virginia. Taylor was a local man from Sevenoaks and of the yeoman class as was reflected in his simple attire distinguished only by large pewter buttons. Too new at his job to know the rules of the Buckhurst Manor household, he had no idea what the bailiff did or did not know. Fortunately for him, Delaware did not wait for an answer, but told Smithers, "Well, you're here now. So what's your name again?"

"Smithers, m'Lord, Jacob Smithers."

"Ah, yes. I remember you now. So speak your business."

Smithers explained that he and his crew had rounded up the required number of recruits.

"Excellent, well done," Delaware assured him. "All sound fellows, are they?"

"As a bell, m'Lord."

"Excellent, excellent. You'll turn 'em over to Captain Brewster, here. He'll tell you what to do with them." On that Delaware turned away to resume his conversation with Chaplain Laurie.

"Ahem," Smithers coughed. "M'Lord, there is, er...one..er..."

"What now?" Delaware snapped.

"It's like this your Lordship. There's a bit of a problem with one of 'em."

"How so?"

Smithers explained that he had trouble with the Jefferys boys and that the youngest was refusing to go and wanted to lodge an appeal. Smither's laughed as though the very suggestion ludicrous. "So I told him, he can appeal all he wants, but it won't do him no good."

"You told him that!" Delaware snapped.

Smithers, not being a very astute man, misread the response, and continued to smile in satisfaction. "Aye, m'Lord, I did indeed."

"Mark me well, master bailiff; no man speaks for me! Any man, even the likes of you, has the right of appeal. You'll do well to remember that."

Chaplain Laurie had moved to a courtyard-facing window and

looked down on the carts below. Only Smithers' wagon retained its human cargo. "Are those your young men?" he asked. The bailiff looked out and agreed that they were. Laurie pressed his nose against the window to better see through the green and bubbled glass of the small panes. "The fair-haired lad at the back," he exclaimed. "I know him. He's the boy I've been schooling. He's good with animals is that one."

Laurie was a lean and seemingly somber figure wearing a long black velvet robe over a black doublet enlivened only by a row of gold buttons. His trunk hose and stockings too, were black. Indeed, his black hair and beard only slightly flecked with gray made him a forbidding figure from head to foot were it not for the white ruff around his neck and his infectious laugh and ready wit. Joining him at the window was Delaware's military captain, Mathew Brewster, who was as robust as Laurie was lean. A soldier of long experience, he had served Sir Thomas's father, and had been with him in Ireland. Brewster's weatherbeaten features and grizzled beard made him look older than his thirty-eight years.

"As these lads may be all that stands 'tween us and the savages, my Lord," Brewster advised, "I say we go down and look them over for ourselves."

"So we shall," Delaware told him as he started down the gallery, his gait awkward, limping slightly from an old wound. To steward Taylor, he muttered, "I don't want to see that feller up here again. Keep him where he belongs. See to it."

From talking with Delaware servants who passed close enough to the cart, Will Jefferys learned for the first time, that their master's voyage was to be no short visit. "Didn't you fools know?" one man shouted back. "He's been made governor of Virginia for life!"

"For life?" Will gasped. "You mean he's takin' us for the rest of our lives?" In an instant his volunteering plan vanished. Now he would have to plead for both John and himself to be allowed to remain at Withyham.

When Lord Delaware invested in the Virginia Company of London he expected to be no more than a shareholder; a substantial investor to be sure, but no more. The first settlers had arrived in Virginia in the spring of 1607, but nothing had gone right, and as time went by and returning reports continued to bring bad news of lost supplies, mounting deaths by disease and at the hands of the Indians, Delaware was persuaded to accept the governorship. But that had not meant that he would have to go there himself; all he had to do was name a good man to serve as his deputy. He found him in the person of old soldier Sir Thomas Gates, and in 1609 he had sent him out with a fleet of seven supply ships under their admiral Sir George Somers. Both Gates and Somers sailed aboard the fleet's flagship, the *Sea Venture*. Though scattered in a July hurricane, the six transports eventually made land, but not the flagship. The *Sea Venture* was lost somewhere in the Atlantic, and all the colony's new leadership with her. When that realization sank in, Delaware had no choice but to mount a new expedition and to lead it himself. That much Will was able to glean from the Buckhurst servants before Virginia's new governor descended into the courtyard to inspect his recruits.

"These are the men we'll have to rely on," Captain Brewster reminded his master as they hurried down the mansion's grand staircase. "Beside the fifty or so we can send from the estate," he went on, "finding even a hundred more good men in London would tax Jehovah himself. All we can expect from the Company, my Lord, will be the refuse dragged from the city's gutters and brothels. To do better will take a miracle."

"Then we must pray for one." said Laurie. "Our Father is ever our good companion, m'Lord."

"'Tis so. And we shall be ever mindful of our prayers. Prayer is our armor, and Christ our sword," Delaware assured him as he stepped out into the courtyard. Scarcely pausing to survey the scene, he roared, "God's blood! These poor fellows are haltered like criminals! By whose orders?"

"Yours, m'Lord," Smithers told him.

"Mine, sirah?"

"Well, mine," Smithers allowed, adding "But on your account.

Else I'd have lost 'alf of them into the woods."

"These are your neighbors, master bailiff. They are also my people, my family. And don't ever forget it. Untie them, I say!"

Grim-faced, Smithers ordered his men to do so, and when one of them snickered, he barely controlled his rage. By the time the last of the ten was off the cart and each had had something to say to him, Smithers's lip was bitten raw.

"Well, now," said Delaware, "which of you young fellers has a mind to miss the greatest opportunity of your lives?" His fatherly smile lit on each of them. "You? You? Or you, maybe?"

"No m'Lord, 'tis me." John went on to plead his case, explaining how his widowed mother would be unable to handle her five acres alone. "She needs us to push the plow and..,"

"And who, pray, is us?"

"Me, my Lord, Will Jefferys." Will explained that he was John's brother, but insisted that he spoke for himself. "Before this lump of horse dung had me trussed like a felon, I was ready to volunteer and serve you like my father did."

"Your father? Should I remember him?" Delaware asked.

"Aye, m' Lord, 'deed you should. He died for you in Ireland."

"I'm afraid a lot of men died for me...for England, in Ireland. 'Twas the price of victory."

"Well, m' Lord, I'll not be volunteering now, not if you be going for life."

"Oh, so that's it." Delaware shook his head. "You have my word — you all have my word that no man shall be required to serve more than seven years. We go to the New World in peace, no warring there – lest it be against the naked savages. And we know how to handle them, don't we Captain Brewster?"

"Like the wild Irish, m' Lord."

"Exactly. Just like the wild Irish, lads. But go you shall. All of you; no exceptions."

He went on to assure everyone in earshot that their homes and loved ones would be looked after in their absence, and that steward Taylor would be charged with assigning a village elder to watch over each family. He went on to say that the fleet would be sailing before March was out, and that until then Captain Brewster would be the young soldiers' father, mother, and if needed, their confessor. He would see each man clothed in Delaware livery, and would even put a few pennies in their pockets. "So good fortune attend us all!" Delaware ended.

"Let's have a cheer for his Lordship, then!" Brewster barked. The response was less than lusty. But Delaware did not wait for a second attempt. Instead, he abruptly turned to reenter the mansion.

"Justice, me Lord!" John Jeffery's voice rang across the courtyard.

Delaware turned, his jaw set and his lips tense. "Justice, boy? What say you of justice?"

"That turd," John shouted, stabbing his forefinger in the direction of Smithers. "That turd shot our dog!"

"Did he, indeed? And what sort of a dog was it?" Delaware asked. "A working dog?"

"Aye, m' Lord. He had been when he was younger. A good old mongrel he was, but..."

"Old curs are two a farthing," Delaware snapped. Turning to Taylor, he ordered "Give the mother a penny to buy a dog that's useful."

"With respect, me Lord," the steward replied, "you can't get much of a dog for a penny, not in these parts."

"Very well. Give her sixpence. And Taylor..."

"Sir?"

Delaware nodded toward Smithers. "Rid us of this fellow. If he ever again sets foot on Buckhurst land or is even seen in the parish, have him whipped until his bones be bared."

On that, Delaware went quickly back into the mansion, followed only by Chaplain Laurie. Captain Brewster remained to give instructions to his new charges, and steward Taylor ordered two of the guards to escort Smithers and his horse out through the gate – which they did at the point of a pike and with evident satisfaction.

That the death of Pilot had cost the bailiff his job was some small consolation to the Jefferys brothers, but Delaware's casual assessment of the worth of the dog who had been the family's friend through much of their boyhood did not sit well. John saw him as a hard man with little concern for the feelings of lesser folk. Will, on the other hand, thought him to be the kind of leader who knew what needed to be done — like dismissing Smithers. That action gave Will considerable pleasure, pleasure that would have been muted had he known that Smithers had his gun.

Neither brother had time to talk nor to exchange more than a few words of resignation before they were ordered across the yard into the banqueting hall where tailors were refurbishing old uniforms to outfit the new generation of Delaware soldiers. The bootmaker from the village had been brought in to see that the recruits were shod, and the blacksmith and his apprentices were working at a portable forge in one of the great fireplaces mending guns, sharpening pikes, and tightening the hilts on rusty swords.

"Where be the arrows?" John wanted to know.

"Arrows?" scoffed the blacksmith. "They's only for savages. You ain't be a goin' to fight the Frenchies at Crecy again. It's guns you be needing." Will, needless to say, agreed.

By the time Delaware returned to the long gallery, his wife had left and only Tom Dowse and the children remained.

"A word if I may, my Lord," Dowse asked.

Delaware assured him that his words were always welcome. "I hope you have garnered a head-full of merry jests to amuse us on the voyage."

"Well, yes and no, m'Lord."

"Need more time, eh?" his Lordship asked. "You've got a week or two yet. We shan't be boarding until the fleet gets round to Portsmouth."

"'Tis about that, sir, " Dowse replied. "I'm hoping you'll change your mind about me going." He went on to plead that he was only a taborer, a drummer, a figure of fun and frolic far better suited to amusing the Delaware children than witless soldiers. But his master would hear none of it.

"Your foolery, good Tom, may be all that preserves my sanity. You'll accompany me, and there's an end on't. Did you see where her Ladyship went?" The words were scarcely out of Delaware's mouth when he glanced out of a gallery window and saw her walking alone down the path between the topiaried yews toward the small brick house of Dr. Lawrence Bohun, the family's resident physician. Wind scarcely noticeable within the enclosed courtyard was whipping across the walkways and scattering piles of dead leaves that should have been burned weeks before. Lady Cecilia knocked on the door and heard a gruff, "Enter!"

The small house, though solidly brick built, offered few amenities. It consisted of two rooms, the doctor's bed chamber and his office-come-laboratory. Dried plants hung on ceiling hooks, and in front of the east-facing window was a large table piled with books and rolls of parchment, some tied with ribbons, but most heaped in loose confusion. On the other side of the room stood the chimney, part of it structured as the firebox for a distillery. As Lady Cecilia entered she found Bohun furiously pumping a pair of bellows to keep fire burning under his distilling apparatus.

"Good day to ye, m'Lady," said Dr. Bohun as he continued to pump. "I need a new cap to my chimney," he told her. "I spend more time trying to get this thing to draw... But sit ye down, and warm yourself. You shouldn't be out in such weather. If you needed me, you could have sent for me, and I'd have been there as quick...as quick as a jackdaw on the wing."

"I know, I know, good doctor, but I wanted to talk to you alone, with none privy to what I have to say." Lady Cecilia knew that Bohun had been with the family for nigh on twenty years, and that having helped her through each of her pregnancies, he was as good a friend as she could hope to find — and infinitely more discrete than any of her waiting women.

Bohun stopped pumping and pulled up a second stool and they sat together in front of the small fire, she with her pale and beringed hands stretched toward the coals and he with his wrinkled fingers extending from knitted mittens that were on the point of unraveling. "I should buy you decent gloves," Cecilia said with a smile.

Bohun patted her hand. "But you didn't come to talk about gloves."

"They say that you're to go with my husband. Is that true?"

"Aye, my lady, that I am. 'Tis an opportunity that will not come again." He stood up and went to the table to pick up a thin book. "This is the record that Master Harriot, Ralegh's man, wrote when he returned from Virginia in '86. 'Tis full of knowledge about plants and roots and earth's that I'm certain I can improve upon once I get there. I have ideas, wonderful ideas of what can be achieved with experimentation. Who knows, I might startle the world with discoveries that..." His voice trailed off as he sat gazing into the fire. Then straightening his back, he said with a smile, "Well, who knows? But with your blessing, good my Lady, I mean to try."

"You have it, dear friend, you know that. But 'tis of my husband I want to talk. I believe he has never fully recovered from the ague he developed in Ireland. Dampness sets his bones aching. I doubt he is well enough to make this voyage. What say you?"

Bohun thought a minute or more before answering. "Good lady, he means to go. Neither you nor I will stop him. Is he well enough? In my professional opinion, no, he is not. But who knows, the voyage may do him good."

"You must tend him closely."

"Have no fear, m'Lady. I shall watch over him — as well as he will let me."

"Had God given me a son sooner," Cecilia said with a sigh, "the death of his Lordship would be tragic but not disastrous to the family. But with Henry only seven, his uncle Sackville might be awarded stewardship, and that, dear doctor, would be a sorry day for us all."

Bohun did his best to assure her that her husband was well aware of his physical condition and that he would be careful to keep his health. Bohun added that he believed that reports of early deaths in the colony were either exaggerated or resulted from the colonists being sickly before they left England. The climate, he assured her, is gentle and its dry warmth could very well rid his Lordship of the ailments that may still linger in his blood.

Lady Cecilia replied that she took some solace from Bohun's words. "But governor for life? Does that mean that he may be expected to remain there until he dies? I've quizzed him a dozen times, but he'll only answer 'We'll see.' And what answer is that?"

The doctor tried to reassure her that *for life* allowed Delaware to appoint a new deputy and once again to govern through him from London. Besides, Bohun added, the Company would want it that way. To make his Lordship Governor for Life was an honor not an order, he was sure of that. "Besides," he smiled, "there'll be nought to prevent you joining him at James Towne once he has the colony flourishing and ready to welcome you."

Lady Cecilia smiled in return, but refrained from declaring that wild horses would not drag her from the comforts of her Sussex home. She was not by nature a selfish woman, but she was practical and a good manager. She would argue that somebody had to stay with the children, and even if her husband wanted otherwise, she would remain as mistress of Buckhurst Manor. And that was that.

While the wind whistled in the chimney and set Bohun's shutters rattling, doctor and mistress remained huddled by the fire watching the slow drip of the distillate from alembic into flask. In marked contrast, much activity continued in and around the banqueting hall. Will Jefferys had done his best to convince his brother that Delaware would keep his promise to see their mother cared for. But John was not easily reassured. In his mind he was indispensable. His mother could not manage the animals on her own, of that he was certain. Will knew that nothing he could say would allay his brother's fears. For his part, however, Will chose to believe that his Lordship's steward would see to it that their mother was given such help as she might need. Now, however, Will had a more immediate concern. His new left shoe was a poor fit and he was sure it would chafe before he walked a mile. As Captain Brewster had announced that the march to London would begin at dawn, finding a shoe that fitted was taking precedence over all else.

Chapter Three

᪥

The march from Buckhurst to London took longer than expected; first one wagon lost a wheel, then two horses a shoe. Only the old soldiers in Captain Brewster's company were trained to march in military order, and no matter how loudly or how often his two sergeants shouted, the new recruits shambled along complaining that their feet were sore. By the time they had covered thirty miles they were belligerently demanding, "Ain't this far enough for one day?" But the Jefferys brothers were not among the complainers. For them every mile brought something new to see and discuss, herds of sheep, churches with spires and churches with towers, estates with great iron gates and, as they got closer to London, villages containing merchants' houses far larger than anything in their own Withyham. Up the old Roman road through Epsom and Ewell, on to Newington, they trudged until finally they were atop the scarp that enabled them to look down to the city. On a summer's day the panorama could be breathtaking, but on a late afternoon at the beginning of March much of it was lost in the smoke from countless chimneys on both sides of the Thames. It being too late to enter the city, Brewster elected to bivouac in St. George's Fields on the outskirts of Southwark. It would provide an opportunity for his men to drill themselves into more marshal shape before making their appearance among the burghers of London. It was also the place to deliver a speech, part exhortative and part warning, against the pitfalls and vices that might beckon once the troops found themselves with free time in the city.

The date of sailing was as yet undecided, much depending on the Company authorities in London being able to charter the ships, assemble crews, purchase provisions, and recruit a two-hundred-man regiment to augment Delaware's fifty-strong personal guard. Privately, Captain Brewster questioned whether his arrival was unnecessarily hasty, and allowed too much time for problems to develop before the fleet got under way. But his Lordship was anxious for the Company to see something happening, and so here was Brewster — and here were his troops awaiting his orders.

"Men," he began, "good fellows all. Before many days have passed we shall be embarking on a great adventure, one that will do honor to our king, to his Lordship, and to you and your families waiting here for your safe return. Rest assured that I am pledged to do all that I can to see that you do. But I cannot do it alone. You have to play your parts, and that means discipline at every level. Last night's attempts to put up tents was a disgrace – and no laughing matter as some of you seemed to think. Today, we shall march smartly across the bridge, through the city and out to Spittle Fields. And when we get there we shall put tents up and down until poles and pegs are as familiar to you as breathing and shitting."

"Where be them fields?" a voice from the back wanted to know.

"'Tis on the other side of the city," Brewster replied. "And if any of you are wondering why there and not here, I'll tell you. What lies in front of you isn't London, its Southwark. Its the place where you can catch every disease known to God, and I'm not about to board a parcel of pox-ridden varmints. You'll stay clear of the stews and the taverns, and keep out of the theaters and cockpits. They are most all on this side of the bridge, and once we cross it, I'll be posting a two-man guard at the bridge house to make sure than none of you has a mind to slip over. If any of you are thinking of renting a boat, take it from me, you don't have the money to pay for it. So keep yourselves clean in mind and body, and if you need something to do, give heed to your souls. There are more churches in London than fleas on a dog."

In retrospect, Brewster doubted that he had chosen the right analogy, but he was a blunt officer not versed in fancy phrases.

"Did he say stews?" John whispered to his brother. "What's wrong with a good stew? Nobody ever got sick from stew unless the meat was bad."

An older guardsman to his left, sniggered. "That's the weft of it, lad. The meat's bad."

John shrugged, and was none the wiser. Not until later was Will able to explain to him that stews were brothels.

By the time that the last of the tents and cooking kettles were stowed and back on the wagons, the bells on St. Mary's Church in Southwark were ringing out their call to matins. In better order than it arrived, the column set out up St. Margaret's Hill toward the bridge. John Jefferys was one of the few who could read names on the corners of alleys, and relished the variety of them: Fryingpan, Mermaid, Blue Maid, Unicorn, Black Spread Eagle alleys and Maidenhead Yard among them. For those unable to read there were signboards hanging in front of virtually every establishment: Black Swan, the Ship, Boar's Head, White Hart, Talbot, Queen's Head; the boards of inns and taverns went on and on, likewise the brothels under the signs of the Cardinal's Cap, Barge Bell, and Swan. By the time the towers of London Bridge came in sight, the road had narrowed and had become so congested that Brewster's column had to break up to get around carriages and to carve a path through the throng of tradesmen, customers, messengers, harlots, and who knew what. For Will and John, this was all new and exciting, and so, so different.

"Phew!" gasped John. "To think that all these people live in one place!" He would soon learn that there would be thousands more to amaze him once he crossed the bridge. Will had heard tell of the way traitors and murderers were displayed as deterrents to others, but neither brother was prepared for the row of rotting heads atop the bridge's south entrance. Some were old and no more than scarcely distinguishable black balls, but others of more recent vintage were still drawing the attention of eye-gouging crows. However, there was no stopping to stare. Riding ahead of his troops, Captain Brewster led the way across the bridge between the small shops and other businesses. In the gaps between the buildings Will caught his first sight of ships, dozens of them moored in the river with rowed boats plying back and forth amongst them. Which one of them would be his, he wondered. Some evidently were larger than others because they had three masts rather than two, but at the same time, being further away it was hard to judge their size. Besides, glimpses caught between the buildings while marching behind a loaded wagon was not the best way to gauge either size or distance.

The continuing march took the procession due north up Fish Street Hill, along Gracechurch and Bishopsgate streets, through the city gate, on past the Bedlam mad house, to an abrupt right turn into Spittle Fields. Indeed, so unexpected was the turn that the horse pulling the last wagon collided with the one in front, causing much consternation and scattering the men marching alongside it. Captain Brewster was not pleased.

Spittle Fields had been chosen for several reasons, not the least of them that Delaware's men could be kept together and trained without too many distracting spectators. It was also an area already set up for musket target practice and also, as John was the first to notice, for archery. The following day he was able to borrow a bow from a boy archer, and with the lad's arrows demonstrated his skills. Will, who was watching, asked Brewster to take note of his brother's prowess.

"Not bad," Brewster allowed, "not bad at all. Let's hope the savages don't shoot as well."

"Was that all he said?" John asked afterwards. "Didn't he think...?"

"I don't know what he thought," Will replied. "But I'll wager you this. He's not of a mind to turn his musketeers into bowmen." Later in the day, on Brewster's order, his senior sergeant, Bill Gideon, uncrated half a dozen muskets and began to instruct his charges on how to load and fire. John was among those chosen – deliberately, he guessed, and so in no mood to learn.

"Now listen ye here, young man," Gideon snapped. "I'm not standin' here for the fun of it. What you learn from me may save your worthless life. So look lively, lad." The guns were far heavier than Will's snaphaunce, and to aim them with any degree of accuracy their barrels had to be supported in a U-topped rest. With a bandoleer over one's shoulder and a dozen wooden containers hanging off it, plus a flask of priming powder and a bag of lead bullets, the kit became a significant incumbrance. "And then there's that stupid length of rope that you have too keep blowin' on to keep it burning," John complained. "Let it go out, and you're done for." Nevertheless, it was Sergeant Gideon's task to turn him into a marksman, and turn him he would.

"When you gets to James Towne, you'll each get your own piece, and you'll put your mark on the butt so as you'll know as its yourn. I expect his Lordship will want to store 'em all in the guardhouse, but it'll still be your job to keep your musket clean and ready. Remember always that your weapon is your best friend. So keep your swords sharp and your guns dry." The sergeant's admonition was uttered with vehemence, but the words came out as though by rote. He had said it a thousand times to more recruits than he cared to recall.

"Remember, always load from your top right flask first, elstwise you may be finding yourselves pouring from one that's empty. Load your powder; insert your ball, and if there's time, add your patch. Then what do you do?" Silence from the class.

"You takes your scourin' stick, and you rams it home like this. Then what?"

"Sounds like you've just made yourself a baby," laughed the third man on the left.

Gideon ignored the joker and went on to complete the drill, opening the pan, pouring the priming powder, blowing on the match and pulling the trigger. Nothing happened. The wind had blown the primer out of the pan before the glowing match reached it. "All right, get your laughin' over," Gideon snapped. "I did that on purpose – just so as you can see what can happen."

John didn't believe him, nor for that matter, did the rest of the class. One thing was clear enough; they all knew that they were being equipped with a heavy, clumsy, and unreliable weapon.

Through the next several days, Gideon's men marched, counter marched, loaded, reloaded, drilled with pikes, and learned to wield cutlasses and defend themselves with round leather bucklers strapped to their left arms. Never having fought with savages, Gideon could only teach from his experience against the Irish. He figured that on balance, they were smarter than Indians because they had the advantage of prior contact with an English army. When questioned, he gave his opinion that he did not expect the Godless savages to fight in a civilized way – rank against rank, volley to volley. "But like as not," he added, "our people have already sent 'em running, and so by the time we get to Virginia, we'll see neither hide nor hair of 'em."

Delaware had been true to his word, and each man was given spending money in the amount of one silver shilling or three groats — with admonitions to spend it wisely. But with ale at a halfpenny a pint, there was little opportunity for riotous living, or so it seemed before the Jefferys brothers decided to visit the great church of St. Paul whose tower dominated the city skyline. They were surprised to find the interior bustling with secular activity, and when they came upon four boys squatting on a tombstone throwing dice, their invitation to join them was hard to resist. Will did not. But to the gamblers' dismay, in the space of ten minutes he turned one groat into three shillings. John, however, had remembered their mother's admonition that a fool and his gold were soon parted, and chose to let Fortuna smile only on his brother.

From St. Paul's they walked on to Newgate, thence to Pie Corner and out into Smithfield market. Once an open space on the edge of the medieval city large enough for horse races and jousting, building construction had greatly reduced its size. At one end a blackened area around the charred stumps of several posts was being loudly touted as the very place where Queen Mary had burned forty-three Protestant martyrs. "Them is the very same posts what are used to this day to burn Papists," declared a ragged youth with a cheeky grin who made a living entertaining bumkins with gory details. "Sometimes, they's boiled alive, but that's mostly for women," he said, spitting disdainfully into the dry ashes. "Still," he added brightly, "there ain't been a woman boiled 'ere in Smithfield since 1541."

"Why?" John asked.

"Why what?" the boy cageyly replied.

"Why do they burn men and boil women?"

"'Tis for poisoners like, and women does more poisonin' than men, don't you see."

"Why be that?" John persisted.

Their guide had been questioned enough. "Well look ye here!" he declared, as he bent down and picked up a small bone from amid the ashes. "If this isn't your lucky day, young gents! Here be a finger bone from the hand of Archbishop Cranmer. It can be yours for sixpence."

But John had seen enough chicken bones. Besides, he'd never heard of Cranmer.

The brothers escaped through the small throng that had gathered to listen to the young showman complete his chronicle of horrors and pass his cap around.

"There's something sort of...I don't know, sort of unchristian about profiting from the suffering of those poor people," John told his brother.

Will laughed. "You stood and listened, didn't you? If country folk like us weren't ready to buy, there wouldn't be lads like him to profit from us." John knew he was right, and said no more on the subject. Instead, they made their way east along Cheapside peering in amazement into the windows of jewelers, goldsmiths, silversmiths, watchmakers, and the sellers of clothing tailored in fabrics woven in gold and silver or trimmed with ermine. There were cordwainers and perfumiers, pewterers and cutlers, glass sellers and vintners, spice merchants, and book-sellers, all mixed together in a kaleidoscope of colors and smells. The throng in the street was no less colorful; Turks in jeweled turbans, blackamoors from Tangier, Venetians in striped hose and short capes, grim men in fur hats from the Baltic, mingling with fat-faced English tradesmen, and merchants with gold chains around their necks. And then there were the women;

women modestly hidden under the hoods of fur-lined cloaks, and women in bold brocaded dresses with jeweled stomachers, lawn ruffs, and breasts immodestly bared. For some, uniformed retainers cleared the way ahead of their employers, but for the most part, wealth and poverty walked side by side. Children in rags, their bare feet blue with cold trod in the footsteps of men with red rosettes on their costly shoes. Girls in woollen smocks and filthy aprons were selling everything from ribbons to live eels. At the corner of Cheapside and Ironmonger Lane, an old blindman was selling caged song birds, and in front of the Exchange a female ballad seller sang her wares in competition with a white haired man shouting that the Judgment Day was at hand and that buying his printed tracts were the only way to salvation. There being no sidewalks, pedestrians took their chances amid the carriages, horsemen, pushers of hand carts, and even the herders of terrified cattle whose excrement fouled the gutters. The noise of wheels on cobbles, the shouts of drivers, and the chatter of foreign languages all blended into a single shapeless cacophony that had John's senses reeling. When he reached the Exchange he told his brother that he had seen enough for one day and was returning to camp. Will, on the other hand, was certain that with his winnings still in his purse, the city had more to offer. He would be back before dusk.

He wasn't, and John supped from the common kettle without him. He had no idea how long he had been asleep in his tent before the camps' night watch pushed his brother in on top of him. But it evidently was long past curfew. "You'll be up on a charge in the morning," barked one of the guards. "So clean yourself up, if you know what's good for you!"

As Will lurched onto his cot he repeatedly muttered, "You be a very nice lady, as good and nice a girl as any feller could...ever..." Moments later he was asleep and snoring.

"You stupid sod!" John sighed as he turned over and pulled his cap over his ears.

Captain Brewster was seated behind his field table at the entrance to his tent when Will Jefferys was brought before him. Behind the Captain stood two lieutenants who Will did not know, and Sergeant Gideon, who he knew all too well. Four or five hours' sleep had done Will some good, but by no means enough. His uniform still stank of stale ale, his eyes were bloodshot, and his walk less than purposeful. "Master Jefferys, you are as sorry a sight as ever I saw," Brewster said in a voice slow and deliberate that made a much deeper impression than it would have had he shouted. "Suppose you tell me what you've been up to."

Will confessed that his memory was a little hazy. He had turned into an alley behind the Exchange and met a lady who asked him where he was from.

"Yes?"

"I told her that I was from Withyham, and she said 'what a coincidence. 'cos I be from thereabouts.' So we hit it off right away like. Then she said. 'seein' as how we're neighbors, how would you...'"

".. like to buy me a pint?" Sergeant Gideon added flatly.

"Right, Sarg. That's just what she said. How did you know?"

"Get on, man! Get on with it!" Brewster snapped.

Shamefacedly, Will told how the woman had taken him into an alehouse. He thought it was called the Pewter Pot or something like that. Once inside she called for drinks, but Will thought she would be ordering ale; instead it was brandy and when he balked at the cost of it, she asked him how much money he had. He told her, and she said that for two shillings she could give him something to remember her by.

"I'll bet she could," Gideon grunted.

"And did she, I mean did you...?" Brewster asked with an encouraging hand.

"Did I what?" Will countered.

"God's blood, man! Did you bed her?"

"Well, no..."

Brewster sighed. "That at least is something."

"We did it against a wall."

Gideon roared with laughter and his captain pounded the table so hard that his ink horn fell off it.

"You know what to do, Sergeant Gideon." Brewster snapped.

"Same as usual, sir?"

"The very same."

The English army's usual and not very efficient cure for the pox was to scrub the offender's genitals with a besom brush and the same kind of lye soap used to scour decks. If it didn't work, it invariably discouraged further dalliance. Will's public humiliation was more painful than the scrubbing, and for several days thereafter he walked like a duck. He got no sympathy from his brother whose only comment was, "quack, quack!" Nonetheless, for better or worse, Will Jefferys had made a distinct impression on his officers.

Ten boring yet arduous days would elapse before Lord Delaware and his retinue crossed the bridge into London. It turned out, however, that his Lordship had come to town only for a last, pre-sailing meeting of the Virginia Company Council. Furthermore, he would not board until the fleet reached Cowes at the Isle of Wight. At the meeting he learned that the Company's two hundred soldiers were proving to be as big a bag of riff raff as Captain Brewster had feared. But they were not Brewster's responsibility. Camped to the west in Finsbury Fields, and under their own officers, they were sufficiently far away to be unable to damage the morale of his Lordship's best. And Brewster had every intention of ensuring that his men were the best. "If they aren't yet," he told his sergeants, "by God they'd better be by the time they land at James Towne."

The decision to keep the Buckhurst company together had been reached even before Lord Delaware's flagship had been named. The men would be loaded onto barges moored at Tower Gate and the nearby St. Katherine's Stairs, and be ferried to the ship lying out in the river. The Finsbury troops, on the other hand, would be marched down to Wapping to board the transports and would have no truck with the rest until all were safely ashore in Virginia. By the time his Lordship's guard learned that on the morrow they would be going aboard, Will had recovered from his ordeal and his confinement to camp was behind him. Once again, therefore, the brothers set out into the city in search of any amusement short of the pox.

In the hope of seeing the flagship, they made their way down to Billingsgate Dock, that being as far upstream as ocean-going shipping could be towed. From the earliest times, Billingsgate had enjoyed the reputation of being as rough and raucous as any area of the city. It was the principle landing place for fishing vessels of all sizes from cod ships to oyster boats, and the men and women who worked there would as soon cut a throat as shuck an oyster. It was, all in all, a very poor choice of entertainment for a pair of country boys decked out in a nobleman's livery.

It being late in the afternoon and the fog settling over the river, nothing was to be seen of the ships but shadows and the tops of masts. The quay on the east side of the dock was long and cobble-paved, flanked by warehouses and taverns. From behind the shuttered windows of the Mermaid came sounds of raucous singing and the scraping of a viol as melodic as the screeching of an alley cat. So many seamen were jammed in the doorway that Will selected, instead, a less popular establishment under the sign of a ship. It was called the Dark-House by reason of its location between two much taller buildings and having few windows.

Picking their way down a narrow, candle-lit corridor and stepping gingerly over the legs of prostrate customers, the Jefferys brothers found themselves in a taproom blue with tobacco smoke and reeking of sweat and vomit. "Pardon me! May I? If you don't mind? May we?" all went unheard as they eased their way through the human barrier preventing them from gaining the landlord's attention.

Someone shouted "Hey, mates! Look at these young farts all decked out in blue and yeller!" The voice brought a momentary halt to the babble and caused a gap to open up that let Will reach the bar. John flushed in embarrassment when he realized that twenty or more, salt-hardened faces were staring at him. Will, on the other hand, was proud of his uniform and responded easily to the laughter. He had decided that going to Virginia was nothing to be ashamed of, and so was happy to let it be known that he was the Governor's man. After the laughter had turned to slaps on the back and good-hearted words of encouragement and well-wishing, the way opened for John to find a vacated table in a corner. Once their curiosity value wore off, the Dark House's habitues resumed their raucous conversations, leaving the brothers to sweep the oyster shells and spilled ale off the table with the backs of their hands and sit down.

"Be this like the room at the Unicorn at Withyham?" John asked.

Will was slow to reply. It hadn't occurred to him that his brother had never been inside it. But before he could begin to describe the difference, a thin, weasel of a man, dirty and ingratiating, came toward them clutching an empty mug. "A very good evenin' to ye, young sirs. The name's Parsons, but you can call me Scotty, me being from north o' the border."

He sat down uninvited, and explained that he was an old sailor whose voyages had taken him to the furthest reaches of the globe. He said he was proud to be talking to two fine young men outward bound for the New World. He added that he had friends among the soldiers assembled in Finsbury Fields, and that he, himself, had sailed to Virginia with good Sir Walter Ralegh . "So, young masters," he said, "just wet me whistle and I'll tell ye everythin' you'll need to know. It's Duppa ale, I be drinkin'."

Had his listeners known that Ralegh had never been to Virginia, they would have been less easily deceived. Instead, Will figured that the investment would be worth it, and called for the refill. "So, what's it like in Virginia? Be there forests, mountains...?"

"Mountains, sir, great mountains what sweeps down to the sea, and forests with trees so huge that six men with stretched arms can't girdle them." Scotty explained.

"And what of animals?" Will asked.

"You name 'em, sir, and they're there. Camels with humps as big as this." He spread his arms. "And elephants bigger 'an them what Hannibal took over the Alps. And tigers, too, with teeth like daggers. Wild, they be." Scotty gulped down his ale, and wiped his mouth with the back of his hand, then pushed the empty pot in John's direction. "Wet me whistle one more time, sir, and..."

Before the request was out, the landlord had stepped behind Scotty and had him by the back of his jersey. "Don't you listen to him. This turd's never been further than the Borough jail, which is where he belongs!"

Amid much laughter and a good deal of pushing and shoving, the landlord and his drawers manhandled Scotty out of the tap room, down the passageway, and out onto the quay. The landlord, having decided the Jefferys brothers were desirable customers, returned full of apologies, offered them a free pint and warned that, "You shouldn't believe half of what you're told. London's a cockpit o' thieves," he added. "Now I've never been to Virginia, not many have; but I've heard tell that its as close to Eden as a man can get. So drink up, and God speed ye."

Will and John gladly accepted the hospitality, and then downed another with the last of John's money. Meanwhile, they made new friends, several of whom were sufficiently inebriated to order more drinks to give the young adventurers a rousing farewell. By the time they were ready to leave, London was a prince of a city and whatever Virginia might or might not have in store was of very little consequence. Their only immediate concern was to speedily empty their bladders into the rising tide.

"Well, well, what have we here?" John was still retying his codpiece as he turned to and saw the speaker silhouetted against light streaming from the doorway of the nearby Mermaid Tavern. Will recognized the voice as that of Scotty Parsons but couldn't place his three burly companions.

"Got me thrown out, did you? Not a nice thing to do to a fellow what meant ye no harm, not a nice thing at all, was it lads?" Scotty asked his companions.

"Nah!" they replied.

"So as they wouldn't buy me a pint, I say we give them a taste o' good old Thames water."

"Yah," answered his inarticulate friends.

"Why don't you just go home," Will told them. "We're not looking for trouble."

"But me and my pals here, we thinks you need a lesson. Allow me to introduce them, 'cos like as not, you'll meet 'em again. They's goin' with you to Virginia, see. This here is Chisman. We call's him 'Twofin' 'cos he's lost two fingers on his hand. And this is Arty, and that's Smiler. Nicer pals you'd never want to meet, but they gets real put out when a friend ain't treated right. Ain't that a fact?"

"Yup," "Aye," and "s'truth," came the replies.

Neither Will nor John had ever learned to swim and this was not the time or place to start. But Scotty and his friends blocked any retreat up the quay into Thames Street, and the other direction led only to the river. "Well, brother," said Will, "there be four of them and only two of us, but three are fat and one's a runt. So the odds be'nt that bad." With that he grabbed a wicker eel trap and lunged with it as Twofin advanced on him. But the attacker caught hold of the trap, and Will at once realized that fat though he was, the man was no easy opponent. A dive into the dock might be the lesser of two evil options. John, meanwhile, picked up a broken oar, swung it, missed, but managed to sidestep the rush of Arty who lunged past him into the black water of the dock. His cry for help coincided with the sound of a whistle and running feet, as half a dozen men in Delaware livery burst out of the darkness. Scotty and his two remaining allies ran off down the quay; but having nowhere to go, they were quickly seized and overpowered. Someone carrying a lantern, held the light up to Will's face and said in a voice that registered both disappointment and amused resignation, "Oh, no, not you again!"

"Aye, sarg. Afraid so," Will confessed.

Sergeant Gideon's six man patrol had been rounding up absentees from riverside taverns when it arrived at Billingsgate with three drunken detainees in tow. Now it had five.

"Looks like I arrived just in time," said Gideon. "Let's hope you're always that lucky."

"We could 'ave taken them." Will assured him.

" As easy as cuckoo spit," John added.

"Maybe. But it's as well they didn't make you prove it." With that Gideon pointed a thumb at the three attackers and then a fore-finger in the direction of the water. "Help these oafs to their boat."

"But we don't 'ave no boat!" Scotty pleaded as his captors rushed him to the quay edge and into the filthy water below. Two more splashes quickly followed.

Gideon had ordered his patrol back into ranks and was preparing to move on when John interceded for the four men shouting and floundering in the darkness of the dock. "We can't leave them to drown," he pleaded.

"What do you expect me to do about it? Jump in after 'em?" Gideon snapped. "Patrol, by the left, quick march!"

So ended the Jefferys brothers' last night out in the fabled City of London.

Chapter Four

CRUSO

O n the morning of Monday, March 26, Will and John Jefferys
went aboard the ship *Delaware* with little but the uniforms on
their backs. It was true that each had been supplied with a canvas
sack containing their exchanged clothes, but they had neither a
spoon nor a mug to call their own. Everything necessary would be
provided soon enough, they were told. But how soon was soon,
they wanted to know. And they weren't alone. The other forty-eight
members of Lord Delaware's guard were crowded with them below
decks, all increasingly vocal as the day wore on and nobody paid
them any attention.

The *Delaware* lay in the stretch of the Thames known as the
Upper Pool that flowed eastward from London Bridge to St.
Katherine's Dock. The fleet's other two ships were moored further
down the river in the Lower Pool. None of the men Will talked with
knew much more than that. One said he had heard that they were
the *Blessing* and the *Hercules,* but nobody was able to confirm it.
But whatever their names or size, there was general satisfaction that
the Finsbury crowd was down there and not aboard the *Delaware.*
Beyond that, for men who had never before seen the inside of a
ship, there was little else to be pleased about.

Will, being taller than John, had not yet learned to stoop to
avoid the overheard deck beams that allowed clearance of less than
six feet. Adding to the sense of confinement was the presence of six
large cannon which, when not run out occupied much of the space
around and over which the passengers had to sleep, either slung in

hammocks above the guns or on palliasses jammed between them. The guns, however, were not the only space reducers. The main mast rose up through the middle, and forward of that was the mounting for the capstan. Then, too, the central area amidships had to be kept clear of the hatch leading down to the cargo hold and to the ballast. Fortunately for the Jefferys brothers, they had been among the last of the guard to go aboard and so had the advantage of the lower deck. Those who boarded first had been ordered further down to the orlop deck which received less of the light and air provided by the midships hatch grating.

Delay in boarding had been occasioned by the need to first load the ship's holds with all the barrels and boxes of supplies that were being carried to the colonists in Virginia, as well as those required to feed and water the crew and passengers throughout the voyage. Rumor had it that the *Blessing* and *Hercules* – if those, indeed, were their names – along with two hundred soldiers, were carrying six cows and several horses as well as quantities of hay and other fodder. It was Will's opinion that those ships would be swimming in shit long before they reached Virginia.

"So how long will it take?" asked Jack somebody-or-other, who Will had met one market day in Withyham.

"To fill the ships with shit?"

"No! How long will it take to get to Virginia?"

Will confessed that he had no clear idea. He had heard ten days or two weeks. But others said that it could take two months or more, an estimate that generated instant dismay at the prospect of being boxed up so long in what one man called a floating coffin. As long as they had been kept occupied in the camp at Spittle Fields, John had been ready to take life day by day, but moments after descending the ladder into their new quarters, his thoughts turned homeward to his mother, their cottage, their livestock, and most of all to the trees and the birds flying free in the sky above them.

There being no immediate supervision, fellow guardsmen either sat buried in their thoughts, or roamed about trying determine the layout of the ship. Astern of them, separated behind a bulkhead, was the gun room that housed two more cannon, all the gunpowder and most of the shot. Through the gun room stretched the tiller, in turn attached to the whipstaff that disappeared up through the ceiling to the steerage cabin. That also contained the candle-lit binnacle with its compass and hourglass by whose sand the ship measured its watches and time traveled. Those details, however, took several days to acquire. For now, everyone was confined below the hatch gratings, and could explore no further forward than the bulkhead and two locked doors separating the lower deck from the bos'n's store and crew's quarters, the latter a cramped space with two more cannon and the shaft of the bowsprit. Above, in the forecastle, was everyone's key to salvation, the cook room with its vast iron kettle and brick-surrounded hearth.

Backus, the cook, was a jovial man, short, ruddy-faced behind a graying beard, with well-fed forearms that man-handled the kettle as easily as spinning a coin. To help him were two boys, the stewards who the passengers grew to know as Big and Little on account of their sizes. As a rule, Big carried buckets of gruel and Little was in charge of the wooden spoons and bowls. Their first descent below decks was received with scrambling joy — until the first diner tasted the contents of the bucket.

"What in Jesu's name, is this?" demanded one man.

"'Tis pork stew," Big replied. "And its fresh. So make the most of it. You won't be seein' much more o' that."

"Not much more," echoed Little.

Above their heads, high in the stern castle, the officers were dining on better fare, most of it brought aboard at their own expense. Seated at the table in the Great Room — space that would later be occupied by the yet-to-arrive Lord Delaware — were Captain Brewster, sailing master Robert Tindall, Lieutenants Fanshaw and Bartram, Isaac Saltzman the cape merchant, chief mate Jim Coolidge, and master gunner Miles Morecomb. Together they represented the ship's officers until such time as Lord Delaware and his entourage would come aboard. Brewster did not know Tindall who would captain the ship when Delaware arrived as admiral, but he had heard that he was a good man of long experience in the Baltic trade. It was Tindall who had been responsible for hiring the rest of the ship's complement, while Saltzman had control of all the supplies being sent to Virginia, as well as serving as the *Delaware's* purser and accountant. Brewster was learning to dislike Saltzman, not because he was a Jew, but because any officer who talked to him with his mouth full and dribbled wine down his chin onto his ruff, was not someone to take into one's confidence. As the officers finished their meal of cold goose washed down with the best of Burgandy – evidently wasted on Saltzman — Brewster reminded them that the *Delaware* would be remaining at James Towne at his Lordship's pleasure, and that any officer who didn't find the place to his liking was free to leave when the *Blessing* and *Hercules* returned to England, providing, Brewster added, that there were sufficient seaman alive in Virginia to man and sail the flagship.

"Alive?" mumbled Saltzman through the last of his goose. "There is doubt?"

"Aye, master purser, there always is doubt when ships sail abroad. You should know that," Brewster snapped. Then he added congenially, "I meant no more by the word than the realities of life and death." He was well aware that his job was to keep morale high and to give the impression that there was naught but sunshine in their future. But everyone knew — at least he thought everyone knew – that Lord Delaware had been made governor because his deputy, Sir Thomas Gates and all his senior officers aboard the *Sea Venture* were presumed drowned. This, however, was not something anyone wanted to talk about, and Brewster hoped that his guardsmen passengers were unaware of it. But they were. For months past, rumors had circulated through the riverside taverns that the rich investors in the Virginia Company had suffered a major setback.

Brewster took Saltzman's question as his cue to emphasize the positive in all things concerning his Lordship and the voyage ahead. "I have served the Delaware's through much of my adult life. No finer soldier treads this earth," he insisted. "Under his leadership, this venture will succeed. You have my word on it."

"And so say we all," added Tindall.

Amid the general mutter of agreement from the lieutenants, mate, and gunner, Saltzman said he had a question. Why, he wanted to know, was there no surgeon on board?

"Because, master purser, his Lordship will be bringing his own physician, Dr. Lawrence Bohun, a scholar of great repute. We can want for none better," Brewster added. He was beginning to expound on Bohun's fame and credentials when mate Coolidge interrupted.

"With great respect, sir, a physician ain't no surgeon. Every ship needs a sawbones more than a doser of physic. Do he have a paper from the Barber Surgeons sayin' he be able to mend heads and lop limbs? Every ship's surgeon has to have a certificate what says so."

"There'll be surgeons on the other ships," Brewster replied. The issue had been discussed back at Buckhurst, and he knew that physicians looked upon surgeons as little more than butchers, while the surgeons scoffed at doctors as pill rollers and potion pushers out of touch with the realities of spewed blood and broken bones. Nevertheless, Delaware had determined that the presence of both the gentle Bohun and a barber surgeon at the same table would not contribute to ship-board harmony. But Brewster saw no point in going into that. "If this arrangement is not to your liking," he told Saltzman, "you have three choices. You can withdraw your services; you can transfer to the *Blessing,* or you can accept his Lordship's decision."

Saltzman shrugged. "I only asked an honest question," he muttered. "There's no need to..." His voice trailed off.

The *Delaware* weighed anchor on the Monday and made a slow and stately progress down river, easing her way amid the other moored vessels. At Wapping she passed the still-moored *Blessing* and *Hercules* and surprised the guardsmen still shut below by firing a salute from her stern chasers. Word of the fleet's departure had spread down river all the way to Gravesend; from large ships and fishing boats came cheers, trumpet blasts, and occasional gun salutes. Meanwhile, back amid the counting houses of Mincing Lane, London's merchants kept their fingers crossed and their prayers prepared.

The journey thus far had been undramatic and provided an opportunity for the passengers to get the measure of life aboard. John had become used to the sounds of sailing, the shouting, the drumming of feet overhead, the creaking of rigging and the crack of sails catching the wind, and the water — its constant swishing and lapping as the bow cut through it. Even the gentle pitching fore and aft that accompanied their progress was far less upsetting to his stomach than he had expected. Were it not for the confinement, sailing the oceans was not nearly as awesome a prospect as Will had led him to expect. But what did Will know? He'd never been closer to the sea than the stream that ran through Buckhurst fields.

Then, on the Wednesday afternoon, complacency was swept overboard as the *Delaware* left the protection of the Thames estuary and plunged into the open waters of the North Sea. The lapping turned to a pounding roar, sea spray came down through the hatch grating, and the wind whistled through the rigging. Sailors and gunners slammed gun ports shut cutting out the principal source of light, and Delaware's elite felt their confinement even more oppressive. The ship plunged first forward and downward and then reared up, sending anything loose rolling and sliding back and forth along the lower deck. A bucket used to swab the guns fell off its hook and hit Will above his ankle. Before he could grab its rope handle, it rolled away to cannon into another man's leg. "God's thunder!" he yelled, as he hopped about nursing his shin, then fell backwards with the next heaving of the deck. The shouting and cursing continued as men clung to hammocks, gun carriages, and anything that kept them from cracking their heads. Then the after hatch opened and down into this chaos came Sergeant Gideon.

"Hold fast, lads!" he shouted. "This'll be over as soon as we clear into the Downs."

Nobody had any idea what he was talking about, but Gideon's presence and evident control of himself was reassuring – up to a point. But he proved right. Half an hour later the heaving decreased as the wave action lessened in the lea of the long shoals called the Goodwin

Sands. From time immemorial outward bound ships had sheltered in the Downs waiting for a fair wind. Many never found it and were driven onto the quicksands and devoured – hence the Goodwins' long-time reputation among mariners as the "shippe swalower." Fortunately, for their peace of mind the Jefferys brothers and their bruised companions were unaware of that, and so relaxed when the movement lessened.

The three ships remained in the Downs for two days awaiting the fair wind that would carry them into the rougher waters of the English Channel, thence to the Isle of Wight and the relative serenity of the Solent. Once there, sighs of relief below decks greeted the turning of the capstan and the sound of anchor chains and cables rattling through hawser ports. Above, the young men called younkers, were already aloft taking in the top sails while the older sailors reefed the foresails and mainsails and ensured that everything was shipshape. With all that done and inspected, the fleet lay ready to receive its admiral. But it was then late in the day and rowing Delaware's party out to his ship against a rising tide was deemed unnecessarily arduous.

"Far better to wait till morning," Delaware assured his chaplain. "If one is to be a presence, it needs to be felt. We'll not skulk aboard unheralded." Laurie had no trouble with that and was happy to spend another night in the comfort of the Tabard Inn at Cowes. But for Will, John, and their companions, it meant another night of waiting.

Still penned below decks, Will and John Jefferys were watching three of their company roll dice and argue over whose turn it was and whether a farthing was true or counterfeit, when Sergeant Gideon came down the after ladder. He called for everyone's attention and then told them, "When his Lordship comes aboard he expects every man on deck, his uniform buttoned and hats on straight. Pikes will be issued for all, and halberds for six." The words had a ring of immediacy about them that Will received with relief. The chance to spend time on deck was already a prospect to be savored.

Finally, late on Sunday morning, the boats carrying Delaware, his staff, and their baggage arrived alongside. Sergeant Gideon was reasonably satisfied that his company had its hats on straight, its pikes and halberds aligned, and its shoe laces tied; alas, none of it achieved without a good deal of shouted invective. The bos'n's whistle piped, the ship's trumpeter trumpeted, the admiral's banner unfurled from the main mast, and his Lordship came aboard his *Delaware* with a flourish of his hat in recognition of the assembled crew. As he walked along the ranks on his way to his cabin in the stern castle, the company had an opportunity to size up its commander. None of the ship's crew had seen him before and knew little or nothing about him. The few of his guardsmen who came from the home farm at Buckhurst had his measure, but others like Will and John had spoken to him only when he addressed them on the day they were conscripted.

A younker perched in the lower rigging decided that he was too short. A sailor thought him too stiff, too haughty. Another saw him as too grim faced. "He ought to look like he's pleased to see us," he muttered. Several guardsmen later said that he looked unwell. Dr. Bohun, however, considered him as well as could be expected. So said Chaplain Laurie who boarded looking appropriately benevolent, and walked behind, bible in hand, smiling to left and right.

"Our father who art on earth," someone snickered.

"Silence, God damn it!!" Gideon hissed from the side of his mouth.

If the chaplain heard the remark, he gave no sign of it, and continued to smile on his new flock. What his Lordship thought of his reception was hard to tell. He was intent on leaving an impression of a resolute leader, reliable, resourceful, and a stern disciplinarian — all of which was true. Smiling was not a prerequisite, and so the single all-encompassing hat wave was familiarity enough. Behind Bohun and Laurie came Sir Ferdinando Wainman whom the Company had named General of the Horse, several more gentlemen, and three of Delaware's personal servants. Bringing up the rear pranced the elf-like Tom Dowse in his medieval style version of the Delawares' blue and yellow livery. He was doing his best to make the best of his misfortune. His tabor (a small snare drum) hung from a cord around his neck, and a flute protruded from his belt. Although none of Tom's musical talents were on display as the little procession paraded across the deck, his dancing gait, winks, and tipping of his cap, left no doubt that he was out of step with the solemnity of the occasion. Intended or not, Tom Dowse's antics served as a valuable counterbalance to Delaware's severe appearance.

Once inside the steerage room, Delaware relaxed and thanked his captains for their smart turn out. "This bodes well, very well indeed," he assured them. To Brewster he added, "You managed to turn our country lads into a pretty smart lot. No easy task I'm sure."

"They clean up and line up," Brewster acknowledged, "but they'll need a lot more work if they're to be ready to fight the savages."

Delaware smiled and nodded. "But I'm sure that by the time we get to Virginia, they'll be as sharp as a Toledo blade. But," he went on, "you must all keep in mind that we go as keepers of the peace, not as invaders or conquerors. I'll be stressing that in all my addresses to the men, and so must you. But first things first."

"Meaning what, m'Lord?" Captain Tindall asked.

"Meaning that we go nowhere until every officer and every man has sworn the oaths of allegiance and supremacy."

"I'm sure the officers have already done that," Brewster replied.

"No doubt they have," Delaware allowed. "But you must all be *seen* to do so. Therefore, you'll do it again." The captains and senior officers of the *Blessing* and *Hercules* who were aboard the *Delaware* to greet their admiral were ordered to return to their ships and do likewise.

That afternoon the crew and guardsmen reassembled on deck to hear the oaths read out. The first required acceptance that the king's highness was the only supreme governor of Great Britain and the Colony of Virginia, as in all spiritual and ecclesiastical causes. The wording was convoluted, but the intent was clear enough, and the Oath of Supremacy made it more so.

"I do truly and sincerely acknowledge, profess, testify, and declare in my conscience that ye pope, neither of himself, nor by any authority of the Church or See of Rome, or by any other means hath any power or authority to depose the King or to dispose any of his Majesty's Kingdoms or Dominions..." Chaplain Laurie was not a strong speaker and much of the language blew away in the wind, but the bit that really mattered came last. "I do make this recognition and acknowledgment, heartily, willingly and truly upon the true faith of a Christian, so help me God." It took more than an hour for each man to place his hand on the Bible and swear, and many of the mumbled responses sounded more like "swelp me Bob" but in the end all but one man had renounced Catholicism, accepting eternal damnation should he be lying. Alonzo Dias, the ship's pilot was the sole hold out. Being a Portuguese, denying his faith was unthinkable and he said so.

Because Spain had been master of the Carribean and most of known America for more than a hundred years, virtually all pilots were Catholics and religiously suspect. But there were times when God and reality parted company. Ships' captains were by necessity pragmatists and unanimous in believing that safe guidance by a Popish pilot was preferable to hitting a rock. Consequently, Alonzo Dias' faith was not an issue, at least in the mind of Captain Tindall. His trust was in Elmo, the seaman's patron saint, and he really didn't know or care whether St. Elmo was Catholic or Protestant. Lord Delaware and Chaplain Laurie, on the other hand, wisely kept their convictions to themselves. Privately, to Brewster, Delaware told him. "'Tis safe enough to assume that this Dias feller won't be Papist enough to sacrifice himself and sink the ship, but once ashore you may bet he'll be King Philip's man again. Lets not forget that."

At home, on Sundays, Will and John went with their mother to the parish church, but religion, as such, was not something they felt strongly about. They accepted that God probably existed in some form or other, but whether the king in London or the Pope in Rome was his spokesman on earth seemed unimportant and probably nonsense. John had asked Chaplain Laurie whether God was in reality the sun, arguing that its light and warmth governed all lives. This, Laurie told him, was heresy and spreading it about could get him into serious trouble. So he didn't, but he did think about it now and then, and wondered about the wisdom of believing something to be so just because a book said so.

"Why," John asked on another occasion, "is it that if Jesus was a Jew, why does everyone hate Jews? Didn't they just kill one of their own? And why, if King James is God's messenger to us English, why does he come from Scotland? And why wasn't Jesus born in London or even in Withyham?"

Laurie admired the boy's inquiring mind, and was troubled by being unable to give him any satisfying answers. He could only respond by urging him to believe and to expel all such dangerous questions from his thoughts. So it was, that when John stood on the deck with his hand on the Bible and gave his oath upon the true faith of a Christian, so help him God, Laurie smiled and quietly told him, "Well said, my boy."

Will Jefferys had no trouble taking the oath. If his betters told him to say that black was white, he'd do so, if he believed that to be his duty. Agreeing that the king was his king and the Pope wasn't, seemed a pretty obvious fact and hardly needed all that swearing. But if that was what his Lordship required, so be it. And his Lordship very definitely did, his belief in the tenets of Christianity being absolute and unquestioned.

Delaware's instructions from the Company were specific. He was to proceed to Virginia *with what speed conveniently you may... and with the first wind to set sail for that place.* And he had done so. On Monday, April 2, after much trumpet blowing between one ship and the next, the fleet weighed anchor, and with a brisk wind blowing from the north east, cleared the Solent and the four towering chalk pinnacles called the Needles and set a course for the islands of the Azores. Now that they were under way, life for Will, John, and the rest of the 'lower deck layabouts,' as Sergeant Gideon called them, became less monotonous. There were drills to be performed, lessons in pike handling, wrestling, and dancing – to the tunes of Tom Dowse. A good deal of grumbling accompanied the order to dance, but Delaware was committed to arriving with a healthy company, and dance it would. And dance it did. He was equally concerned that his people should arrive rich in the grace of God. It mattered to him not one whit that his reluctant congregation found Chaplain Laurie's sermons more tiresome than Dowse's drumming. But woe betide any man caught yawning. Deck scrubbing and latrine emptying were the price of inattention.

On their twelfth day out the fleet reached St. George's Island in the Azores without incident, the weather having stayed fair and the seas gentle. Rumors had spread through the ships that while there to take on water, the passengers and crews would be allowed ashore at the town of Velas. But the next day being Friday the 13th, a ferocious gale sprang up that set the ships to tossing and rolling far worse than they had in the North Sea. The guardsmen's hope to tread on land vanished as they clung to each other and to anything still tied down. Captain Tindall's suggestion that the fleet should run to the lea of Graciosa, the northern most island, proved not to be a good idea. The wind shifted again, and though riding in forty fathoms, the *Delaware*'s anchor failed to hold. Both the *Blessing* and the *Hercules* lost anchors, and aboard the *Blessing* twelve men were injured when the capstan broke. By the morning of the 15th, with the gale still raging, the *Hercules* had disappeared.

Soon after the remaining ships cleared the Azores, the seas abated, the crews repaired the damage, and both Will and John claimed to have benefitted from the experience.

"Thought we were gonners, didn't you little brother?" Will laughed.

"I thought no such thing," he replied.

"Liar! Liar! Liar!" The shout was not in John's ear, but came from above where a sailor had been tricked into telling an untruth. The 16th of April being Liar's Monday, it was an old sea-going tradition that the first man caught in a lie would be condemned to spend the next week doing the dirtiest job aboard ship; namely, the daily cleaning of the beak head along which ranged the crew's latrines. It was also a dangerous job, there being no solid flooring under the prow. No one remembered how the tradition got started, but it served the useful purpose of getting a foul task done with the fewest complaints.

Lord Delaware, too, heard the shouts, and had to have them explained by chief mate Coolidge who was taking his turn at the helm. "A relief, Master Coolidge, a relief indeed." Delaware sighed. "Naught is worse than disorder among the men. There's no telling where it may lead." On that he turned and retired to his cabin. The mate shrugged, nodded to himself, and continued his watch at the whipstaff.

Leaving the Azores the fleet struck westward into the mid Atlantic on a course that should bring it in sight of Bermuda. For three weeks there would be nothing to see but sea, and as the days passed neither drilling nor dancing could eradicate the boredom or the shortening tempers. On the lower deck, dicing and griping were the principal pastimes; so much so that Gideon reported it to Brewster, and Brewster to Delaware.

"Discipline, Captain. Discipline and prayer." he snapped. "They're the only remedy for loose minds."

Brewster wouldn't have called either a remedy, but he wisely refrained from saying so. Two days later, the problem took care of itself. Storm clouds, freshing wind, and mounting seas kept the crew busy aloft and the passengers clinging to whatever was handy. The storm lasted little more than an hour and was over as suddenly as it came up, but the guardsmen's scrapes and bruises again gave them something new to grouse about.

On May 28, the strong winds that had made the voyage satisfyingly short, dropped away, leaving the two ships becalmed under a scorching sun. An ideal moment, Delaware decided, to deliver his Virginia homily to the assembled company.

"Perhaps, m'Lord, the cool of the evening might be preferred..." Chaplain Laurie began. But Delaware cut him short.

"Now is best. If the wind freshens we can be on our way."

Bohun, too, expressed concern about the heat, but his suggestion was as abruptly dismissed. "Prayers to follow, Master Laurie," Delaware told him. "Something uplifting. The twenty-third psalm might be good. I think that's the one that says something about still waters."

"Indeed, it does my Lord," Laurie assured him. "If I might say so, a most appropriate..." But Delaware had already left his cabin on his way to the quarter deck.

"Company and crew, stand to!" Brewster ordered. "Give ear to his Majesty's Lord Governor and Captain General of Virginia, the right honorable Sir Thomas West, Lord Delaware."

"Give a cheer to his Lordship, lads!" Sergeant Gideon's instruction generated a few reluctant hurrahs, and more shuffling of feet.

"Hurrah, my arse!" someone muttered. "Sod this for a game of sailors!" added another. But his Lordship was already mounting the stairway to the quarter deck, his mind fixed on his oration.

"Men, countrymen, fellow venturers into a great new world of opportunity," he began. "Our journey is near done. Within a very few days, with God's grace, you'll see our promised land of Virginia." The hurrahs were more heartfelt, but Gideon beat the deck with the butt of his halberd to silence them, and Delaware held up his hand and smiled benevolently down on his people.

"We know not what awaits at James Towne," he allowed. "You may have heard rumors that all has not been well there. But rumors are rarely right. I'm confident that we shall find the makings of a fine city which, with our help — your help — will thrive and prosper and make us the envy of all Mankind. That you come as soldiers is but a warning to the king of Spain that any attempt to unseat us will be futile." Then followed his standard condemnation of Catholicism, a warning against the insidious works of the Devil, and the assurance that heathens would be consigned to the pit that was bottomless. All this took a good ten minutes, and before he was through, most of his Lordship's sweating listeners were wishing him the same fate.

"We must recognize, however," Delaware went on, "that the savage Indians we shall confront in Virginia, may not speak our language and have yet to hear the words of our Lord. Though they are not as we, they are all God's children who can, with gentle instruction, be brought to his love and their salvation. In your dealings with the savages, remember always that we are civilized men. Now let us join our chaplain in prayer."

"Caps offs!" barked Gideon, and then in a lowered voice, "Down on your knees every goddam one of you!"

Chaplain Laurie was sweating like the rest. His ruff was sagging, and he wiped his forehead with his sleeve before beginning. "Oh merciful and gracious Lord in whom all things are perfect, look down upon your servant Sir Thomas and all who journey with him in the righteousness of England's cause, and bless our endeavor to bring thy love into the hearts of the ignorant savages so that they may dwell forever in thy grace." Laurie's pause prompted a smattering of "Amens," but he was only getting started.

"Let us pray, too, for the health of his Majesty King James and all his ministers, and also for the well-being of the noble Virginia Company, and all who..."

Suddenly a breeze tickled the limp sails, and Delaware interrupted. "Enough, Master Laurie. Well spoken; but enough."

"But the psalm, m'Lord, I haven't..."

"Another time. You're prayers are answered. We have a wind!" Then to Captain Tindall, "The ship is yours, sir."

As the trumpet blew and orders rang out, the congregation scrambled to its feet to avoid being trampled by running top-sail men and sailors. Canvas dropped and billowed, and within minutes sufficient sails were set to get the ship under way. Down below once again, John laughed and said, "We can thank the Lord for that!"

"Amen," Will added. But although it was slightly cooler out of the sun, the heat soon built up between the decks and around the sweating bodies. Before long men were calling for water and several collapsed onto their pallets gasping for breath. What conditions were like below on the orlop deck, Will hesitated to imagine. The stench rising up through the hatch grill was appalling, but probably no worse than the odor of the lower deck to which its inhabitants had long become accustomed. Daily swabbing with sea water and vinegar helped hardly at all.

Mercifully, the voyage was almost over. On Tuesday, June 5,

experienced crewmen detected a sweet smell in the air that reminded one of them of the scented aroma that wafted thirty leagues seaward from the southern coast of Spain. "It be land, to be sure!" he exclaimed. "I'll bet my britches on it!" No one took the wager, and a few minutes later the *Delaware's* lookout sighted twigs and other forest debris floating in the water. Pilot Dias estimated that the ships were ten or twelve leagues east of Cape Hatteras, and before long the air was filled with screeching gulls, welcome sounds audible below decks even over the rushing of the water. Three of the guardsmen laid low by the heat were still sick and being treated by Dr. Bohun, but the rest had come through their ordeal with nothing more than scratches and bruises. On Thursday, Sergeant Gideon called his men on deck in groups of eight. Will and John were among the first, and arrived to find the barrels they had seen earlier being hauled up from the hold contained the armor: breastplates, backplates, and helmets. "These ain't your cheap pot helmets," Gideon announced with pride. "These are morions, and although they don't have no plumes, they sets you apart from thems as is back of us." He pointed with a thumb in the direction of the trailing *Blessing*.

Although the morions were in the Spanish style and had wider brims than the ordinary pots or cabassets, they would prove harder to wear. But these had been provided from Lord Delaware's own store to ensure that his personal guard could parade as a presentable unit. The body armor, however, had been purchased by the Company, and in characteristic penny pinching it had bought some previously classified by the Tower armorers as 'unfit for modern service.' One size had to fit all, much of it ill matched and rusting. "Humph," said Gideon as he surveyed it. " Looks like there goin' to be a lot o' buffin' an' polishin' afore you gets ashore."

He was right. But no amount of shining could revitalize cracked leather and missing rivets. When that was reported to Delaware, he cursed the Company, unjustly blamed the cape merchant, then decided that for ceremonial purposes the guard would parade without its body armor. For Will and John who had donned it for the first time, that decree was a blessing. Their enthusiasm for wearing armor had quickly waned when they found how heavy it turned out to be. Standing in the sun encased in steel was not a happy prospect. But those of the guard who had seen service in Ireland said that they preferred its weight to an arrow in the chest. John, however, hoped that the American Indians would prove less hostile than the wild Irish, and said so.

"You wanna bet?" laughed one veteran. "You mark me well, young friends, savages are savages the world over. They'll be shootin' at us, sure as there's pips in apples." That had come to be known as guardsman Chris Bailey's pet phrase, and had earned him the nickname Pips. He hailed from the village of Hartfield north of Withyham, but had served the Delaware's as a cooper since he was fourteen. He was now forty or more, and though so much older than both Will and John, he had become their friend and military mentor. "Stay 'side old Pips," he'd say, "and you'll be safe as the Tower o' London." And they never doubted him.

Passing well to seaward of the Hatteras shoals, the fleet sailed north out of sight of land for a day and a half, and when Tindall ordered the helmsmen to steer three points to nor' nor' west, the shoreline still remained hidden by a wall of low-lying mist. Not until three hours after sun up on June 7 did it clear. "Land to!" came the shout from the main top, and by then the ribbon of the shore was high on the horizon.

From the poop deck Delaware had an opportunity to use his new toy, the telescope that Galileo had invented only two years earlier. Purchased in Holland, the scope was of shining brass with the eye-piece cradled in silver. It came in its own leather sleeve, with a cap held in place with woven gold threads. "There," he said passing the instrument to Sir Ferdinando Wainman, "now you can see what the eye can't see."

"Would that our guns could shoot as far," Wainman replied with less enthusiasm than his admiral would have liked. Sir Ferdinando was suspicious of gadgets.

"The telescope will be as important to the future of navigation as the compass or the astrolabe," Delaware insisted. "Mark me, it'll change the world." An hour later, his glass picked out the promontory of Cape Henry.

"Why not let Jenkins, our top man, use your glass?" Captain Brewster suggested. "He can see much better from up there."

"Certainly not!" Delaware snapped. "If he dropped it, where would I be?" With that he thrust the telescope into its case and marched back to his quarters.

Brewster let out a deep breath. His Lordship was a fine man, but he could be mighty waspish and petty when his head hurt. Dr. Bohun had heard the exchange and knowing the signs, followed his master back to the Great Cabin. A testy arrival would be in no one's best interest; he was sure of that.

"Eight fathoms!" called the lead man. "Five!" then "Fowle water!" as the ship's passage stirred the sandy bottom.

The date was June 8, and Sir Thomas West, Lord De La Warr and Governor General for Life, was about to assume control of what he hoped was already a successful and burgeoning dominion.

Chapter Five

❧

M id afternoon found his Lordship rested and in a better mood. "Tell the carpenters to build me a cross," he ordered. "I shall plant it here at the cape as a memorial to this historic day, and Master Laurie will lead us in a prayer of thanksgiving for our safe arrival."

Captain Tindall suggested that as they were about to go ashore, trailing a seine to catch fish might be a good idea. Delaware agreed.

"We'll be wise to take a few musket men with us," Captain Brewster advised. "Just in case."

Delaware agreed to that too, but added that he didn't expect any trouble from the savages. "If there are any hereabouts, they'll surely run off when they see us coming," he confidently declared. Nevertheless, Brewster chose four of his guardsmen, two of them being Will and John Jefferys. If asked why he chose them, he would have answered that theirs was a name he could easily remember. However, the brothers naively supposed that they were selected because of their recognized worth, and when others who were not to be the first to land, guessed at the real explanation, they dismissed it as understandable jealousy. But no matter the reason, getting off the *Delaware* into the longboat and feeling the sea breeze, was a joy to be savored. Disembarking and waiting with them for the arrival of their Governor, were Chaplain Laurie, Dr. Bohun, pilot Dias, and Captain Brewster, as well as six oarsmen, two of whom would do duty as fishermen. When, eventually, Delaware descended the ladder, it was very evident that he was dressed for prayers and not for fishing.

As neither of the elected fishermen had ever cast a net, the first try wrapped it around the tiller and the second got it caught on the hilt of his Lordship's sword. On the third attempt a weight hit Dias behind the ear as the boat drifted northward on the rising tide. The fourth was more successful in so far that the net landed in the water. It also drew attention from the shore where several Indians had emerged from the woods to witness this demonstration of the strangers' art of net casting.

As the boat neared the beach the Indians retreated to the edge of the woods and watched as the netters disembarked and began to haul it in. Meanwhile, all but two of the oarsmen waded ashore, Delaware in the lead followed by Will carrying the cross and John two spades. While his Lordship dropped to one knee and doffed his hat, his chaplain said a prayer calling on the Almighty to bless him and those who served under him. The net-pullers then brought their seine to shore and to the amazement of all, had landed a remarkable number and variety of fish. Delaware called it a gift from God and the best of all omens, and three of the evidently impressed savages cautiously approached the catch.

"We come in friendship," Delaware announced with a flourish of his hat. "In the name of our Savior our Lord Jesus Christ, we bid you share his bounty, for he, too, was a fisherman."

"I don't think they understand English," Laurie volunteered in a half whisper.

"*Matakennowntorawh*," replied the lead Indian.

As neither knew what the other was saying, Lord Delaware's first encounter with the native population was conducted with smiles, friendly gestures and shared fish. The Indians watched with interest as John dug a hole and Will erected the cross, and recognized that some sort of ritual accompanied its setting up. Before returning to the boat Chaplain Laurie blessed the savages and welcomed them into the family of civilized men. As the boat pulled away the amused and at the same time puzzled Indians gathered round the cross, one repeatedly prodding it with his forefinger. Others gathered up their share of the still-flipping fish out of the sand.

"An excellent beginning," Delaware exclaimed. "Fish in abundance, and simple people ripe and ready to hear the Word. A fertile field, Master Laurie, a fertile field!"

"I dare'st hope so, my Lord," Laurie cautiously replied.

Before the longboat reached the *Delaware*, more good news appeared on the horizon. The missing *Hercules* was catching up, having been blown off course after leaving the Azores. By nightfall all three ships were reunited and at anchor off Point Comfort at the mouth of the Chesapeake. Yet more news reached his Lordship the next morning with the arrival of Captain James Davies who had been rowed out from Fort Algernon.

The approach of the Captain's shallop had been sighted almost as soon as it left shore, and by the time it reached the fleet Delaware's guards were in parade order on the main deck. Not being sure of the visitor's rank, he and his officers assembled on the quarter deck. From there, if warranted, they could graciously step down to add further emphasis to the grandeur of the greeting. But because none of them knew Davies, he had first to give his name and state his business to the boatswain who called them out in the redolent tones of a town crier.

"Welcome, good Captain," his Lordship declared, as he descended the steps to the main deck. "You are a face most heartily welcome. Have you news of the *Sea Venture?*" he quickly asked.

"Indeed, Sir. Governor Gates and Admiral Somers and all their company are safely landed."

"Do you hear that?" Delaware called to anyone in earshot. "Thanks be to God, the *Sea Venture* is safe arrived!"

"Well, my Lord... Her people are safe arrived, but the ship is lost."

"But at James Towne? All is well there, I trust?"

"Sir, I have much to tell you..."

"Indeed, you do. But first a cup of wine," Delaware said, as he ushered Davies into the Great Cabin. As he poured the wine, he enthused over his first meeting with the Indians. "Simple, honest fellows, almost as naked as the day they were born. But we mustn't hold that against them, eh?" he laughed. "Adam and Eve entered the

Garden of Eden without raiment, and look what God's love did for them. Drink up, and tell me all."

As Davies did so, the smile faded from Delaware's cheeks. "Leave? They plan to leave, to abandon his Majesty's colony?" he gasped. "Treason, sir! That is naught but treason! And you?"

Davies replied that he was ordered to destroy Fort Algernon, and stand ready to board the *Virginia* pinnace which even then lay rigged and ready to sail. He added that he was expecting Gates and Argall to bring the remaining ships down to rendez-vous with him at the entrance to the Chesapeake. "In a tide or two they'll be here," he predicted.

"The devil they will!" Delaware, rasped. "I'll see them sink first!"

"But, my Lord, they have no choice," Davies pleaded. "The savages are as fast killing us without as the famine and pestilence do within."

"No choice, man? Of course, they had a choice! They could have done their duty!" Delaware told Davies, before dismissing him and calling his officers to the cabin.

"Remember your health," Dr. Bohun begged him.

"Damn my health, sir!"

The repetition of Davies information was received with protestations of amazement, and with even more surprise when Delaware said that he would sooner sink the fugitives in the river than have them escape. "Master Gunner," he ordered, "see that we are prepared. Captain Tindall, get under way as soon as wind and tide will let you. Now leave me, all of you."

Dr. Bohun was the last to do so. He stopped to say something, and then thought better of it. His Lordship needed time to compose both his thoughts and himself.

Delaware paced the cabin floor several times, thumped the bulkhead with his fist, and then sagged dejectedly onto his cot. To have come so far only to find this situation, it seemed that God was laughing at him, maybe at all Englishmen for attempting to challenge Spain in the New World. Ralegh had tried and failed three times in Virginia. His colony in New England had lasted less than a year, and the reports from James Towne had never been as encouraging as the Company gave out. Was he now doomed to follow in Sir Walter's footsteps? And in spite of all he had said, in the final analysis would it not be he who would be blamed for this latest fiasco? It wouldn't be Gates or Somers. Oh no, not they! They were more likely to be lauded for having saved the crew and passengers from the *Sea Venture*. But, compose himself he would. Before leaving the cabin Sir Ferdinando had advised caution, and maybe he was right. Virginia's new governor drew in a deep breath and stood up. Keeping an open mind, he decided, had to be better than one already closed.

The order to prepare the ship for battle produced a rush of overhead activity that quickly descended to the lower deck as gunners mates and quarter gunners took up their stations, unlashing the britchings and running out the guns.

"Anyone down here smokin' tobaccy?" the gunner's mate demanded. "If you be, douse it now!" He wanted no sparks anywhere near the powder cartridges being brought forward from the gun room. Four and one-half inch solid iron shot for the demi-culverines were ready in troughs beside the guns. However, it was not yet time to remove touch hole covers, to pour the priming powder or ignite the match. But it *was* time to wonder who they would be shooting at. The consensus had it either that Spaniards had been sighted in the river or that the message from Fort Algernon was that the Dons were already in control of James Towne. To the gunners, knowing whether the enemy was ashore or afloat made all the difference. Broadsiding the enemy's ships should be within the guns' 830 yards' point-blank range, but firing from the river at the land would mean elevating the muzzles and rendering them much less effective at their maximum range of 5000 yards. In answer to a question from Will, one of the gunners replied, "It cuts both ways. Broadside to broadside, there's a lot o' wood flying, and a lot of blood runnin'. But at long range their shot will likely lodge in our timbers and do us no harm. You can waste a lot o' powder that way," he added.

About half an hour later, the gunner's mate came below with

news that no one was ready to believe. Delaware was preparing to fire on English ships reported to be moving down river toward him.

"Fire on our own people," guardsman Pips gasped, "why would he want to do that?"

"You must have gotten it wrong," another insisted. "No Englishman would do that!"

"Just tellin' you what I heard," the mate replied. "You can take it or leave it."

Above, on the quarter deck, master gunner Miles Morecomb reported that his ordnance was ready. However, the wind was not. Blowing from west south west it favored the departing colonists already aboard their four small ships. They were the *Deliverance* and *Patience* constructed in Bermuda by the *Sea Venture* survivors, Captain Davies' *Virginia* built by the northern colonists in 1607, and the *Discovery*, the smallest of the original expedition's three ships. Rather than again risking all their leaders in one wreck, Gates was to command the *Deliverance,* Somers the *Patience,* and George Percy the *Discovery.* Together they had agreed to head north to the Newfoundland fishing banks hoping to fall in with other less laden English ships. Meanwhile, still out of sight near Point Comfort, longboats of Lord Delaware's fleet ferried messages of instruction – and surprised responses – between the flagship, and the *Blessing* and *Hercules.*

A worried Captain Tindall approached his admiral on the quarter deck. "My Lord, if the winds stands as it does, we'll not be able to move with any deliberation before dark. There'll be every chance that the James Towne ships'll slip by us in the night."

Delaware knew him to be right, and instructed Captain Brewster to man the *Delaware's* skiff and head up river to intercept.

"And what am I to say?" Brewster asked. "It's not for me to arrest the governor."

"Well, tell him..." Delaware wasn't sure what to tell him. "Tell him... that we are here to assist him, that we are...er, joyful in the news of his salvation, and that... Oh, just tell him to heave to and drop anchor!"

As he had before, Brewster chose the Jefferys brothers as part of his escort. With the *Delaware's* bos'n at the helm and eight of her oarsmen rowing, the skiff made slow progress up river against a fast falling tide. Although the light boat was rigged with a spritsail, the contrary wind made it of little use. Nevertheless, eighteen miles later, they came to Mulberry Point on the north shore, and just around the three English ships riding at anchor. Brewster immediately ordered the admiral's banner unfurled and fired a pistol to attract attention. But he had no need to do so. From the poop deck of the *Deliverance* Sir Thomas Gates saw the boat the moment it rounded the point.

By the time Brewster's skiff came abreast of the moored fleet and slid alongside the *Deliverance*, departing colonists were hanging over the sides of all three ships. Those fit enough to do so were scaling rigging to get a better view of what was afoot. When word passed from one ship to another that Lord Delaware had come, a few cheers went up from *Sea Venture* people only to be matched by the cursing of James Towne evacuees who saw their hopes of escaping to England vanish. Aboard the little *Discovery* the widowed Maggie Beale quietly wept.

What had passed between Captain Brewster and Lord Delaware's deputy governor aboard the *Deliverance* remained a mystery to the crew of the skiff, but when Gates and Somers stepped down into it, John Jefferys was surprised by their joviality. These, after all, were men whom his Lordship stood ready to sink in the river. Nevertheless, Sir George Somers with great good humor, urged the crew to bend to their oars. "Row, row, good fellows!" he laughed. "You are a crew of angels, so carry us swiftly on your wings!"

Surveying his sweating companions, Will thought them a singularly scruffy bunch of angels. Neither he nor John could hear what was being said in the stern of the boat, but from all they could see, the conversation was animated, even festive, with much slapping of knees and loud laughter. Brewster, however, appeared reserved, though answering the laughter with polite smiles and nods. Meanwhile, aboard his flagship, the Governor for Life steeled himself to receive his old friends with all the grace he could muster.

The trumpeter blew, Tom Dowse beat his drum, and the rest of his Lordship's elite provided an impressive guard of honor for visitors who looked anything but impressive. Their hair was long, their beards unkempt, and their clothes torn and dirty. They looked, as indeed they were – two men who had endured incredible hardships. But Gates' and Somers' steps were firm and their smiles expansive. Laughed Gates, "My good Lord, we are well met!"

"Sir Thomas, well met indeed," Delaware declared loudly for all to hear. "And you, worthy Sir George, you are thrice welcome." Then to the ship's company, he added. "The Lord of Hosts has delivered our noble friends from the jaws of evil. What greater manifestation of His blessing can be lighted upon this Christian colony than is shown to us at this historic moment? God's blessing upon us all!"

"Three cheers for Sir Thomas Gates and Sir George Somers!" Sergeant Gideon shouted. And this time the response was loud and unanimous.

Delaware led his guests into his cabin, but when Sir Ferdinando and other officers moved to follow, he waved them away. Only Dr. Bohun and the Reverend Laurie were to hear what was about to be said. "Be seated. Be seated. A glass, gentlemen, to make your story the more smoothly told?"

Gates and Somers readily accepted, as did Bohun who was relieved to see his patient so cordial. "Now," said Delaware, "tell us everything. Omit nothing."

"Well, my Lord," Gates began, "your fleet had made a good passage until July of last year when we saw a hurricano approaching from the north east. The skies darkened, the wind grew to full gale and..."

"Yes, yes, I know all about that," Delaware snapped. "Get to the point."

Gates looked puzzled. "The point, my Lord?"

"The point, sirrah, the point!"

"The point was that we were wrecked, and by God's grace..."

"James Towne, Sir Thomas." Delaware drummed his fingers impatiently on the table. "Get to James Towne! How was't when you got there?"

"Dire, my Lord, most dire."

"Dire indeed," Somers added.

Gates had sensed that Delaware's initial cordiality was more tactical than real, and so he now launched into a graphic defense of his actions. He told how on his arrival he was horrified to find that out of the five hundred souls brought out by the rest of his fleet, only sixty survived. All the others had died of starvation or had been cut down by the savages. "And of those which were living were so meager and lean," he went on, "that it was lamentable to behold. Many through extreme hunger had run out of their beds naked, so lean that they looked like anatomies, crying out we are starved. Others we believed to have gone to bed in health were found dead the next morning." Gates vehemently assured Delaware, that there was nothing he could do to improve their lot. The supplies sent out in 1609 were all gone, and coming from Bermuda he carried only a few hogs and turtles to feed his hundred as they continued to Virginia.

"But 'tis spring time. What of their plantings?' Delaware demanded.

"They were too weak to work and had eaten their seed corn."

"There are fish in the river, are there not?"

"They were too starved to man their boats," Gates assured him, "and unable to leave the fort for fear of the savages."

"Unable?"

"Unwilling, then," Gates allowed. "But you have to remember, m'Lord, that these people were at the point of death, walking cadavers. Indeed, many still are."

"So, ill provisioned though you were, you thought it best to abandon our colony and take your chances on the ocean?"

"We did. In council, we so determined," Gates replied, carefully spreading the responsibility in his answer.

"You did not think it prudent to await our arrival?" Delaware's voice was ice cold.

"We had no certainty when you might arrive, or even that you were coming," Somers explained. He went on to point out that Sir Walter's colony on Roanoke Island had sent for supplies in '87.

Three years later they still had not been shipped, by which time the colony had vanished.

Delaware knew that to be true, but he was in no mood to concede anything. Instead, he charged that James Towne's governors should have put duty before dishonor. Nothing, he thundered, was more dishonorable than failing to defend one's fort to the last man. "Get you back to your ships. Return them whence they came. See that they are unloaded and your people back in the fort by noon tomorrow. Have them stand to, and await our coming. Your council and all your commissions are hereby canceled pending my review."

"But, my Lord we..." Gates began.

"That is all, gentlemen. I bid you good day." Delaware waved them away, and the two men left the cabin with dismay and astonishment writ large on their faces. Will and John were still in the skiff ready to escort the lieutenant governor and his admiral back to their ships, but were ordered back aboard the *Delaware* leaving only the rowers in the boat. Although Captain Brewster escorted Gates and Somers to the rail, he was charged to accompany them no further. So ended Lord Delaware's first meeting with his new subordinates. They had come aboard exuding relief and gratitude; they were leaving humiliated and despairing.

From the rail of the *Virginia*, Maggie Beale and others watched anxiously as the long boat returned. Although, given the chance, most of the survivors would vote to go home, they felt sure their officers would think differently. Thus, when Gates and Somers returned with no expressions of joy, several optimists read the omens as meaning that Lord Delaware had agreed to abandon the colony. But their hopes were soon dashed. Word passed quickly from ship to ship that at dawn, everyone would disembark and return to their former places in the fort. Cover against a possible Indian attack would be provided by musketeers from among the *Sea Venture* survivors.

Maggie, like so many of her companions, lay down on the afterdeck to sleep, taking such respite from the day's heat as a light wind afforded her. Staring up at the stars she questioned why God had made her suffer so long, then allowed her a glimpse of salvation one day only to snatch it away the next.

For Will, John, and their fellow guardsmen, there was to be no sleeping under the stars. All they had to stare at was the deck planking over their heads. But almost to a man they, too, were nervously wondering what the unexpected turn of events would mean for them. Their officers had told them little, but the gunners drawing back and securing the artillery, assured questioners that the need had passed. No ships would be challenged, no broadsides fired. Will was disappointed; he had wanted to hear the guns roar and share the excitement of action. John, on the other hand, had no desire to be deafened or run over by recoiling carriages. Above, in the Great Cabin, Lord Delaware's consultation with his three sail captains and his principal land officers stretched late into the night. When they left no one was in any doubt about their commander's intentions. No matter what might face them in the fort, there would be no abandonment, no failures condoned, no feigned sickness forgiven, and no revisionism tolerated.

The Lord Governor's word would be law, and woe betide anyone unwise enough to think otherwise. "This," he declared, "I shall make publicly clear on the morrow."

Dr. Bohun shook his head and hoped that the morrow would be cooler. "Amen," added Chaplain Laurie. If, however, he uttered up such a prayer, it was not answered. The morning of Sunday, June 10, dawned hot and humid, with very little wind to stir trees or fill sails. Nevertheless, by noon, Delaware's order had been obeyed. Everyone was ashore from Gates' three ships, and most of the scant supplies were back in the fort by the time the arriving fleet anchored off James Towne Island. Delaware viewed the activity through his telescope, but could not distinguish between the healthy *Sea Venture* survivors and the supposedly sick and starving settlers.

"Right you are, me lads," Sergeant Gideon shouted. "Now's the time for you to shine. This what you're here for; so let's see you be a credit to me and our captain." The guardsmen were to land ahead of the officers, and stand in file on either side of the approach to the fort gate. This they did — for an hour and a half before his Majesty's Governor and Captain General stepped down into the long boat to be rowed ashore. With him were Sir Ferdinando Wainman, sailing Captain Tindall, Captain Brewster, two more land captains and as many lieutenants, along with Bohun and Laurie. Behind them rowed boats from the *Blessing* and *Hercules* carrying more naval and military officers. By the time all three boats had beached and their passengers were ashore and had sorted themselves into hierarchical order, the honor guard was wilting, its helmets so hot as be scorching to the touch.

"Nice weather we're 'aving, eh?" grinned Pips.

"Always the funny one," John whispered.

"Well, at least it ain't rainin'."

"Stand to!" Gideon ordered as the procession moved forward from the sandy shore. A short stretch of grassland separated the beach from the fort's wooden palisades. The grass was long on either side of the heavily traveled track and was dotted with shrubs and young trees growing where others had been cut down. The fort itself was built from the trunks of small trees set side-by-side in the ground, and lashed together by vines and a few tree-nailed boards that appeared to be repairs necessitated when some of the poles had began to yawn. Its open gates were fashioned from planks, but their weight had caused the supporting posts to lean, thereby making it difficult to open and close them. Had Delaware arrived three weeks earlier, he would have found them off their hinges altogether. All this he took in as he stepped ashore to survey his inheritance.

Sir Thomas Gates and his senior officers were waiting at the gates. Among them was George Percy, who had been in command before his arrival; George Yeardley, aged 23, who had served with Gates in the Netherlands; and Captain Samuel Argall, who had arrived with the 1609 fleet after sixty-nine days at sea. Aged 30, Argall was both an experienced navigator and a seasoned soldier. Furthermore, he had a potentially useful link to his new governor by virtue of being the brother-in law of Lady Cecilia Delaware's uncle. Connections could be important.

Another *Sea Venture* survivor, the 38 year-old William Strachey, a man ever anxious to ingratiate himself, had been appointed the colony's secretary by Gates after the previous incumbent drowned. Now he was given the honor of carrying Lord Delaware's standard, and he made the most of it.

Before approaching the waiting leaders, Delaware doffed his hat, went down on his knees and silently prayed— and at some length. Everyone present, therefore, had the opportunity to recognize that the new governor was a devout Christian and, they hoped, a man of compassion. They had the first right and the second completely wrong.

His praying done, Delaware brushed the dust from his knees, adjusted his cloak, put his hat back on, and marched purposefully up to the fort gates. Strachey, with an extravagant bow, dipped the standard and swept the ground with it in greeting.

"Welcome, my Lord Governor," said Gates loudly. The settlers standing around at the entrance watched the arrival with looks both resentful and suspicious. Had Delaware taken the time to evaluate his reception he would have recognized that he would have much work to do to win the trust and loyalty of his people. But winning popularity was not in his Lordship's mind. What he saw was a rag-tag gaggle of colonists and the carriages for several cannon standing abandoned at the gates. "Why, sirrah," he demanded of Gates, "are your pieces not mounted on these carriages? Are they still aboard?"

"No, m'Lord, We buried them."

"You did what?"

"We buried the guns in the ditch...to keep them from the enemy."

Delaware removed his hat and fanned himself with it as he grew purple and then white with rage. "You buried our guns to keep them from the naked savages?"

"No, m'Lord, from the Spaniards, should they come."

"And come they would, Sir Thomas. Oh, yes, they would come! And do you suppose they wouldn't have the wit to find the guns in a freshly filled ditch?"

"My Lord," Gates explained, "the guns are heavy and our men

sick unto death. The best they could do was to run them out into the ditch. Indeed, Sir, few had the strength to dig enough dirt to cover them. We did all we could."

Delaware had only to look about him to see the truth of that. Grudgingly, he admitted that such might be so, and added that retrieving the guns and repairing their carriages would be one of the first duties of his arriving troops. "The fort has a bell, does it not?" he asked.

"Aye, my Lord," said Yeardley.

"Then in one hour, ring it! I want every living soul, no matter how sick, out in this square or whatever you call it..."

"'Tis the market place."

"Is it indeed? And on market days who comes to buy and sell?"

"The savages used to m'Lord." Yeardley replied. "'Tis just a name, an English name."

Delaware replied with a derisive snort as he set off around the fort on his first inspection. Meanwhile, his guard had broken ranks and with their sergeant's permission were commandeering empty houses as their quarters. Will and John surveyed the options, none of them very appealing. The thatched roofs of some had collapsed inward under the weight of winter snow; several had been stripped of boards to repair others; some had burned, and more stood empty, robbed of anything portable in the hours when Indians overran the vacated fort.

"How about this one?" John asked as he pushed open the door of a single-room dwelling. The space was a little less than their attic bed chamber in England, but it had a chimney built from from sticks and mud, and beside it a bed frame constructed from charred wood and nailed firmly to the wall. A couple of Indian pots lay unbroken beside the hearth. Will concluded that the savages weren't interested in carrying away pots of their own making. "Aye, this'll do right well, providing Gideon'll let us keep it."

"Why wouldn't he?" John answered. "We got here first." The words were scarcely out of his mouth when a dark figure appeared silhouetted in the doorway.

"This be my house! Get you out of it!" Maggie Beale had returned. A ragged blanket slung as a sack over her shoulder contained the few belongings she had been able to take with her when Gates ordered the fort evacuated. "This is mine. My hubby built it. So get you gone!" she snapped.

"We're right sorry, mistress," John began. " But we were told..."

"I don't care what you were told," Maggie replied. "This be my house. 'Tis all I've got, and no well-fed young louts is goin' to take it from me!"

Together, the brothers assured her that they had no such intention. "If you'll pardon us, we'll seek another before they're all taken," Will told her.

They would have been out of the door and on their way had Maggie not been standing there. "Wait," she said. "What say you to sharing?" When Will demurred, she demanded to know why not. "You'll be better in here than a tent. As for me, I'll be better off with two of the governor's men to watch out for me than I would be on me own."

"But it wouldn't be proper for us..." John began.

"Proper, my eye!" Maggie told him. "You keep your hands and your eyes where they belong, and we'll get along like bread an' cheese... if I 'ad any. You do men's work, and I'll do mine. You'll find that I'm good with me needle. And if you bring me aught to cook, I'll show you that I'm good at that too."

So it was that the lives of Margaret Beale of Bermondsey and the Jefferys brothers of Withyham became fatefully entwined.

Chapter Six

❧⟨❧⟩

L ord Delaware's progress around his domain was watched in silence by the old colonists, none wanting to be the first to bid him welcome. He, in turn, said nothing to them; no smiles or waves of encouragement. It was as though they did not exist, so intent was he in focusing on what he considered to be the essentials. What he saw were the conditions that had prompted his predecessor to pack up and go home. Sir Thomas Gates, however, had had no supply-laden fleet to enable him to remedy his inherited ills. Consequently, the new Governor and Captain General's outlook was fundamentally different. He was not there to commiserate but to lay blame and to correct, and he intended to make both very clear. The small troop of officers following him on his tour was ready to answer questions or offer explanations, but none were sought. Indeed, not until Delaware returned to the market place and entered the church did his emotions get the better of him.

"God's blood! Have you men no shame, that you should let Our Lord's house come to this?" He waved his hand around, pointing in disbelief at the breached roof and the scattered remnants of benches dismantled to be used as firewood. In the empty chancel mud and wattle walls damaged by ice and winter storms had been reduced to bared stick lathes and piles of powdered clay in which weeds were already growing. Like the rest of the settlement, the ruinous church spoke loudly of nature's regeneration and Man's neglect.

"Gentlemen, your renewed labors begin here," Delaware declared in a voice that brooked no argument. "I want this church rebuilt, repaired, renovated, and made pleasing unto Our Lord. And I want it done now. At this juncture our spiritual needs far exceed our temporal. The Lord our God is looking down upon us, and he is not pleased. Until we are manifestly worthy in His eyes, we shall not prosper." Then to Gates, "How oft are divine services held here?"

Taken by surprise, Gates stammered, "Well, I'd say...I don't know...I think the good Reverend Buck is the man to answer that." But he wasn't.

"Under the circumstance, m'Lord, I deemed it best to let each man pray as..."

"Did you, indeed?" Delaware snapped. "Then, sir, you contributed to the malaise of mind that allowed this place to fall into such disrepair. Shame upon you, sir, shame, shame!"

He went on to say that his own Chaplain Laurie would help and provide the luckless incumbent with instruction that would bring the flock firmly back into the fold. The church bell would be rung every morning at ten o'clock to summon the settlers to prayer and again at four. Sermons were to be delivered every Thursday and twice on Sundays. The word of God would henceforth be in every mouth and praise in every heart — or his Lordship would want to know the reason why.

It came as no surprise, therefore, that the new governor began his administration with prayers and a sermon from the still-trembling Reverend Buck. That was followed by the reading of his commission by his usual standard-bearer, Ensign Anthony Scot, a lengthy exercise that had many feet shuffling and several frail colonists passing out in the heat.

"We, the said council," Scot read, "having considered the great and zealous affection which you Sir Thomas West, Knight, Lord De La Warr, have in many ways manifest unto us and for the furtherance and advancing of the plantation..." Scot proved to be a better flag holder than he was a herald, and his reading of the handwritten document was halting, often incoherent and lost to those at the back of the crowd. However, the wording made clear, for those who could hear it, that no matter what Delaware might think of Gates's prior performance, he was to be confirmed as lieutenant governor, and that Somers was to be chief admiral, and Wainman master of the horse. That brought a laugh from somewhere in the crowd, everyone being aware that apart from those now arriving, every horse had been eaten.

"And master of the ordnance," Delaware hurriedly added.

The event was being further prolonged by the formality of Gates surrendering his commission and having it returned naming him to be what he had been already, the colony's lieutenant governor.

"It be past lambing time at home," John Jefferys sighed. "I wonder how our Ma be faring?"

Before Will could answer, Lord Delaware's voice penetrated to and beyond the edges of the crowd. His irritation at the length and quality of the reading, coupled with the growing inattention of the sweating assemblage, was all too apparent when he began his own oration. He was never the kind of speaker who began with an icebreaking joke. On the contrary, he was not there to be loved but to be obeyed, and for that no honeyed words were necessary. "Gentlemen, and fellow Englishmen, you have heard my commission read to you. You will know that I am your governor and shall be so as long as the good Lord chooses to spare me. And, if you will recall, the closing line of that commission empowers me to deviate from it as circumstances may warrant. That means that in all things I am the law, the jury, and the judge. I know that some of you," he went on, "have suffered mightily and I commend you for your fortitude. But others, many others, have put all at risk through their idleness and vanities, and may well be to blame for the calamities that has befallen this colony. If I find this to be so, I shall be compelled the draw the sword of justice, to cut off such delinquents." A sword, he added, that he would much prefer to wield in their defense.

It was evident from the faces in front of him that the prospect of the sword of justice flailing in their direction was not one to savor, and the tag line about it being used in their defense failed to register the wielder as a man of compassion forced against his will.

Commented one old settler, "That means he can 'ave your head 'afore breakfast and nobody can say him nay." Delaware would have been pleased to have heard him, because that was precisely the impression he intended to leave.

In the days that followed, Will and John grew to appreciate their good fortune in finding Maggie Beale. Although she had been at James Towne less than a year — she had come aboard the battered 1609 fleet — she knew everybody and everybody knew her and admired her ability to survive. Food brought by Delaware's ship was strictly rationed, but with three shares to work with, she managed to keep them fed, made more palatable by the inclusion of herbs and roots, knowledge gained from the Indians in days before the great falling out.

"What falling out?" John had asked.

"'Twas that John Martin what had been our president," Maggie explained. She told how he had gone down river in the fall to trade with the Nansemond Indians who lived on the other side of the river. But instead of trading he seized their chief, took their village and set himself up in it, violating their temple and burial monuments. Before long the Nansemonds rallied, saved their king, and took away a thousand bushels of corn. "That would have fed us for months," Maggie said bittery, "but that rat-livered Martin didn't go after them. He just let it go. Then he came back and left a nice young lad, Lieutenant Sicklemore, I think his name was... left him down there to guard whatever they'd built."

Maggie went on to confess that she didn't know what happened next. "But 'twas said that some of his men mutinied and took a boat away to England. And that poor Master Sicklemore..." She stopped and shook her head. "It was 'orrible, right 'orrible what they did to him."

Pressed by Will, Maggie went on to tell how Sicklemore had abandoned the Nansemond outpost and crossed the river to buy food from the previously friendly Kecoughtan Indians. But they must have already known what Martin had done to the Nansemonds and so murdered Sicklemore and all his men, stuffing their mouths with bread and leaving their corpses to be found by the next party that came down from James Towne to trade for food. "So we had bloody John Martin to thank for that," Maggie said in disgust. "Them savages get to know things far quicker than we do, and so by winter none of them would truck with us. It pleasured them to watch us starve."

That same first evening as John and Will squatted on the floor – they had yet to make any furniture – they urged Maggie to tell them all she knew about the Indians. Across the market place, on the other side of the settlement, Lord Delaware was asking the same question. "This Powhatan, what's he like?"

"Old," replied George Percy, who was of the few remaining at James Towne who had met him. "For a savage he's unusual tall, but well proportioned. He looks as though his body has been toughened by hard labor, but his gray hair and his beard are so thin that they're hard to see. He is old, maybe in his sixties. Or he could be seventy. 'Tis hard to tell with savages. They tend to look old early. But whatever his age, he's still dangerous. He'll cheat us if he is able, and kill us when he can. He is sly as a fox, but when he chooses he can coo like a dove."

"An interesting combination of talents, Master Percy," Delaware replied. "Tell me more."

Percy thought for a moment. "He's not above sending one tribe to attack us and claim that they did it on their own. He has a passion for blue beads. John Smith had a good relation with him, gave him weapons..."

"Did he, indeed," Delaware coldly observed.

"...and he gave him an English bed and sent Dutchmen to build him a house. Captain Smith even gave the bastard a red robe and put a tin crown on his head. Made him a king. It was really very funny."

"Not to me," Delaware snapped. "The next time there's to be a ceremony, it'll be when he comes here and kneels in submission to me. So what of the Dutchmen?"

Percy shrugged. "They never came back." He went on to explain that several Englishmen who disappeared during the starving winter were thought to have run away to join them. "But we don't know whether Powhatan took them in or had them killed."

Delaware grunted and muttered that, "We must hope...or *they* must hope that he did." Then out loud to Percy, "You spoke of this savage cheating us. An example?"

Then the governor and his aides sat in silence as Percy told them what had happened to council member John Ratcliffe when, in the fall of the previous year, he had gone to buy corn from Powhatan at his village on the Pamunkey River. With a party of thirty men, Ratcliffe sailed a pinnace up the river to Orapakes where Powhatan and his people received them graciously. They feasted him and gave him lodging. The next day, Ratcliffe and a few others were taken to Powhatan's food store and there bartered for bushels of grain. The exchange was going amicably until one of Ratcliffe's party whispered to him that Powhatan was cheating.

"How so?" Delaware demanded.

Percy went on to explain that as the baskets were being filled, the Indians holding them were pushing up the bottoms to make them appear to be holding more than they were. Ratcliffe challenged Powhatan. Powhatan denied it. Ratcliffe persisted. Powhatan walked out. The deal was off.

"I see," Delaware was unimpressed. "So the savage cheated. Many a villain in England has given short measure. So that was the end of it?"

"Would that it were," Percy answered. "When our people were making their way back to the ship, the savages picked them off one by one, until only Master Ratcliffe was left. They seized him, tied him to a tree, and lit a fire at his feet. Then women — women, mark you, with sharpened shells and reeds, they began to flay the flesh from his face. And when they were done, men cut off his limbs and threw them into the fire while he yet lived. He has yet to be avenged," Percy added.

"A foolish fellow not to have guarded his flanks," was Delaware's first response. "But how know you all this, if no one lived to tell of it?"

Percy explained that Captain Newport had given a thirteen-year-old boy named Thomas Savage to Powhatan in exchange for a trusted servant named Namontack, each to learn the other's language. Newport took Namontack to England and brought him back, but he had gone a second time and had not yet returned.

"That's not entirely so," Gates interjected. "He was aboard the *Sea Venture* with another, the Indian Machumps, when we struck. 'Tis said that there was some falling out betwixt the two. I know not what 'twas, but some say that Machumps killed him."

"So where is this Machumps now?" Delaware demanded.

"He returned at once to Powhatan, m' Lord."

"There is something you should know about our relations with the savages," Percy volunteered. He went on to explain that almost from the outset, in an effort to woo the Indians the Council had set aside a native-style hut for the accommodation of visiting Indians. Until the previous winter there was frequent commercial exchanges conducted within the fort. "'Twas to the advantage of all," Percy insisted. "And we still have a tame savage of our own. His name is Kemps – or something that sounds like it. Although he's no longer accepted in his tribe, he's tolerated as a go-between. Besides, he's a good hunter and tracker and has taught us much."

"I would see this fellow," Delaware grunted. "Bring him to me."

"I shall, my Lord. The next time he comes to the fort," Percy replied.

"He comes and goes as he pleases, does he?"

Percy decided to skirt the question, and replied that the Indian was on a hunting trip to the territory of the Kiskiak while at the same time trying to determine the level of that tribe's allegiance to Powhatan.

"My question, Master Percy," Delaware snapped, "requires but a one-word answer. Does he or does he not come and go as he chooses?"

"Aye, my Lord, he does."

"And others? Do others of these savages come and go as...?"

"Sometimes," Percy admitted. "They come to trade with us, just to trade."

"Why not trade outside the walls where they cannot spy on us?" Delaware demanded.

Percy lamely replied that they preferred not to do that.

"I doubt it not! But no more. The practice will not continue."

"No, my Lord," Percy replied. He knew that there would be no point in trying to explain that trade depended on an appearance of friendship.

"Now about the boy with the unfortunate name, this Savage. What of him?"

"Still with Powhatan, at least as far as is known. There is, my Lord, a second boy," said Percy, returning to his explanation. "He's Henry Spelman, and he also was traded, not to Powhatan but to his son. And he, too, is still with them. Both English boys were there when they tortured and killed poor Ratcliffe."

"A terrible death, to be sure," Delaware allowed. "But vengeance is not our purpose. Those who did it are but heathen savages who know no better. 'Tis our charge to win them to Christ. You have heard the words of my commission, and they're clear on this point. I am to exercise diligence in converting these natives and savages to the knowledge of the true God, and to keep ever in mind that their redemption in Jesus Christ is the most pious and noble end of this plantation."

Nobody disagreed, but the skepticism on several faces spoke louder than any words. Had their opinions been invited, most would have replied that friendly persuasion would have no more success than the crusaders had in winning the followers of Islam.

"I am resolved," Delaware went on, "that from the outset, their king must be made to know that on the one hand we come in peace and mean him well, and on the other that we carry the sharp sword of righteousness and will not be denied."

He went on to explain that he proposed to send an emissary to Powhatan with a written message of greeting and friendship. It would require proof of the savages' willingness to trade with us, he added. He would be commanded to return all prisoners and runaways, and all English tools and weapons now in the Indians' possession.

"Do you really expect him to do that?" asked John Martin with a sneer. "I know these bastards!"

"I've heard that you do," Delaware replied coldly. "And I have also heard that you learned little from that knowledge."

Even by candlelight, anyone could see that Martin had gone bright red in the face. Given as he was to delivering one-sided reports to the Company, he was almost certainly thinking how best to undermine confidence in its new Governor and Captain General. It had to be galling, too, that nobody reacted to the rebuke. Indeed, it was though his presence was tolerated but unrecognized.

"And what of the sword, my Lord," Gates asked. "Where and when shall it fall?"

Delaware replied that he hadn't made up his mind, and would be open to suggestions at a later time.

"About the emissary to Powhatan," Percy asked. "Let me go to him. Give me forty men and a ship, and I'll make sure he knows what's what."

"No doubt you would, Master Percy," Delaware replied. "But tell me this. How would your expedition differ from the ship and forty men that Master Ratcliffe took to treat with him?"

Without waiting for an answer, Delaware announced that he had something quite different in mind. He explained that a high level deputation would be seen as recognition of Powhatan's power and prestige, and could risk the loss of yet more English lives. He had been led to believe that the Indians were curious people, and sooner or later they would send their own emissary to the fort. "When they do," he said, "I shall send only two worthy gentlemen to their king with my demands. No, on second thoughts," he added, "not two gentlemen, but one ordinary fellow. His vulnerability will display trust, but his lowly status will deny Powhatan the satisfaction of receiving a supplicant delegation. Yes," he said, rubbing his hands in satisfaction, "I like that idea much better."

"You have someone in mind?" Somers asked.

Delaware replied that he did not, but that it had to be someone strong, healthy, sensible, and able to read.

"I think I know the very man," said Brewster. "He's one of your own guard, John Jefferys, the lad who wanted to appeal against his coming."

"Humm," Delaware grunted. "I remember him well. He'll probably want to appeal again," then added with a short laugh, "but it'll get him the same answer."

There the matter rested, the discussion turning to immediate concerns regarding the state of the palisades, how food was to be stored and distributed, and where the troops still aboard the *Blessing* and *Hercules* were to be quartered.

The following morning Will and John awoke from an uncomfortable night's sleep on Maggie Beale's dirt floor, and went outside to allow her the privacy to leave her bed and to dress. If there was any washing to be done, and there usually wasn't, it meant a trip out of the fort and down to the river. Maggie had warned that lone people washing themselves made good targets for Indian bowmen, and that she preferred to be dirty than dead. But once people were up and out in numbers, the savages were long gone. "Back into the woods they'd be, hidin' like the animals they is," she said with disgust wrapped around every word.

For the next several days Will and John found themselves in a squad singled out to erect and work a pit saw in a cellar hole left open after the hut over it had burned. Rain had washed the clay sides down into it, rendering the bottom a waterlogged morass and home to countless mosquitoes who resented the intrusion. Although each man took only fifteen minute turns as the bottom sawyer, the work was hard, the sun hot, and the mosquitoes hungry. But by the first day's end, the team had cut seventeen fifteen-foot planks for use in building a new palisade. Section by section the old, rough hewn poles were being replaced by vertical boards secured with lateral stretchers between large adzed posts, for which other poor devils were digging four-foot holes into the hard-baked clay. Like most of the construction work going on inside the fort, the palisade building was in the charge of carpenters and seamen from the ships, although the design was based on plans previously employed around English settlements in Ireland.

Shortly after noon on Tuesday the 12th, the first of the Finsbury Fields troops came straggling through the fort hauling some of their supplies on borrowed carts, but much of it on their backs. Tents, kettles, spades, shovels, axes, bedding materials, crates of muskets and armor, all had to be transported in through the river gate and out through the western postern to the open field between the palisade and the burial ground. Although parts of the field were low-lying and patched with marsh grasses, it was the only large open space for a hundred Londoners to pitch their tents. Already encamped were some of the *Sea Venture* survivors, there being too little room inside the fort. Old hands thought it appropriate that this four-acre space had been named Smithfield after the place outside London's city wall where the Jefferys brothers had seen the execution ashes. Indeed, the comparison went further, for here, close to the river's edge, were the ashes and pyre of a colonist who in the winter had killed his pregnant wife and ate all but her head before being arrested. George Percy, as acting president, had the man hung up by his thumbs with weights on his feet until he confessed, then had him staked and burned as a warning to others. But according to Maggie Beale, many people died and never went to burial. "We all knew, but weren't talkin'." she explained. "After all, if it had been me and not my hubby had died, I'd have wanted to feed him a little longer, now wouldn't I?"

"But he died, and you didn't do that." John reminded her.

"Because... well, I just couldn't, that's all." she snapped, quickly changing the subject.

While John was taking his turn in the saw pit, he looked up and saw four soldiers pulling a cart piled with canvas and poles. He could only see the wheels of the cart and the lower halves of the men, but the sight of one of them made him stop sawing and get shouted at from above. The man had but two fingers on his left hand.

Both John and Will knew to expect "Twofin" Chisman and his cohorts to be aboard one of the transports, but as Will said, there was always a chance that they might have died or been thrown overboard on the way. But they didn't and they weren't, so keeping out of their way was the only sensible course. Maybe time and the

Indians would take care of them.

Of more immediate concern to the leadership was the arrival of these 250 additional mouths to feed, as well as the 148 from the *Sea Venture* and sixty more who had survived the winter.

"Nigh on five hundred souls, and not an ear of corn planted!" Delaware ranted. "Why aren't your people fishing, Sir Thomas? Smith told us that the river's so full of fish you can catch them in a frying pan."

Gates took in a deep breath before answering. He was tired of hearing what the bombastic John Smith had or had not said. "M' Lord, my men have put out nets four or five times each day through the past two weeks, and drawn in almost nothing. They cannot catch what is not there."

"We've but one recourse," said Somers. "I'll take the *Patience* back to Bermuda and lade her with hogs and turtles. 'Tis barely two weeks sail. I can be back in a month. And if you can spare the *Discovery* too, so much the better."

Delaware agreed that with the food he had brought, the colony could last a month or more. "We shall miss your counsel, Sir George. But we'll wish you God speed, and pray for your safe return."

On June 19, therefore, Somers set sail as captain of the *Patience,* with Captain Samuel Argall following aboard the *Discovery.* Maggie Beale was among the little throng of women who watched the pinnaces disappearing down river. The Bermudas, once thought to be the island of devils, had become an Eden in the minds of settlers who heard tales of the easy living that the *Sea Venture's* people had enjoyed there. "Sir John weren't no fool to get away from this place," Maggie told anyone in earshot. "He knowed what's what, did that one."

"Aye, and I doubt he'll ever be back," added another of the women.

At James Towne, eleven days went by with no attacks by the Indians. The only report of a sighting came from a gang of lumbermen cutting trees on the back side of the island. They claimed to have seen four – it could have been five – in a canoe crossing the waterway they called the Back River that separated the island from the mainland marshes. The island was, in reality, a tidal isthmus, linked by a causeway to the land at low tide and isolated at high. To protect it, a small log block house had been erected to detect and prevent incursions across the causeway. And there had been several such attempts in the previous year, all of them easily repulsed.

On the sixteenth day a runner sent back from the blockhouse reported that three Indians were there asking to see the English Lord. Here was the news Delaware had been expecting. His letter to Powhatan had been written and rewritten, pored over, debated, and written again. But in spite of Chaplain Laurie's hesitant suggestions that perhaps this or that was a little strong, his Lordship knew what he wanted to say and how he wanted to say it. The rewriting and consultations were merely a courtesy and possibly an opportunity to share or shift blame if something went wrong. In truth, the only person of importance omitted from the deliberations (other than the untrustworthy John Martin) was the messenger.

The arrival of the Indians necessitated the hasty rounding up of an escort, and it being Sergeant Gideon's watch, Will and John were two of the six guardsmen chosen. For the first time, with Gideon at their head, they marched out of the fort's west gate and made their way down the path that led to the graveyard, but which also divided the military camp into two blocks of tents and some hastily constructed stick-built huts. Being the first arrivals, the *Sea Venture* people camped closest to the palisade with the Finsbury recruits in the field beyond them. Of the one hundred ninety who had survived the voyage, most were sitting, squatting, standing in small groups talking among themselves, but doing nothing constructive. No officers were in sight, and Will got the impression that the governor had yet to decide what to do with them. If so, he thought, the camp might prove a seed bed for future trouble. However, he had no time to develop that thought. The escort file was already past the camp and nearing the blockhouse whose sentries were standing talking to one of the Indians.

It was the Jefferys brothers' first sight of the indigenous Americans. John had imagined them as diabolic monsters seven feet tall, painted every color under the sun, devils with nothing but murder on their minds who spoke only in grunts. He was surprised, and almost disappointed to find that they were no taller than he, wore no war paint, and that one talked in English with the guards and even laughed. Lieutenant Puttock, commander of the blockhouse, introduced him to Sergeant Gideon as Machumps, Powhatan's emissary. His companions evidently spoke no English.

John's surprise at finding Machumps speaking English was not shared by the governor who already knew about his voyages to England, but even he was surprised that the Indian had such a firm grasp of it. Later he would tell Wainman that the damned savage spoke better English than many a bumpkin in the wilder regions of Britain. "And I include Ralegh's Devon kinsmen among them," he added.

Sir Ferdinando happened to be friends with Sir Walter and several other Devon men, and so did not join in the sycophantic laughter. A quiet man of middle age, he knew his place and intended to keep it. He was convinced that before long, his leader's autocratic approach to government would breed factions and renewed rivalries, and he wanted no part of either. Nevertheless, he, too, was impressed by the Indian's bearing and command of the English language.

Machumps stood in front of Delaware in the market place, straight backed and proud, making no bow or nod of subservience. Nor was there the slightest hint of deference in his delivery. "My lord, the noble *weroance*, Powhatan, ruler of all the several peoples of the great rivers, sends greetings to the English King James and his captains now lodged in our land. He extends the hand of friendship and regrets past differences, and as proof of his trust and good faith, he will provide many baskets of corn from this year's harvest."

Standing at the doorway to the still dilapidated storehouse that served as his civic center, Delaware attired in a velvet doublet under a half suit of armor, and draped in a scarlet cloak, looked every inch the commander, admirably contrasting, so he thought, with the vulnerable nakedness of Machumps in his deerskin loincloth. Machumps, on the other hand, thought that wearing all that steel and thick fabric in late June was something that only the stupid Christians would do.

"You may tell your master," Delaware replied, "that we welcome his greeting as we shall his corn. I shall prepare a reply in good time. Meanwhile you and your..." Unsure whether to call Machumps's companions Indians, and certainly not savages to their faces, he settled for the most diplomatic word that came to mind. "...your escort, will remain here as our guests..."

"As prisoners, then?" Machumps's retorted.

"As you will," Delaware told him. "I shall prepare my response and send my own messenger to carry my letter to your king. You will guide him and see that he comes to no harm either going or returning." Then to Brewster, "Captain, see that these men are fed, housed, and watched over." With the meeting over, Delaware turned and went into the storehouse followed by Gates, Somers, Wainman, and the rest. It was an impressive exit into the darkness of the long building that left Machumps standing in the bright sunlight unable to see into it. Nor could he see Delaware and his retinue immediately exit through a side door and take the few steps to his house. Two halberdeers remained at the storehouse doorway, their weapons crossed to prevent the Indians from following. But Machumps had no intention of doing so. His months in London had taught him much about the English taste for empty pageantry, and he was not impressed. He was resigned to spending time at the fort – time that could be put to good use in sizing up the capabilities of the colonists and gauging the morale of the rank and file. He was convinced that sooner or later, his people would have to root out the English cancer, and that sooner would be better than later. He had already said as much to Powhatan.

Powhatan had been paramount chief of all the Tidewater Virginia tribes for more than half a century. When still of warrior age he had led the attack that destroyed Ralegh's 1587 colonists as they moved north from Roanoke Island. But by 1610, the excitement of battle was a fading memory. It suited him best, indeed it amused him, to let the English destroy themselves. Every deserter who came to him, every shovel or gun that could be bartered or stolen, added one more nail in their coffin. Christopher Newport, captain of the first Virginia fleet, had once traded twenty swords for as many turkeys, a coup that prompted Powhatan to offer the same deal to John Smith who turned him down. Nevertheless, dissident and hungry colonists had stolen most of the tools and weapons from the storehouse and clandestinely traded them for food. The Indians had discovered, too, that when ships were moored off James Towne, their crews could be responsive to offers of furs in exchange for stolen food ferried ashore to upstream villages under cover of night. All these transgressions served to generate friction between the sailors who would be leaving and the colonists who wouldn't.

Powhatan's old home village of Werowocomoco on the north shore of the York River had been ideally suited for keeping in close contact with the tribes to the north and south. But raids by Smith and his men early in 1609 had prompted him to retreat out of reach of the English. Thus it was that he moved his capital inland to Orapakes on the Pamunkey tributary of the York, a distance of about seventy-five miles from James Towne. From there he was safe from surprise, but could still control his vassal tribes, both by land and by water. But for his Lordship's chosen messenger, unlike the fleet-footed Indians, the trek to Orapakes would be long and arduous.

On the afternoon of June 30, John and Will were part of a ten-man detail sent out to fell trees in the forest northeast of the fort. All ten took turns hewing, two pairs felling and six men guarding. Nobody had seen or heard anything but the thud of their own axes, the rasp of saws, and the occasional crash of a falling tree, until suddenly there came the swish of an arrow that struck the tree that Will was cutting. It stuck quivering in the bark barely six inches above his head, its quartz point buried half its length into the tree. "Time to go, lads," whispered the corporal in charge. As quickly as they could, they rounded up their clothes and tools, expecting at any minute to hear scores of arrows winging toward them. But none came, nor did they see or hear any Indians as they warily and silently retreated out of the forest.

Once into the cleared area in sight of the fort, everyone broke into energetic conversation, each man trying to outdo the others in dramatizing their narrow escape. That they were still in bow-shot range of the woods went unnoticed as one story topped another. When the "phewing!" and "Praise be to God-ing" had subsided, John Jefferys quietly offered his opinion. "That arrow hit the tree so straight and so deep, it had to have been fired from very close range. If the savage had wanted to kill brother Will, he'd have done so. That only one arrow was fired says to me that 'twas a warning, no more."

"I think the lad's right," said Pips Bailey. "The buggers just wanted to remind us that they're still here — watchin' and waitin'."

"I vote we leave it to them lazy sods in the camp to go fetch the wood," said another man. The remark was unnecessary as fellers were not draggers, but as the squad marched back along the ridge behind the fort and returned to the perimeter of Smithfield, resentment about the lack of discipline and control being exercised among the soldiery was a prime topic of conversation. To demonstrate the difference the corporal had his squad march in parade order down the avenue between the tents, their axes and saws carried as they would muskets. Will had just muttered that he thought they looked stupid when small groups of soldiers began to emerge from the rows of tents to tell them so.

"Playin' at soldiers, are we? One, two! Left, right! Present your saws, little darlin's!" The shouts, punctuated with cat calls and ribald laughter, got louder as more soldiers came out to join the fun.

"Well, well, will you look at that! Ain't them a sight for sore eyes?" John recognized the voice before he saw the face. It was Twofin Chisman with his two Billingsgate bully boys. "We got your number, ain't we mates?" he laughed as he walked alongside. "You think you're so special, bein' in his bloody Lordship's guard an' all. But you ain't no better than the rest of us." Chisman poked John in the ribs as he marched. "You listenin' to me, mate? 'Cos we'll get you sooner or later. You mark my words."

John was tempted to swing his axe at his tormenter, but wisely resisted the impulse. Instead, he stayed in step, looked straight ahead, and pretended not to hear. Will, being on his brother's right, could not hear the words, but knew their taunting tone. Both brothers recognized, as they had already feared, that the enemy at the fort gate needed to be watched as closely as any in the forest.

Maggie was waiting for them when they got home, as was a borrowed cauldron of water kept hot in the ashes of the fire. She had done this every day since the brothers had been put to manual labor in the fort. She helped wipe the sweat and sawdust from their backs and dried them with rags salvaged from an abandoned hut. For John, Maggie Beale was becoming a surrogate mother, but for Will she stirred different feelings that he found hard to define.

They had stood in line to collect their evening rations and were back sitting at the makeshift table Will had built, when there came a loud rap on the door. Sergeant Gideon did not wait for a response, but entered and then apologized for the intrusion. "'Tis on his Lorship's business that I'm here," he explained.

"What can we do for him?" Will asked.

"It's not you, Will. 'Tis John I'm wanting." Gideon went on to explain that the governor had honored him by selecting him from all the others to be his ambassador to the Indian king.

"To Powhatan?" John gasped.

"The very same." Gideon told him that he was to carry a letter and read it when he got there. "You will listen carefully to what the savage replies and try to remember every word so that you can report them to his Lordship on your return."

"Then I'll go with him," Will announced.

Gideon shook his head. "No, 'tis his Lordships insistence that only one of us is to go." Then to John, "You'll be guided by the Indian you brought into the fort. His name is Machumps. His English is good and he can translate for Powhatan if he cannot understand your words as you read him the letter."

"But, sir," Maggie asked. "Who's to say that them varmints'll let him return? They's none of them to be trusted further than a lass can spit."

Gideon replied with a smile, saying that although he had no

knowledge of lasses' spitting range, he could guarantee that John would not be harmed. "Powhatan will be as anxious as will his Lordship to see that his answer is received. No, yon lad will be safe enough," he added. "You're to report to me at the corps-du-garde at first light. Be wearing his Lordship's uniform and your strongest shoes. You'd best sleep sound tonight."

But John could not.

Chapter Seven

Had there been a cock left to crow, John Jefferys would have been up before it could have uttered a sound. Excitement at the adventure ahead, the responsibility that was to be his, coupled with fear of the unknown had kept him awake most of the night. Neither Maggie nor Will had been spared his questions and pleas for reassurance, and no counter requests begging "for the love of Mary, let us sleep!" could silence him. He heard the changing of the watch at the fort bulwarks at twelve and four, and from time to time the howling of a wolf somewhere on the island. Maggie had so often expressed her opinions of the ungodly savages that she was of no comfort to him. As for brother Will, he thought he should have been chosen and was in no mood to be sympathetic. Nevertheless, both he and Maggie were up to wish John well as he downed his gruel breakfast before heading for the guard house.

"Over slept, did we?" Sergeant Gideon barked as John entered. Then with a conciliatory smile, he added, "Sit ye down, lad. A good night, I trust?"

John did as he was ordered, but refrained from admitting that he had slept hardly at all.

"You know what you have to do," Gideon went on. "You carry his Lordship's message to Powhatan; you read it to him, remember his reply, and come back. 'Tis that simple. The Indian Machumps will..."

Gideon's instructions were interrupted by the arrival of Captain Brewster. "Good morrow, sergeant," he said, "and to you young

Jeffreys. Be seated." He then extracted several sheets of paper from a leather pouch and laid them on the guard house table. "Let me hear how well you can read," he demanded.

John looked at the first sheet and drew in a deep breath. "I be versed in printing, but reading from writing, I'm sure I don't know. The letters look different and run together."

"Try," Brewster ordered.

John took up the first sheet and carried it to the small window, the guard house being dark and the sun scarcely risen. "In the name of our something lord King James the..."

"Sovereign. The word is sovereign."

"In the name of our sovereign lord King James the First of Great Britain, France, and Ireland..." John stopped in mid sentence and looked over to Brewster. "France? Our king is king of France?"

"Get on with it," Brewster snapped. "'Tis a convention, no more."

"Do the French know?" John muttered half to himself.

"Read, boy!"

" ...France and Ireland, I Thomas West, Lord De La Warr, Governor of Virginia Britannia, send greetings to the emperor Powhatan, and wish him long life and much..."

Brewster interrupted. "That's good enough. You'll do, lad." Then to Gideon he added, "See that he's properly equipped and mindful of his duty. Then take him to Machumps and send them on their way. There's one more thing. One of the savages will be carrying a sack of trinkets as gifts to Powhatan. The neck is tied and secured with his Lordship's seal. Break it only in Powhatan's presence. Otherwise he'll suspect you robbed him. And now, God speed you, young Jefferys." With that, Brewster left the corps-de-garde and headed for the governor's house.

Gideon advised John to read the whole of Delaware's message and do so a sufficient number of times that he could deliver it almost from memory. "Deliver it with authority, no stumbling and mumbling, mind. You'll be the voice of civilized men, and the savage king must respect it."

John said he would do his best, but wondered whether he was

old enough and tall enough to be the voice of England and of Christendom. Gideon next told him to select armor from among the corselets and helmets hanging in rows along one wall of the guard house.

"Why would I want armor?" John countered. "I be promised safe passage, be I not? So who is to attack me? 'Tis only useless weight."

Gideon knew he was right, but told him to take it anyway. The breast plate would make him look larger and more robust than he was, and shining armor would impress the Indians. That was the theory, but in truth they looked on the wearing of it as just one more English idiocy. Nevertheless, Gideon insisted that John take it, but conceded that he could let Machumps's companions carry it. "But gird on a sword, a falcheon, or whatever blade best suits you," he added.

"Why so?" John replied. "I'm a messenger, not a soldier. 'Tis just something to get tangled in the vines."

That, too, was true, but Gideon's patience was wearing thin. "You're being a very contrary young man," he snapped. "You will take a weapon, and that's an order!" Whereupon, John shrugged, and selected a hanger, a short single-edged blade akin to a seaman's cutlass. Gideon carefully returned the governor's pages to their leather bag and instructed him to "keep it always about your person." He also handed John a canvas bag containing a small loaf of bread and a flask of beer, while assuring him that the savages would be feeding him far better than he could hope to receive at James Towne.

Machumps and his two companions had been housed in the small guest lodge close to the fort's west gate, and were squatting outside it when Gideon led John to them. Greetings were exchanged, Machumps telling John that he remembered his face from their encounter at the block house, and assured him that he would be well looked after. "Have no fears," he said. "You are the great Lord Powhatan's honored guest. The son of Lord Delaware is the son of Wahunsenacawh."

When John looked perplexed, Machumps explained that that was his king's personal name and that Powhatan was a title derived from the tribe of his birth. "But you will greet him as the great lord Powhatan," Machumps added.

"Well, has he gone?" were the first words from Lord Delaware when Captain Brewster entered his house. "You're sure he's the right man for the mission?"

Brewster reminded him that it was by his own choice that a simple servant had been selected in preference to one of the governor's councilors or a member of the gentry. Grudgingly, Delaware allowed that it was still a good idea to put the savage in his place; but in saying so his voice hinted that he was having second thoughts. Both Gates and Wainman had questioned his decision, and had advocated a show of force. Might it not be better, they suggested, that his Lordship should travel up the Pamunky River to Orapakes by ship, and land there with the trumpets blowing and drums beating? The danger in that approach, as Delaware pointed out, lay in the possibility of an angry confrontation from which neither side could gracefully retreat. "We make our demands, and the savage refuses them. What then?" Delaware had asked. "Our only choice would be to walk out of the meeting and appear rebuffed and defeated in their eyes. No," he added, "a common messenger has no authority and can commit us to nothing. But the Jefferys lad *is* worthy and loyal, is he not?"

"He's one of your own Buckhurst tenants," Brewster answered.

"To be sure; to be sure," Delaware muttered before turning to his favorite topic, the regeneration of his church. "This has to be completed by Sunday," he said. Percy assured him that it would, adding that he was taking personal responsibility for the work. Rightly or wrongly, Percy believed that a whispering campaign had been launched by John Martin and others that he, Percy, was solely responsible for the decline of the colony in the past winter and for the deaths resulting from it. He thought it imperative, therefore, that he should make himself indispensable in the eyes of the new governor. Although Gates was superficially cordial, Percy guessed that he, too, would be reporting to London that it was under his leadership that so many died and the fort fell into such disrepair. Rebuilding the church, therefore, seemed the best means of gaining Delaware's approval.

Sir Thomas Gates, too, had his own agenda. As deputy governor he wanted to make his military mark on the pages of the colony's history. The savages needed to learn an unforgettable lesson, and he was the man to teach it. The Indians at Kecoughtan remained a threat to Point Comfort's Fort Algernon, he said, and should be eliminated. "My Lord will remember what they did to Lieutenant Sicklemore and his men. We must avenge them," he insisted. "And soon."

But Delaware was unconvinced, and told Gates to be patient. It would be better to hear Powhatan's answer to his messenger before doing anything that might tip the political balance.

Will Jefferys and Maggie Beale had watched the messenger leave through the west gate, and got a parting wave of his cap as he did so. John was wearing neither his helmet nor his armor, and was followed by a none-too-happy Indian carrying both in a canvas sack. More jeering from the Finsbury soldiery punctuated their passage between the tents leading to the causeway that connected the island to the mainland. Machumps had set out at a loping pace, but slowed to a walk when John convinced him that there was a difference between traveling seventy-five miles barefoot while wearing naught but a loin cloth, and going dressed in a woolen shirt, velvet doublet, trunk hose, and heavy leather shoes.

The tide was rising as they crossed the causeway, and John's shoes were waterlogged before he reached dry land. As he squelched his way along the narrow trail, he was already aware that the *naturals*, as some people called them, were better suited to being Virginians than were the English. He guessed that Machumps and his two Indian escorts were thinking the same. That they went barefoot regardless of the twigs and pebbles that littered the trail was an amazement to John whose feet would have been torn and bleeding before he had trotted a mile.

The trail led northward into territory occupied by the Paspahegh Indians, and John was aware that of all the savage tribes the Paspahegh had been the most persistent in their attacks on the settlers. John hadn't forgotten the arrow that had flown so close to his brother's head only a few days earlier, and so wondered whether refusing to wear armor had been a wise decision. However, he was not about to change his mind and let his guides assume that he did so out of fear.

The Paspaheghs lived on both sides of the Chickahominy, the Great River's largest tributary that snaked its way inland as far as Orapakes and beyond. The Chickahominy Indians, too, were foes of the English, and as they lived largely independent of Powhatan and his vassal tribes, their behavior could be unpredictable. Machumps, however, assured John that he had nothing to fear from either the Paspahegh or the Chickahominy, as any harm done to the Great Lord's messenger would result in war. "They've not forgotten what happened to the Chesapeakes," Machumps told him with a wry laugh.

John knew nothing of the Chesapeakes' fate, and it was not until evening when he and his companions stopped to dine on a scrawny, spit-roasted rabbit that he asked Machumps to say more. Between mouthfuls, small and sinewy as they were, Machumps explained that a few years before the first English arrived, Powhatan's priests prophesied that from the mouth of the great bay would come a foe who would destroy his empire. It wasn't the Kecoughtans because they were ruled by Pochins, one of Powhatan's several strategically placed sons. So it had to be the Chesapeakes, the tribe nearest the bay on the south side of the Great River.

"So what happened to them?" John asked.

"Wise leader that our emperor is," Machumps answered, "he chose to strike first. He took them by surprise, killing them all, *weroance*, family, every man, woman, and child. The Chesapeake people are no more. 'Tis as though they never existed. Only then did Powhatan feel secure."

"And was he?"

Machumps smiled. "And you should ask that?"

"Why not?"

"Because, my friend, 'twas not the Chesapeakes, but you who

are the fulfillment of the prophecy."

John sat back on his haunches and stared into the fire before asking, "And does Powhatan believe this to be so?"

Machumps replied that he wasn't sure. His king had not said as much. To have done so would have been to admit that he had slaughtered his neighbor by mistake. Not only that, he would have to say that his priests had given him bad advice, and it was on the validity of their words that Powhatan's entire social structure depended. "But," Machumps added, "if I know the truth, he who is so much wiser, must know it too."

John looked across the fire at its reflection in the eyes of his three Indian guides, and replied more as a statement than a question, "So he... *you* will kill us if you can?"

Machumps stirred the ashes with a stick, then answered with a smile. "In due time our gods will decide. But not tomorrow."

"When, then?"

Machumps spread his hands, looked up into the night sky, and shrugged.

That same evening Maggie Beale and Will Jeffreys risked a walk out of the river gate and down to the water where a cooling breeze was blowing from the southwest. They, too, talked of the future, though the prospect of a Chesapian-style massacre was nowhere in their vision. Will's focused on going home to Buckhurst, but Maggie confessed that she could see no further than tomorrow. "When Sir Thomas told us we were leavin' this accursed place and going back to England," she said, "I dared hope that..." Then she stopped and shook her head.

"Hoped for what?"

"Oh, I don't know. That fate, luck, God, might have something better in store. But with me man dead, I had nowhere to go, no one to go home to. I only knew that this island was no place for me, nor for any woman, or for *any* Christian body for that matter. But now here we be, Master Will, and like as not we'll die here."

"Not me," Will told her. "Not me, Maggie, not me! Seven years is all."

"Be there a maid waitin' for you?" She asked the question without any hint of personal interest. She could have been asking whether his roof was thatched or tiled.

"Never had no time for dilly dallying," he told her. "'Sides, if I had, I couldn't expect her to wait seven years, now could I? So it's just as well I don't."

For several minutes they sat watching the fireflies darting overhead and the lights on the moored ships shifting with the tide. When Maggie broke the silence she was staring out across the water as she asked, "You know what they'll be sayin', don't you?"

"Sayin'? Who? Sayin' what?"

"About us." Maggie turned to Will and laid her hand gently on his sleeve. "With John away, it'll be just you and me. But I'm not a whore; I want you to know that."

Will pulled away. "I never thought... I swear, I never thought..."

Maggie smiled. "I know, I know. You're a good man, Will Jefferys, I know that. But others will talk just the same."

"What would you have me do?" he asked. "You want me to find another roof till John gets back?"

"Nay, Will. You're my..." She groped for a word, then lamely whispered, "You're my friend."

"Aye, I am that." After a pause, he added. "And so is brother John. There's not a day goes by that he doesn't say how lucky we are to..."

Maggie smiled and took Will's hand. "To be sure, I know that. But answer me this, Will Jefferys, would you want to bed me if I'd let you?"

Before Will could answer, a gun shot from the army camp brought the fort suddenly alive, and sent Will and Maggie hurrying back into the safety of its palisades. Moments later, Captain Brewster and his two lieutenants ran from the guard house calling the duty detail to follow them out through the west gate. Settlers ran from their houses, some gathering at the gate and others climbing up on to the palisades' parapet step to try to see what was going on. Numerous camp fires cast an orange glow among the tents, not because the soldiers were cooking but because their smoke kept the mosquitoes at bay. Silhouettes of men could be seen moving about between the rows of tents, but there seemed no urgency or sense of danger in their coming and going. When nothing exciting happened the settlers in the fort began to lose interest and drifted away to their homes. Ten minutes later Brewster and his detail returned, half leading, half dragging a soldier between them.

The governor, Gates, Wainman, Yeardley, and several others were waiting in the marketplace when Brewster's men threw the man at their feet. He had shot and wounded a tent-mate after a dispute over a card game.

"The victim is not bad hurt?" Delaware asked.

"No, m'Lord," Brewster replied. "Merely a shoulder wound, nothing serious."

"Get him to his feet," Delaware ordered. "What's his name?"

Brewster didn't know, but quickly found out. "Thompson, m'Lord. Jack Thompson."

"Indeed," Delaware replied coldly. "Then Jack Thompson, you shall have the honor of being an example to all your fellows. Tomorrow, after the roll is called, you shall hang."

"But, my Lord..." Yeardley interjected. "Surely..."

"He will hang, Master Yeardley, hang like a pheasant till it be ripe, hang for all to see and be warned."

Yeardley persisted. "But the man he shot was but nicked."

"The shot was fired. The intent was there. The result, fortunate thought it was, is immaterial. The law, *my* law, ordains that any common soldier who discharges a firearm with the intent to harm another is condemned to die. And so he shall." With that Delaware returned to his house, and the luckless Thompson was led away and locked in the cell behind the guard house.

Gates, Wainman and Yeardley had followed Delaware, and as they sat smoking at his table, they began to share their concern that the idleness and lack of discipline in the army camp might quickly become a serious problem. Wainman noted that the close on two hundred men had but one commander, Captain Jeremiah Douthitt, and two lieutenants, both young and neither with any experience. He didn't remember their names , but considered Douthitt an officer of questionable quality. "Leave his men with nothing to do, and with little drilling to keep them respectful," he said, "I fear they may do us more harm than the savages."

Dr. Bohun had been listening to the conversation and added his own warning. "Some are already falling sick," he said.

"Of what cause?" Somers asked.

"As yet I know not. But like as not, 'tis the result of drinking from the brackish river. But if, as I suspect, 'tis to be a contagion, we should build a pest house beyond the fort and quarantine the sick before it can spread." All should be prevented from drinking from the river, Bohun advised. "I'm told that there are fresh springs not a mile away on the mainland," he added. "The healthy should be put to bringing it here in barrels."

"Easily said, good doctor, but not so easily done," Gates replied. "Put the ailing away in the woods and the savages will surely kill them, as well they may the water carriers."

"How many are sick?" Wainman wanted to know.

"About a dozen," Bohun replied.

"Then it will be no hardship to set up several cabins to one side of the camp and build a fence around them," Wainman told him. "As for water, properly armored and with scouts attending, soldiers can make themselves useful hewing a wide trail to the spring."

"A good plan, Sir Ferdy," Delaware told him. "I leave it to you to see it executed." Then, setting aside his pipe, he pushed back his chair and stood up. "'Tis late, gentlemen, and tomorrow I have an unpleasant duty to perform. So I bid you a good night." Stopping at the door to his apartment he added, "Neglect not your prayers."

Chapter Eight

It had rained in the night, and the riffraff of soldiery emerging from leaking tents stank like a kennel of wet spaniels. Whatever discipline they had acquired on Finsbury Fields evidently had deserted them. The drum beat calling the men to muster hurried them not at all. Half-hearted orders to "step lively, lads!" were greeted with curses as Lord Delaware's army ambled out onto the parade area beside the river. News of Thompson's impending execution had spread through the camp late in the previous evening, and had been grist for mutinous talk throughout the night. It wasn't that many had much sympathy for the man, and certainly none for his firing a gun at a fellow soldier, it was simply that those bastards in the fort had the power to take a life without the decency of a trial. It also galled that their general, Lord Delaware, had been too preoccupied inside the fort to care about conditions outside it in the camp. The soldiers had watched the efforts being devoted to repairing the palisades and had seen the results as symbolic of a distinction being made between those within and those without. None of this had real validity, but men with too little to do were fruitful ground for the seeds of discontent sown by the likes of Twofin Chisman and his Billingsgate cronies. Their senior officer, Captain Douthitt, had been a sergeant in the Earl of Essex's army in Ireland where a charge of willful and reckless disregard for orders was dismissed when Essex abruptly returned to England. The Company's decision to appoint Douthitt had resulted in his recruiting several old friends of equally questionable reliability. It was small wonder, therefore, that the Governor General's army left much to be desired.

It was true that Delaware had not yet inspected the camp, but reports by Wainman, Brewster and others, had kept him aware that something needed to be done. Indeed, his decision to make an example of private Thompson had much to do with his intent to restore discipline. "Discipline and morale," he told Sir Thomas Gates, "are two tines of the same fork."

"Just so, my Lord," Gates replied, thinking it unwise to disagree with his leader's dubious premise. It was true, nonetheless, that without discipline there could be no morale. But Gates was experienced enough to know that morale depended more on trust and popularity than it did on hangings. It had been his example that had kept the *Sea Venture* survivors sufficiently optimistic to build two ships and escape the foam-capped reefs of Bermuda. In hindsight many were now thinking that they had been much better off on the islands than in James Towne, but no one was blaming Gates for that.

Will Jefferys had been awakened early by the last of the night watch informing him that he was to parade with the rest of his Lordship's elite at eight o'the clock, or more specifically at the tolling of the church bell, for no one of his status owned a watch. Not until he reported to the guard house did Sergeant Gideon tell him that he and five others had been singled out for a special duty that required very specific instruction.

This was to be Delaware's first full dress muster, and every officer from Lieutenant Governor Gates and General Wainman down to the lowest corporal were to be in attendance. Assembled in the market place, the halberd- and pike-carrying fifty-man guard was down by eight: John and the five assigned to special duty, emissary John being somewhere up country, and one man sick. A delirium, Dr. Bohun called it. But the rest were smartly at attention in their helmets and body armor waiting for the order to march. The sun was up, the wind had dropped, and it was getting hotter, but his Lordship was in no hurry. He had no intention of moving out until he was sure that the camp was on parade and ready to welcome him. Besides, he needed to be sure that his oration would strike the right notes and strike them hard. A quarter of an hour later he was still shuffling papers, writing, scratching out words, and rewriting with growing irritation. "God's blood!" he finally snorted. "I suppose this'll have to suffice!"

The Company had stipulated that English common law was to be the basis for any legal requirements and consequences in the colony, but it also gave the governor expansive leeway to supplement as he should see fit. And Delaware was attempting to do just that when Captain Douthitt arrived at his door to report his troops ready and waiting.

Sergeant Gideon had brought Thompson from the guard house and stood him, hands tied behind him, amid the six-man escort to march between the first and second column of the governor's guard. In front went Gates's drummer in company with his Lordship's own Tom Dowse, and behind them, Captain Brewster as guard commander. After the guard columns marched three ensigns as standard bearers to Delaware, Gates, and Wainman, and behind them the governor and the rest of the officers and gentry. A third guard contingent completed the procession. It was an undeniably impressive turn out – or it would have been had the troops been in a mood to appreciate it. Instead, they saw it as further proof of the hierarchical gulf between them and the folks in the fort.

Delaware took a deep breath, forced a smile, and set out to inspect his army. Carefully ignoring untied shoe strings, sagging shirts, or that most were parading without their helmets, he made an effort to appear warm hearted. "Ready to fight for your king?" he asked one man, and "you look like a lusty young fellow," he told another. The first grunted and the second grinned, but neither expressed delight at being singled out. For his part, Delaware was satisfied that inspecting one motley rank was more than enough.

Standing on an up-turned tub, with his back to the river, and with only the standard bearers behind him, Delaware launched into the first major speech of his administration. "Fellow Christians and Englishmen," he began. "As your governor, I welcome you, and congratulate Captain Douthitt on your turn out. As always," he added, "there is room for improvement, and I know that you will strive to achieve it, as shall we all." For ten minutes he talked about the rich fruits that all who diligently labored would enjoy. He told them that he was sure that mines of gold and silver waited to be discovered, and promised that every man would reap the benefits. "Serve your country well, and it will do the like for you," he declared. Then, with the sugar spread, Delaware turned to the substance of his address.

"The rule of law – God's law and our own, are the tenets that separate us from the heathen savage. It is necessary that we all understand and abide by them. It is my intention, therefore, to prepare a code of regulations that will be read to you by your officers at each and every muster, so that there can be no doubt in anyone's mind as to what is permissible and what is not." Delaware then reached into his pouch and extracted his unfinished notes.

His first edict charged *all captains and officers, of what quality or nature soever* to diligently frequent morning and evening prayers and ensure that their subordinates did likewise. His second ordered that no man *speak impiously or maliciously against the holy and blessed Trinity,* or any of the three persons; that is to say, against *God the Father, God the Son, or God the Holy Ghost— upon pain of death.* The same went for blaspheming God's holy name, taking the name of God in vain, or uttering traitorous words against the king. Taking an *oath untruly* or bearing false witness would be punishable by death, and so would sodomy. So, too, would stealing an ear of corn.

Surprising to those close enough to hear were their governor's concerns for the protection of the Indians. Anyone breaching any alliance or treaty would die, as would anyone who, without orders, should set fire to any Indian house, temple, or grain store, or steal, ransack, or ill treat *the people of the country...shall be punished with death.* The list was long and much of it was lost in Delaware's reading of it. Invariably, however, the tag line *punishable by death,* came across loud and clear.

Left to last was Delaware's freshly phrased, but yet to be polished order that any man, who in a quarrel with any other, should take up a firearm with the intent to do bodily harm, should be put to death. Jack Thompson, he declared, was such a man.

Three trees had been left standing beside the river's edge, one of them having a dead limb projecting about eight feet from the ground. A pulley lashed to it testified that this was not the first time that the oak had served as a hanging tree. But today, there was to be no delay while someone fetched a ladder and threaded a rope. Up and over it went. As the grim-faced troops watched in silence, Delaware stepped down from his tub to allow it to be placed beneath the tree. Then Thompson was lifted up onto it. It fell to Will Jefferys to be the one to put the noose around his neck. "I'm right sorry to have to do this," he whispered.

"Aye, I'll bet you are," Thompson sneered, and spat in his face.

"God rest ye," Will answered as he stepped back.

The drums rolled. Captain Brewster gave the order: "Detail, do your duty!" Three men pulled on the rope and a fourth kicked the tub away. Looking neither to left nor right, Lord Delaware walked briskly away, followed by the standard bearers and officers. "Company, attention! Files, by the left, quick march!" Orders rang out from sergeants and corporals as the governor's guard hastily shifted from awe-struck silence to military smartness. Will Jefferys and his five companions joined the tail of the departing column, each in his way, reliving the moment they would not soon forget.

Maggie Beale was waiting at her door. "I saw it. We all saw it from the palisades," she said.

"It was awful," Will muttered as he went inside and sat down on the bed. "To think that I..."

"'Twas justice. Somebody had to do it."

"But to kill a man I didn't even know... He spat in my face."

"There's no blame, my dear. You did your duty."

But Will was unconvinced. "There's still his spittle on my collar," he said. "I can still hear his sounds, still see his eyes. I can still see him kicking. His face will haunt my dreams, I swear it."

"No, it won't," Maggie assured him. "But if it should; well, I'm here to drive away the goblins."

Back at his house, Lord Delaware felt no remorse. He had done what had to be done, and that was that. But he was concerned about the wording and order of his edicts. He was sure they needed a wordsmith's hand. He explained to Chaplain Laurie the importance of putting God's will before all else. "There must be no room for doubt or misunderstanding," he added. "The ungodliness of our people brought us to where we are."

"True, my Lord. True, indeed," Laurie replied.

"That Strachey fellow, the one we made recorder. Might he not be the man to do it? What do you think?"

Laurie agreed. "He has some experience in politics, I'm told. He was secretary to our ambassador to the Levant."

"So why is he here?" Delaware wanted to know.

"There was some falling out, I know not what," Laurie added. "He'd been something of a gallant, mixed with players, and thinks himself a poet."

"A poet, by God! What use has Virginia of poets?"

Ten minutes later William Strachey was standing before the governor's table wondering why he had been summoned. He was thirty-eight, thin, pale faced, and of a nervous disposition. "You...um...summoned me, my Lord?" he asked.

Delaware looked him up and down and wondered why such a man should have chosen to come to Virginia. "I'm told you have some talent as a scribbler. Is that right?"

"Some slight...yes."

"And hob nob with those London playhouse people, I hear."

Strachey allowed that that was so.

"Share their views, do you?"

"Views, my Lord?" Strachey cautiously countered.

Delaware explained that he had seen the Dukes' Men perform something called *Titus Andronicus* and thought it the kind of nonsense that gave the groundlings republican ideas. "So what do you say to that, Master Strachey? Are you one of those radical thinkers?"

Strachey replied that he had taken the oath of supremacy and was as loyal to the Crown as any man in England.

Thus reassured, Delaware assigned him the task of taking his notes and all the other directives and laws and working them into a document of *Laws and Orders, Divine, Politique, and Marshall for the Colony in Virginea*. Strachey was delighted. The task gave him even more stature and the very private thrill of being able to write prescriptions for chained imprisonment, running the gauntlet, whipping, years as a galley slave – or death.

Death on paper was not on John Jefferys' mind as he trudged along the trail with the two mute Indians hurrying him from behind. Machumps was leading, but seemed to be looking warily from side to side as he walked. If, as he had said, John had nothing to fear from the tribes whose territory they were to pass through, why the hesitancy? John remembered that John Smith had been shot at and captured by the Chickahominy though accompanied by an Indian guide. Might this not happen to him too? How would the Indians know that Machumps wasn't a renegade allied to the English, or, for that matter, that John wasn't a scout rather than a messenger? These were all thoughts that passed through his mind, but remained there because Machumps was too far in the lead for idle conversation. Besides, the Indian's English was sometimes intertwined with his own words, making it difficult to understand unless talking face to face.

Suddenly Machumps stopped. "*Momonsacqweo!*" he said, holding up his hand to halt.

The word meant nothing to John until a black bear cub ambled out of the bushes and crossed the trail. Machumps made no move. A few moments later a crashing in the underbrush preceded the arrival of a huge female bear followed by another cub. She sniffed the air, saw the men, and reared up on her hind legs, her teeth bared and her claws extended. John had seen a brown, dancing bear hauled on a chain through Withyham village, but it was nothing like this majestic black beast. Had he been alone, John knew he would have turned and fled, but Machumps stood his ground. For what seemed far longer than it was, Machumps and the bear stood eye to eye not twenty feet apart. The bear made the first move; she let out a deep-throated growl, hunched her shoulders as though about to lunge, but instead dropped to all fours, and followed her second cub off into the forest.

"Whew!" John gasped. "If I'd been alone I'd have bin half a mile away by now."

"See that big tree back there?" Machumps asked. "You wouldn't have gotten that far before she had you. Never run from a bear."

"But why didn't one of you shoot her?"

Machumps smiled. "That be the trouble with you *Tassantasses*, you English, you shoot without thinking. So we kill the bear, what then? We have to stop to gut her and skin her. The carcass would be good vittails in the winter. But not in the summer; we have no need. Would you want to carry a carcass for another three days knowing that it would be bad by the time we got to Orapakes. And as we are still on Paspahegh land, would you want to be the one tell them that you shot their bear?

John shook his head. "I wouldn't have shot. But my brother would, that I know."

"Then your brother is a fool." Machumps grunted, and added, "But all *Tassantasses* are fools." Before John could think of a response, the Indian turned and headed on up the trail.

At the fort, two more of the starving time survivors died, and several more soldiers in the camp fell sick. Dr. Bohun reported that he had set up his laboratory in a hut behind the store house and was experimenting with concoctions distilled from local plants and a cordial made from the sap of a white tree. "I'm calling it *Terra Alba Virginiensis*" he told his master.

"And what does it cure?" Delaware demanded.

"Nothing yet my Lord, but I am hopeful that it'll attack some pestilential and malignant fevers. But 'tis too soon to tell." Then Bohun asked, "Did you know that Sir Ferdinando is unwell?

Delaware answered in surprise, that he hadn't noticed him to be so. "Did he say as much?"

The doctor replied that he had not, but that he had been watching and could see for himself that the man was unsteady and sweating.

"Good doctor, we are all sweating and ere each day is through, most of us are unsteady. I bid you watch, but say nothing," Delaware told him. At that point the conversation was interrupted by the arrival of the lieutenant governor.

"My Lord," said Gates, "we would speak with you on the matter of..."

"We?"

"We, my fellow officers, Sir George, Sir Ferdy, Captain Brewster, Percy, and others, on the matter of our response to the savages. It is imperative that we do something before they convince themselves that we are unable," Gates insisted.

Sir Thomas West, Lord Delaware and governor for life, was not a man who responded well to being pushed, and even less at being told what he should do. "Prayer, Sir Thomas, will be our guide, as it is in all things. The officers will assemble in the church at eight in the morning and pray for Divine guidance, at which time everything will be discussed and, God willing, the right decisions will be reached. But before you go, let me remind you once again of our Company's very specific instruction." Picking up the by now much thumbed copy of his orders from London, Delaware began to read:

It is very expedient that your Lordship with all diligence endeavor the conversion of the natives and savages to the knowledge and worship of the true God and their redeemer Christ Jesus as the most pious and noble *end of this plantation.*"

"Remember this above all else," he added.

As previous governor, albeit lieutenant governor, Gates had heard all this before. More to the point was the Company's advice to him that Powhatan was not to be trusted, that he had been responsible for the slaughter of the Roanoke colonists, and that if he could not be captured he should at least be made to pay tribute. That was the kind of order a soldier understood. God would bless whatever it took to control the savages, and Sir Thomas intended to say so on the morrow.

Dusk found John Jeffery and his escort at a small Paspehegh village on the east bank of the Chickahominy River where they were greeted by its elderly *weroance,* whose name sounded like

Annawingopo. The old man was small, bent, and walked with the aid of a daughter. He spoke no English, but smiled and nodded in response to whatever Machumps was telling him.

This was John's first encounter with the Indians on their own ground, and he was surprised to find that their settlement was not laid out as he expected; no rows of houses side by side as in an English village. Barrel-roofed huts covered with reeds and walled with mats were situated under trees and set widely apart from one another. The inhabitants were mostly women and children, and John could count only half a dozen men of warrior age.

"You are welcome, son of the great lord Powhatan," the weroance told Machumps. "But we are poor and have very little food to spare." Nevertheless, women provided bowls of boiled fish that smelled to John as though it had been around a little too long. They, too, smiled encouraging him to eat. But the men stood watching from a distance, and they did not smile.

Chapter Nine

M aggie Beale was astir at dawn, and by the time she returned to her house to wake Will, she had news. At James Towne nothing remained a secret for long. She heard it from Sara Fielding, another of the winter's survivors. The governor was about to call a war council and every man able to stand and hold a musket would be ordered to be ready to march against the savages. "We'm goin' to kill every last one of them," Sara had added, "And about time too!"

Will's first thought was for his brother's safety. If this was true, it made no difference what message John was carrying to Orapakes. As like as not, the savages would slaughter every white man they could lay their hands on.

"There's naught you can do, my dear," Maggie told him. "It's yourself you must look to. Do what they say you must, but be no hero. Nobody will thank you, and if you're dead... if you're dead there's only one person'll cry on your grave."

At eight o'clock the church bell chimed thrice summoning the officers to the council meeting. Gates, Wainman, Yeardley, Martin, and Percy were all attired in their military finery, as were Brewster and two more captains, Thomas Holcroft and George Webb. Consequently, to the watching "other sort," Jeremiah Douthitt's late arrival from the camp generated much amusement. He evidently had just gotten out of bed. Hatless, his britches were untied, his stockings wrinkled, and his shirt defied his efforts to tuck it in. There was, however, no hint of amusement on the face of his Lordship who glared at the apologetic Douthitt in silent disapproval.

The interior of the church, as Percy had promised, had been greatly improved since the governor's first dismal assessment. The crumbling clay walls had been repaired. New shutters had been hung on the windows, and more importantly, pews cut from sweet-smelling cedar were in place. So, too, was the governor's own green velvet chair and a stool with a velvet cushion for him to kneel on. The communion table was rough hewn and the pulpit yet to be constructed, but the improvements were substantial and pleasing to the eye of his Lordship — which was all that mattered.

The awkward relationship between Delaware's Chaplain Laurie and Gates' Reverend Buck had been resolved. They would take turns conducting the services and delivering the twice daily sermons. That seemed fair enough, Buck agreed — until he learned that whenever the governor was present, Laurie would be at the spiritual helm. And he was to be so again today.

"Oh, heavenly Father," he began, "we are gathered here today in thy sight..." Unlike Buck whose perorations often rambled their way along the road to eternity, Laurie knew to keep it short. "And as God hath made you instruments for the enlarging of the Church militant here on earth, so when the period of your lives shall be finished, the same God shall make you members of his Church triumphant in heaven. Amen."

"Amen," replied the tiny congregation.

"No sermon this morning, thank thee, master Laurie," Delaware told him. "Now, gentlemen, Sir Thomas wishes to make a statement. Is that not so?"

Gates got to his feet and thanked his governor for the opportunity, and did so with florid courtesy. Privately, however, being subordinate did not sit well with him. To be lieutenant governor was an honor and a good post as long as the Governor for Life remained in London, but with him living next door and controlling everything from when to pray to where to "do the necessities of nature," the job was becoming increasingly onerous. But on this June morning he was intent on accomplishing something important on his own.

The savages must be made to fear.

Gates told his audience that in his view the Indians were becoming increasingly bold. Ever since they ambushed Ratcliffe and his men, they had ceased to trade with James Towne. They had learned the limitations of musketry and so sound and smoke held no terrors. Nothing but a massively destructive strike against them would teach them that submission was their only salvation.

Delaware liked the sound of that, and said so.

Though a soldier to the bone, Gates was as shrewd a politician as any pale-handed courtier. Quoting from the wording of his own instructions from the Company, he declared, "We shall never make any great progress in this glorious work nor have any civil peace as long as their priests are left to poison and infect the minds of the ignorant savage. Furthermore," he added, "we must be mindful that our enemies are two sorts, natives and strangers whose ships may even now be at our gates."

He was referring, of course, to the bogey men of Spain who lurked in the dark corners of every Englishman's subconscious. Ever since Harry VIII defied the Pope and Mary brought him back, Spain had succeeded France as the national enemy. The Armada attack on England in 1588 and the failed Gunpowder Plot as recently as 1605, were reminders that Spain and Catholicism were still an ever present threat. So there could, indeed, be strangers at the door to the Chesapeake. Fort Algernon, Gates insisted, was too puny a structure to be anything more than a place of protection for lookouts watching for enemy sail. "Behind it, lies Powhatan's son, Pochins, and his large settlement of Kecoughtan. My Lord, as long as that exists our flank cannot be safe. Give me leave, therefore I say, to remove that cancer from our breast."

"Anatomically, Sir Thomas, your flank and breast are not in the same place," Delaware told him and drew polite laugh from his officers. He then called for discussion and found unanimity in the responses. Wainman spoke in favor of an attack sooner rather than later, and the murmur of "ayes" left the Governor in no doubt. All that remained was to work out the timing and the strategy.

"We'll surprise them by night," Gates explained. "By day they'll be watching for us."

"We've only to stir from the fort, and they know it," Percy added.

"Which is why we'll board the barges after dark on a falling tide," Gates replied, "It should take about two hours. We'll land upstream of our fort. If the savages have scouts out, they'll be watching it and not us. We'll advance through the woods from the west, then draw their men out from their village and put them silently to the sword. Musketeers will hold their fire until silence is no longer our ally."

"Draw them out, you say. But how are you to do that?" Delaware wanted to know.

"Ah, m' Lord, that's where I crave your help," Gates replied with a knowing smile.

"You're not expecting me to...?"

"No indeed, m'Lord," Gates assured him. "No, I have in mind to borrow your taborer, what's his name."

"Dowse? You mean you want Tom Dowse? He's naught but a comedian. He bangs his drum, plays his pipe, and tells droll stories. What possible use can he...?"

"That precisely, m' Lord." Gates replied. "The savages are beguiled by music. We'll send him out ahead into their corn field. He'll bang his drum, toot his flute and sing and dance until they come out. Then he'll back away drawing the savages toward him. And when they're far enough into the field for us to encircle them..." He stopped and clapped his hands together for dramatic effect. "We have 'em!"

"Clever, Sir Thomas, very clever," said John Martin with a hint of a sneer. "Suppose they don't come out? Suppose they're cleverer than you think? Suppose only one comes out? What then?"

"And suppose they shoot Master Dowse?" Delaware argued. "I wouldn't want that. No, indeed, I wouldn't."

"In war, my Lord, anything is possible," Gates allowed.

"'Tis a bold plan. I like it," Wainman declared. He could see that once the governor expressed doubts, others would be emboldened to raise more objections. It was time to halt discussion before the plan was committeed to death. "It only remains, does it not, to decide which men to send?"

"I shall lead the expedition myself," Gates announced. "If it fails, you'll know who to blame," he added with a laugh. "I'll need men who are healthy, sensible, and courageous; forty or fifty of them."

"My men are ready!" came an unfamiliar voice from the rear. Captain Douthitt stood up and offered his assurance that not only were his troops ready, they were eager to kill savages and would do so with such will that in future no Indian would ever dare oppose them. The officers sitting in the front pews turned and stared at Douthitt as though he was an intruder from some undiscovered land.

"Thank you, Master...er?"

"Captain, Sir Thomas. Captain Jeremiah Douthitt, commander of the first, second and, and..."

"Yes, thank you, Captain," Gates told him. "Now, please sit yourself. If I need your men you may be sure that I shall call on them." There was no point in telling Douthitt what others thought of them. In an unusually candid moment, Preacher Buck had declared that "many of the men sent hither have been murderers, thieves, adulterers, idle persons, and what not besides. All which persons," he added, "God hateth even from his very soul." Gates wasn't about to go that far, but neither were Douthitt's men of the caliber he wanted on a raid whose success depended on strict adherence to the plan.

Captain Brewster had listened in silence to Gate's proposal, but now felt compelled to speak up. "My Lord, gentlemen, this bold plan will wait, will it not, until our messenger returns with Powhatan's answer?"

Delaware looked to Gates. "Well, Sir Thomas, how say you?"

"I say we do not wait," Gates replied."Our surprise will be the greater."

"But we put a young man's life at risk," Brewster persisted.

"Aye, but a risk worth the taking." Gates turned to Delaware. "My Lord, the fate of the colony rests..."

Delaware held up his hand to stop him. "Enough said. The command is yours Sir Thomas, and so is the timing."

The meeting ended with a closing prayer but no stated decision on which troops to use or which night to send them. In reality, Gates knew very well that the only troops he could rely on would be the governor's own guardsmen – as Will Jefferys found out later in the day.

Around mid-morning on the 3rd of July, John and his escort came within a mile of Orapakes. Several Indian women were gathering berries from the bushes and vines alongside the trail. The first to see him ran away calling on her companions, "*Awassew, Bauqweuwh! Awasseu!*" but stopped when Machumps shouted to them that John came as a *netab* – a friend.

First cautiously, and then at a trot they came back, all talking at once. Three of the women wore their hair short and two wore it in a long braid but shorn at the front. All were tattooed in black in rows of dots and chevron patterns, some around their calves, others around their biceps, and some around both. Their only clothing were skirts of deerskin or silk grass, and like John's escort, they went barefoot. He had no idea what they were saying, but all were smiling and laughing. With a broad grin, Machumps told him that they were telling each other that he was more comely than the other *tassantasses* they knew. "The Dutchmen with Powhatan are a filthy lot," Machumps added, "and the English who came in the winter were walking bones. You're a much better stranger, they say."

"Thank them for that – I suppose. And tell them I wish them well."

Machumps's translation seemed to take much longer than the English words necessitated. But whatever he said, it pleased the women who then invited John to take berries from their baskets. However, the first fruit he bit into was so tart that it made his eyes run.

"They're better boiled," Machumps assured him.

By the time John reached the cornfields marking the outskirts of Orapakes, his procession had grown to a dozen or more women and girls and two or three near naked boys of six or seven. The noise of their approach had preceded them, although Machumps assured John that their journey from James Towne had been watched all the way and that Powhatan knew exactly where they were at any time in day or night. The news was not particularly reassuring to John who had neither heard nor seen anyone but the few people he had encountered in the villages along the way. Had he not stopped in those villages, the city of Orapakes would have been both a surprise and a disappointment. It was simply more of the same, only more so. Many of the barrel roofed dwellings were larger, some with their side mats removed, and many had fenced gardens around them, but as in the other villages, they were scattered amid the trees and faced in all directions. There was, however, a central area cleared of trees which John took to be the Indian's version of an English village green. Beyond it stood a yet larger mat-walled building that Machumps said was a lesser palace of the Great King. Flanking its small entrance were two red-painted wooden figures, one somewhat resembling a mountain lion and the other a huge bird.

John half expected Powhatan to emerge to greet him, but no one appeared. Instead, half a dozen lesser dignitaries awaited him in the middle of the cleared area. Two, who John took to be the most senior, were swathed in mantels coated with turkey feathers – mantles so enveloping that the men appeared to be birds. The effect was further dramatized by headdresses that looked a cross between an eagle and a cat. Around the men's necks, but largely hidden under the mantels, were strings of cowry shells interspersed with blue glass beads.

Speaking in English in a voice that seemed to grip the words deep in his throat before uttering them, the oldest of the feathered Indians told John, "You are welcome in the home of the Great Lord. I am Werowough, *weroance* of the Mattapani, and I greet you in his name."

John was uncertain how to return the greeting, and so settled for a formal bow, something he had seen lesser officers do before addressing Delaware. "I am here to speak unto the great Powhatan with words given me by the Lord Delaware, the Governor of Virginia," he said.

Werowough smiled and nodded. "Then you may tell me the words and I will convey them."

"Well..er..no," John stammered. "I am instructed..."

"No?" The *weroance's* voice was cold.

John explained that the words were in writing and had to be read — and read only to Powhatan.

"That may not be possible. The Emperor is unwell and sees no one but our priests. He is in the hands of the *Quioughcosoughes*." Werowough went on to tell John that he was welcome at Orapakes and could remain as long as he liked. And maybe, just maybe, Powhatan would recover enough to grant an audience. In the meantime, a guest house was available and every comfort would be provided. On that the *weroance* ordered a male servant to show John to his quarters, and then turned away. The meeting was over.

John looked to Machumps for advice, but got no response. Instead, he followed Werowough in the direction of one of the larger houses. Clearly Machumps had obeyed his orders to escort the English messenger safely to Orapakes, and that was where duty and friendship ended. The arrival formalities had been watched by twenty or thirty chattering women and children, and with the ceremony over they were emboldened to come closer and to mill around the visitor. Several were smiling and making small hand movements of greeting. As John waved back he noticed one young woman standing behind and apart from the others. She was better, or rather *more* clothed than the rest, having a deerskin robe pinned at one shoulder. A string of blue beads glistened in the sunlight. Her hair was short, and John noticed that her face was less tawny than most and unscarred by tattooing. Whoever she was, he assumed her to be the wife of someone important. But when his eyes met hers, she abruptly turned away.

The mat covering the door to John's lodging had been rolled up, and the servant stood aside to let him pass. Behind him came his two Indian escorts, one carrying the sack containing his armor and the other with the much heavier sack holding Delaware's gifts to Powhatan. Having dumped them on the dirt floor, the Indians departed as silently as they had remained throughout the journey from James Towne. Left to himself John had nothing better to do than to examine his quarters. It took no time at all, there being nothing in the single-room house besides bunk beds on either side that had been folded back against the walls. On the ground beside them lay bearskin rugs that still smelled of what he took to be bear but could have been any other animal that had shared his space. A circle of river rocks defined the center of the dirt floor and within it were the ashes of a fire whose smoke had escaped through a round hole in the roof. That, and the open doorway, provided the room with its only direct light, though more filtered in through chinks in the mat-covered walls.

John had been walking since dawn, the sun was hot and the humidity high, and he was tired. Although a midday nap was unthinkable amid the duties and bustle of James Towne, to do so while awaiting Powhatan's pleasure seemed an excellent idea. He unhooked one of the beds, spread a bearskin over its sagging vine lattice, and sat down, half expecting the cot to collapse. When it didn't he opened his knapsack and extracted the leather flask that Sergeant Gideon had given him. He removed its stopper and tried to drain the last drop from it. In truth, he already knew that two days earlier he had consumed what had been left of his beer. But it seemed worth a try. Machumps had told him that Indians traditionally drank nothing but water, preferably slightly warmed, and so beer would have to remain a memory until John returned to the fort. On the way, he had drunk from streams along with his guides, and welcomed the water as cold as the springs allowed it to be. Why the Indians would prefer it warmed, was beyond him.

"You *tassantasses* drink strange waters that cannot be good for you," Machumps had told him. "Sailors from your ships have traded what you call usquebaugh to our people in exchange for furs. It is a water that burns the throat and makes the drinker mad and falling down. They trade it in bottles with the face of a devil on their necks, and devil's water it is." John knew that trading liquor to the savages was banned and could get you hung, but he also knew that the laws on land seemed not to apply to the seamen aboard the anchored ships. Be that as it was, John had never tried spirits or cordials. Beer was his drink, and now he had none. He was also hungry. The loaf he had been given when he set out had been eaten before dark on the first day, and the food killed and cooked by Machumps and his companions left nothing for storage. But Werowough had told him that he would be looked after, and food being part of hospitality, John went to the doorway and waved to a group of women who were cleaning something about fifty yards away. They waved back, and when he made hand gestures toward his mouth, they appeared to understand. Yet nobody moved.

Rather than stand in the doorway looking stupid, John retreated into his lodging and sat down on the bed. Moments later an old woman entered, a wooden tray in her hands and on it a loaf of bread and a handful of purple berries. She laid the tray down in front of him, said nothing, and departed. He found the silence unnerving. It was as though he had entered another world in which, to its inhabitants, he did not exist. On reflection, however, he concluded that as he did not speak the Indians' language nor they his, there was little point in saying anything. So they didn't.

Satisfied with that thought, John ate his loaf, lay down on his cot and closed his eyes. Minutes later, the sound of an attention-getting cough made him open them.

"Just got back and heard you were here," said a figure silhouetted in the doorway. "Welcome to Orapakes."

Shielding his eyes against the sunlight, John saw that his visitor was wearing clothes as English as he sounded.

"I'm Harry Spelman. And you are?"

John told him, and added that he had never been so pleased to see anybody. Spelman replied that not having been to the fort since Lord Delaware arrived, he was anxious for news. Questions and answers batted back and forth, as they brought each other up to date.

"And you are happy here?" John asked, the surprise evident in his voice.

"Happy, no. Content, yes. 'Tis my lot." Then with a laugh, Harry added, "At least I'm alive and well fed – which is more than can be said for most of the folks who came to James Towne." Harry Spelman was now fifteen. He had been a favored trophy in Powhatan's household for nearly two years, during which time he had learned the several Algonquin dialects of the tribes in the emperor's chiefdom. For their part, a surprising number of Indians had learned the rudiments of English. "They pass the learning from one to another, the word sounding stranger with each telling" he added.

"Tell me," John asked. "How sick is Powhatan?"

"Sick? I saw him this morning," Harry replied. "He's not sick. It pleasures him to keep you waiting, that's all."

"For how long?"

"Who knows? A day, a week; could be more. It depends how eager he is to hear the words of Delaware's message and receive his gifts." Harry went on to explain that Powhatan's priests had told him that the English were no longer a threat. That they had been prepared to abandon their fort – and, indeed, had done so – was a sign from the gods that in time they would defeat themselves and die of disease and starvation. There was no need to do anything but sit and wait.

"Do you believe that?"

Harry answered that if a fleet filled with supplies didn't soon follow the arrival of Delaware and his three shiploads of mouths to feed, then, yes, they would all be dead by spring.

"And you?" John asked.

Harry shrugged. "I live my life as an Indian, I suppose. But I'll tell thee this. If the opportunity arises, I'll high me to the Potomacks." He explained that they lived on the waterway of the Chesapeake Bay and had been friendly toward John Smith and Captain Argall when they traded tools for corn. Harry had grown sick of Powhatan's caprice and the uncertainty of his favor. "One wrong word, and he'll have my head," he added. "You asked, am I happy? My answer is this: Living in fear of what the morrow may bring be no path to happiness. But take Tom Savage now; he's been here longer than I. He'll tell you he be content to live like an Indian and think, well – like a savage."

"And where is he now?" John wanted to know.

Harry told him that Powhatan used Savage to carry messages between villages, keeping their elders abreast of new developments at James Towne. Both Percy and Gates, and John Smith before them, knew of Tom Savage's dual role and were satisfied that he provided more valuable information about the Indians than they got about the fort.

From their first meeting onward, Harry Spelman became John Jefferys' friend and mentor, and it was Harry who told him that come the evening they would be the guests of a *weroance* more to be feared than Powhatan himself. Opechancanough was king of the Pamunkey tribe and the oldest and most influential of three brothers. It was he who had captured John Smith and taken him as a prisoner to Powhatan. "You must be careful what you say in his presence," Harry warned. "He understands English very well and is quick to take offense though none be intended."

Throughout that afternoon John Jefferys and Harry Spelman talked and talked, Harry wanting news of England and the Spaniards, and John wanting to learn everything he could about life among the Indians. All he knew of the Spaniards, John confessed, were the rumors he had heard in his brief stay in London. Their spies were everywhere, and the English Catholics were all heretics. Thwarting the Gunpowder Plot conspiracy had shown Londoners how unprepared they were for another such attack, and hatred of all strangers was rampant. From Harry he learned that like James Towne, the Indians, too, were facing food shortages. Both last summer and this spring had been unusually dry, stunting last year's corn crop and arresting its growth again this year. The English, on the one hand, had responded to attacks by burning Indian fields, and on the other by bartering for corn that could ill be spared. "Beads, copper, and iron tools be hard to resist," Harry said with a sigh of disbelief. "But 'tis so."

Late in the afternoon in the hour before dusk, a noise like a hundred wailing banshees broke the relative quiet, backed up with a high-pitched piping and the din of rattles. Though nothing new to Harry Spelman, for John the sounds came as a complete surprise. Thirty or maybe forty men and women were dancing in a circle, stamping and howling, and bending back and forth like birds pecking at the earth. Beyond them mats were being laid out in the form of a square with two stools, one facing the other across it. These, Harry explained, were for Opechancanough and for Lord Delaware's son. He said the word with a broad grin adding that he, too, was a *son* — the son of Captain Newport who had traded him. To be less than a son of a *weroance* was to belong to the "other sort," and to have no social standing but that of a serf. "Kings don't feast commoners," Harry added, "so play the part as 'twere your birthright. Be his equal. If he pays you a compliment, don't appear grateful, but return it with one of your own. 'Tis but a game, but a game in which there must be no loser."

John thanked him for the advice, and wished himself home at Withyham with nothing more on his mind than a mean bailiff. By the time two women came to escort him to his stool, a fire was burning in the middle of the mat-defined square, and lesser nobles in feathered capes and shell encrusted robes were squatting down on opposite sides, evidently taking places made familiar by protocol. A few acknowledged John's presence with a nod and a smile, but most ignored him, all eyes focusing on the empty stool at the far side of the square.

Amid more rattling and chanting, Opechancanough finally made his entrance. Guarded by six bowmen, he made his way to his stool and sat down. Only then did he raise his eyes to look at John across the smoking fire, and make a gesture of welcome. Even seated, he appeared taller than most of his lesser *weroances*. Like them he wore his head shaven on the right side and the hair at his crown greased to stand erect. The left side was uncut and was twisted into a plait that reached to his waist and was stuck with feathers and pieces of copper that glinted in the fire light. His ears were pierced and threaded with thongs from which hung animal claws and what appeared to be the feet of turkeys. Around his neck were strings of shells and black pearls as well as the ubiquitous blue glass beads. But below them he was clothed only in a deerskin skirt fringed with the tails of small animals. To the apprehensive John Jefferys, and seen across a smoking fire, Opechancanough looked for all the world like a demon from the depths of hell.

Once the Great King had seated himself and said a few words to the *weroances* on either side of him, first one and then another rose and launched into speeches that grew louder and more frenzied the longer they spoke. They waved their arms and stamped their feet, and from time to time their words – at least to John's ear – dissolved into howls and yells, all of which evidently were appreciated by the guests who howled back. Only exhaustion brought the orators to a panting and gasping halt. Throughout John did his best to sound interested and impressed, though he could not understand a word of it. He looked around for Harry Spelman who had not been invited and had wisely gone about his business.

"They are telling you about the great deeds our King has done." The voice was female and little more than a whisper in John's ear. He looked over his shoulder and saw the young woman he had noticed at the back of the crowd when he first arrived. She smiled but said nothing more. Other women had moved up to stand behind each of the seated *weroances*, and on a signal from Opechancanough they handed each a wooden bowl of water in which they washed their hands. While that was going on a procession of both men and women moved into the firelight carrying trays of food that ranged from roasted venison and wild turkey to boiled fish, beans and cornbread. To John, the feast looked large enough to feed several times the number of guests, and he wondered what the hungry hundreds at James Towne would think of such a spread.

As the food was brought in and dishes and bowls distributed, the chanting and rattling began again from the gathering darkness; but on somebody's cue it abruptly stopped. Then each *weroance* reached to the food nearest him, took one bite, spat it out, and threw it into the fire while muttering what sounded like a Christian grace. That done, everyone dove in, stuffing meats and handfuls of cornbread into their mouths, and washing it down with gourds of walnut milk, a favorite Pamunkey drink that John later learned was called *powcohicora.* Whatever its name, he didn't like it; but remembering Harry Spelman's warning, he did his best to pretend that he did. Nevertheless, had he thrown up, nobody would have taken any notice. Belching, it seemed, was taken as evidence of gastronomic delight.

Once the feasting was done and the dishes removed, John understood why so much food had been served. Each of the guests instructed his servant to remove whatever remained uneaten and to dole it out to the people who had accompanied him on the journey from his home village. John watched all this with interest, while smiling and nodding when anyone looked in his direction. If any of the assembled lesser lords spoke English, they kept it to themselves. Indeed, none said a word to him until Opechancanough called across the square, "You are well fed, English son, I trust?"

John answered in total honestly that he had been extremely well fed. He thought it unwise to add that he had greatly overeaten, was dead tired, and wanted naught but his bed.

"*Vhpoocan?*" asked Opechancanough holding out a clay tobacco pipe that an aide had already filled and lit for him. "You will drink *Vhpooc* with me in friendship with your Great Lord?" The question sounded much like an order, and John who had never smoked tobacco was afraid that in doing so now he would disgrace himself. "Er, yea...gladly," he replied with as much bravado as he could muster.

Several of the younger guests had departed as soon as the feasting was over, and those remaining were evidently of senior rank and certainly older. Each sucked on the pipe as it was passed from one to another, drawing the smoke deep into his lungs and then expelling it through his nose. John watched intently to see what the result might be, but the precaution told him nothing. Four or five sat back contentedly with mouths agape, and two coughed, spluttered, and spat on the ground. John was sure that he would belong to the latter group, but as he reached to take the pipe a commotion at the far side of the square caused his host to rise angrily from his stool. He shouted something in John's direction and strode away into the darkness, followed by the rest of his surprised guests. Within seconds John was alone staring at the square of vacated mats. Servants scrambled to clear away the debris and began rolling up the mats, all the while casting curious glances in his direction. He was still there when Richard Spelman reappeared.

"What happened?"

Harry replied that he wasn't sure. But a messenger had just arrived from Paspahegh warning that the *tassantasses* were up to something.

"Like what?" John wanted to know.

Harry didn't know, but he said he'd do his best to find out. "But I would guess that the Governor has decided to do something decisive without waiting for you to return with Powhatan's answer. If so, you may well find yourself more a hostage than a guest." Harry added that he thought the best thing John could now do was to make himself invisible. "Take my advice," he said. "Go to your lodge and stay there. By morning I may know more."

The center of the Orapakes village was almost deserted by the time John reached the doorway to his house, and he was surprised to find the entrance mat rolled down and light coming from inside. Looking back he realized that all the occupied dwellings had light seeping from them. He would later discover that it was a woman's duty to keep tapers burning and fires alight, not for warmth but through the summer to keep mosquitoes at bay. He lifted the mat and slid under it, and saw tapers burning in wooden brackets anchored to the roof supports. In the shadows something moved.

"Who be there?" John demanded as he drew his sword.

"It is I, Taropoto," came the answer as an Indian woman rose from squatting in the darkness beyond the bed. "I am to be yours this night," she said. "I am the gift of the Great Lord to his honored *Uttassantassowaih*." With that she untied the thong that secured her mantle at its shoulder, and let is slip to the ground. Not until she moved into the light did John realize that this red-painted and oiled body belonged to the young woman who had served him at the feast.

Unlike Will who had gained his carnal experience in London – if not before, John had never been with a woman, nor had he seen a maid unclothed. "I don't know, I mean...I'm, well, I'm not really..." he stammered.

Taropoto held out her hand. *"Neighsawhor"*, she said.

Chapter Ten

ᕙᕗ

When John Jefferys woke the next morning, the sun was already up and light was streaming through the smoke hole in his roof. His fire was out; so were the mosquito repelling tapers, and his companion of the night had gone. It took him a few seconds to convince himself that all the events of the previous evening had been more than a dream. He was still pulling on his britches when Harry Spelman peered around the edge of the door cover.

"A mite slow this morning are we?" he asked with a laugh. Without waiting for a reply, he rolled up the mat and entered.

"She was here when I fell asleep," John muttered. "Where did she go?"

"Home."

"Home? But isn't Orapakes her home?"

"She didn't tell you who she is?" Harry asked.

"She told me her name. 'Twas something like potato."

"Not potato, Tarapoto. She's a sister of the queen of the Paspahegh."

"She is?" John gasped. "You mean I...we...but..I mean, why did she...?"

Harry explained that to the Indians a noble visitor merited a noble bedfellow, and when Powhatan ordered, lesser *weroances* obeyed. As John already knew, Wowinchopunck, king of the Paspahegh, was the most dangerous enemy of the English, and in Harry's view, it probably amused Powhatan to put a serpent in his guest's bed. "If you weren't here under the Emperor's protection,"

Harry added, "she'd like as not cut your throat before she left."

"And I thought..." John began, then settled for an embarrassed smile.

"Well, look at it this way. When you get back to wherever your home is, you'll be able to tell 'em you bedded a princess. You did, didn't you ?"

John nodded.

"There you are then. Something to remember." In answer to John's questioning, Harry reported that the messenger whose news had taken Opechancanough so angrily from the feast was that the English at James Towne appeared to be readying barges to carry troops on some unknown mission. He had reported, too, that men with pieces (guns) had been seen shooting at targets, something they rarely did when powder was in short supply. According to the messenger it all added up to an attack on someone. Harry thought that the Paspahegh village at the mouth of the Chickahominy was the most likely target. He added that he had not detected any sign that John was in immediate danger of being harmed.

"Thank thee for that," John replied. "Do you think Powhatan will summon me today?"

Harry shrugged. "You'll just have to wait and see. Maybe he will; maybe he won't. There be no telling."

The report of military activity at James Towne had taken a little more than a day to reach Orapakes. Meanwhile, at the fort, Gates, too, was waiting – waiting for the top of a falling tide after dark and for a moonless night. Both conditions would be met on the nights of July 9 and 10; but Gates being eager to get on with the business, chose the ninth. In the previous days more men had fallen sick. Several were from the ranks of Delaware's guard, but many more were ailing among the troops billeted beyond the palisades. Dr. Bohun called their sickness "strange fluxes and agues" and confessed that the prospect of an epidemic was more than he could handle. "We must have physicians more skilled in these matters than am I, and we need the right kinds of medicines. We've barely three weeks more of what we have. I beg you, my Lord, send the *Blessing* home to bring us what we need."

But Delaware was unwilling to do so. He replied that with the *Discovery* and *Patience* gone, he could not – would not release another ship. "Be assured, good doctor, that when they return, Sir Thomas will be eager to sail." With that, Bohun had to be content, or so Delaware insisted.

For Will Jefferys waiting to be called to arms was becoming increasingly galling. When he heard that two water carriers had been wounded, he was loud in his irritation at the lack of response from his officers. "If 'twere my say," he told Sergeant Gideon, "I'd be out after the bastards and kill every one of 'em!"

"Fortunately, it ain't your say," Gideon told him, "elseways you'd have more of us dead." Later that morning, Gideon decided to cool him off, and so sent him and three more hotheads fishing. Though they cast their seines again and again, they caught nothing, and returned in no better mood. Maggie was waiting for them when they beached the boat, "'Tis tonight," she told them. "Gideon says you're to rest 'til the bell."

As Maggie gave Will his supper of bread and bean soup, he told her, "I don't know why you look after me so well."

"Because you be my man, that's why," she replied.

Maggie's answer nudged at a door Will was reluctant to open. The question she had put to him as they sat that night beside the river, had not been answered nor repeated. He was grateful for her kindness and affection, but he had never thought about the future beyond tomorrow. They were two people thrown together by circumstances and mutual need. But to go beyond that to being Maggie's man implied a commitment that scared him. "Oh, I don't know about that," he replied with a self deprecating laugh. "I'll wager you'll find someone better ere long."

There was no laughter in her reply. "Will, dear heart, I doubt I'll be lookin'," she told him. "Eat your supper."

A single toll of the church bell was the signal that everyone had been awaiting, some eagerly, some apprehensively, and some, like Tom Dowse, in abject fear. Darkness held terrors of its own, and rumors that the savages were capable of summoning demons out of the depths of hell made the timorous even more fearful. Marching against the enemy in broad daylight with drums beating and colors flying helped make one feel invincible, or at least convinced that if anyone was going to get killed it would be someone else. But in the dark, one would be alone, robbed of sight and reliant on untrained senses. Will had talked about this with other guardsmen ever since they learned that the attack was to be by night, but if there were any such fears in his heart, they were hidden deep inside. The bell had tolled, and now, at last, it was time to end hiding like a turtle in its shell.

Lines were already filing in and out of the corps-du-garde when Will crossed the market place expecting to receive his musket along with its support rest and all the other equipment needed to load and fire it. Although he had no intention of admitting it to his brother, ever since drills at the Spittle Fields camp he had been aware that military issue matchlocks were far more unwieldy than was the snaphaunce musket he had left at home. He was surprised and relieved, therefore, to be issued only with a sword and a short pike called a partizan. Sergeant Gideon later explained to his men that the success of the first assault would depend on speed and stealth. Musketry would follow once the initial surprise had been lost. Gideon's own file was to be the first to attack once Tom Dowse's antics had drawn the savages into the open.

"Only officers will be wearing armor," Gideon explained. "It makes too much noise, and is too easily snagged by vines. Remember that though the savages may have the advantage over us in daylight, they're no better than we are in the dark. Keep low and keep moving, and you'll come back safe and the better for the exercise. And one more thing," he added. "our general says there's an extra ration in it for any man who captures their king. So watch for him."

Will's enthusiasm for the coming adventure was somewhat tarnished when he found that the ailing in his ranks were being filled by a file of ten musketeers from the camp. He was even less pleased when he saw that Twofin Chisman and his friends, Arty and Smiler, were among them. However, he might have been happier had he known that Captain Douthitt had selected the three trouble makers in the hope that they'd get themselves killed.

At a few minutes before eight-thirty Gates bade leave of his Governor, and with Captains Yeardley and Brewster and Lieutenant John Earely they made their way out of the fort and down to the waiting barges. Much against Gates's better judgment, he allowed William Strachey to join the expedition. He had insisted that as James Towne's officially appointed recorder, it was his duty to witness so important an event. "Otherwise," he added with an ingratiating smile, "how can you expect me to properly describe your victory?"

Sir Thomas was not a man who warmed to flattery, but he knew that Strachey was right, and so let him aboard. "I wouldn't wear a cloak, if I were you," he grunted.

"It may get chilly," Strachey replied, as he clambered over the thwarts to the stern and sat himself down beside an already shivering Tom Dowse. "This is going to be great fun, don't you think?" said Strachey brightly.

Dowse was a small man, and appeared even smaller as he sat, his shoulders hunched and his arms wrapped around his drum. "Some idea of fun," he mumbled. His talent was to amuse, and he deeply resented being conscripted into what he was sure would end before dawn with his precious drum broken and his hide bristling with arrows. "I never, never, never should 'ave let his Lordship bring me here, and that's the truth," he whined.

"I'll see you go down in history," Strachey told him. "You'll die a hero."

As he had been from the moment they left Buckhurst, Will Jeffery was in Sergeant Gideon's file, and sat with his fellow pikemen in the first of the five-man rows. Without turning round, he estimated that there were twenty-five or so men behind him. The rest, including Captain Douthitt's ten, were in the second barge. In each were six rowers, their rowlocks wrapped in canvas, augmenting a small foresail which, if a wind should comply, would carry them silently downstream. Lieutenant Governor Gates and Captain Brewster commanded the lead boat, and Captain George Yeardley and young John Earely, the second. One behind the other, they slipped away from James Towne Island. Only the muffled dipping of the oars and the gentle lapping of the water as the bows cut through it broke the silence. And when a man in the second boat coughed it seemed as loud as a pistol shot.

Gates had wanted a dark night, and with no moon and a light mantle of clouds he had a blackness as stygian as a Newgate dungeon. He was certain that no savage would see the boats glide by. In any case, the plan was to go ashore about four miles upstream from Kecoughtan, and they did so without any evidence that they had been seen. But the darkness that had been their friend on the water deserted them once they were ashore, and the crunching of underbrush, the cursing that accompanied every tripped-over root or entangling vine made nonsense of Gates' aim to "approach as silent as the grave." Whispered calls for silence went in vain. Twice Dowse dropped his drum, and several musketeers lost their rests. Only the soldier carrying the dark lantern that would be used to ignite the musketeers' match fuses could see where he was going.

Brewster whispered to Gates that he was sure the savages would have heard their approach and that he should be prepared to be attacked before they reached the village. But Gates replied that he had no alternative but to press on and hope its inhabitants were deep sleepers. While still in the woods, but about half a mile from the target, the faint odor of smoke from village fires warned that they was not far away, and shortly thereafter the first of Brewster's column reached the cleared and planted acres that surrounded it. He held up his hand to halt the advance, but few saw it and several pikemen ran into each other before the word passed successfully to the rear.

The order to "Charge your pieces," resulted in even more confusion, as the musketeers fumbled with their powder tubes and groped in their bullet bags. The dark lantern man had to open it to ignite the length of niter-soaked cord that had to be passed from man to man as each lit his own fuse. In retrospect, Brewster wasn't sure that his commander's order not to march with loaded guns had been such a good idea. However, he was aware that the pin points of glowing

fuses provided the enemy with useful targets, and with the musketeers as clumsy as they had proved to be, he supposed it likely that
someone's gun would have discharged and blown the kneecap off
his nearest companion. Worse, it would have aroused the village.

Nevertheless, that hadn't happened, or if it had, the savages
were silently laying a trap.

"Bring Dowse up," Gates ordered. The word passed quickly
back into the woods where Tom Dowse was hoping he had been
forgotten.

"Up you go, good fellow," said Strachey. "Remember, I'll be
watching for you. Toot away!"

The reluctant Dowse found himself roughly passed from soldier to soldier until he was propelled to the front. "You know what
you have to do," Gates told him. "Go out there into the field and
when you think you're close enough to the village to be seen, start
banging your drum and tooting your flute.

"I'm not sure I've the spittle to play. My throat's parlous dry,"
Dowse complained.

"Then beat your drum and sing!" Gates snapped.

"But if I can't play, I'm sure I can't sing," Dowse pleaded.

"You'll find a way. Now get on out there! And if you know
what's good for you, keep moving. Dance your jig!"

Someone shoved the luckless taborer out into the open. He
hesitated and made to turn but thought better of it when a voice
behind him hissed, "There's a pistol pointed at your arse!" Step by
step as though walking on glass, Lady Delaware's favorite fool edged
out into the Indians' cornfield. Behind him and to his flanks, Sergeant Gideon's file crawled forward through the ripening corn. Will
wished he wasn't dragging his pike alongside him, but he was glad
not to be doing it in armor.

"Start drumming!" Gates shouted in as low a voice as he could
manage. "Why doesn't the damn man start drumming?" he demanded
of anyone in earshot.

Captain Brewster's response was not without sympathy. "Because the poor fellow's scared to death, sir."

Rat a tat tat! Dowse had begun to play – and dance. Somewhere in the village a dog barked.

"Louder! Louder!" Gates had ceased whispering and was now bellowing at his decoy. "In the name of sweet Jesu, bang it louder! Go closer, man!"

Sergeant Gideon and his file were the furthest into the field, and when the hint of dawn lightened the eastern sky, they were the first to be able to see the village. An under-construction palisade of saplings prevented Will Jefferys from seeing what, if anything, was going on behind it. He had heard that Kecoughtan had as many as a thousand inhabitants living in three hundred houses, a town more than twice the size of Withyham. If true, taking it with only sixty men was going to be a bloody business.

As the sky continued to lighten, Will could see the palisade's open gateway and from it emerged first one Indian and then another.

"Dance, Dowse!" Gates shouted. "Go closer!"

The Indians at the gateway were soon joined by several others. At first they stood there peering into the gloom trying to locate the source of the noise, but moments later one pointed in its direction.

"They've seen him," Gideon hissed. "Stand by."

Hesitantly at first, and then with bows drawn, the Indians advanced down the lane dividing two cornfields.

"Now back away," Gates shouted. "Keep playing and back away." But Dowse had seen enough. He either failed to hear the order or decided that self preservation took precedence, and so turned and fled back toward the woods. An arrow whistled past him as he ran.

"Now!" shouted Gideon. Instantly, Will and the rest of his file rose out of the corn with swords drawn and ran at the surprised Indians. The second file under Lieutenant Earely rushed out from the other side and cut off their retreat. It was all over in seconds. Armed only with bows and arrows, the Indians were no match for swords and pikes. Five lay dead or dying, but three escaped and ran back into the village pursued by Gideon, Will, and several others. Simultaneously, the rest of Gates's force came out of the woods and converged upon the village from two sides.

Gideon was first through the gateway, and as he shouted, "Come on, lads!" an arrow pierced his throat. He stumbled, dropped his sword, clutched at his neck, and fell backwards into Will's arms, blood spurting from his severed temporal artery. "I fear I'm done," he said. "Leave me."

"Not as I live," Will told him, as he lowered him to the ground. The arrow had passed through Gideon's throat at an angle and emerged under his left ear. Will tried to pull it back but couldn't without doing more damage, and so broke the shaft and pulled the barb through. He stripped off a stocking and tried to stem the blood, but couldn't do so.

"'Tis an order, Will lad, there's no..." Gideon's voice trained away into a blood-drenched gurgle.

"Hold fast," Will urged. "We'll get you back." Meanwhile, more of Gates's men were pouring into the village, none stopping to help the dying sergeant. Yelling louder than the Indians, they surged amid the reed-built houses intent on slaughtering any who stood in their path.

"Leave him, lad." The voice was Captain Brewster's. "There's naught more you can do."

The Indians put up very little resistence, and instead fled with their women and children into the forest to the north and west, with the English soldiery in pursuit. A few were run down and wounded. Not until later did Gates learn that Pochins, Kecoughtan's *weroance*, was away at a meeting with his father. The expected thousand population proved to have been vastly over estimated, as were the three hundred houses. Thirty was closer to the mark, and in the space of twenty minutes all were burning. Silhouetted against the flames, soldiers ran back and forth carrying baskets and pottery bowls of corn, beans, and other foodstuffs. A wooden figure standing outside the largest of the houses was tossed into the fire as the looting went on, and Twofin Chisman and his friends chased a terrified woman into the woods, but lost her. Clouds of black smoke billowed high in the morning air, and the stench of destruction was everywhere as Gates and his officers surveyed their handiwork.

"Too bad about your sergeant," Gates told Brewster. "A good man, was he?"

"The best," Brewster replied. "We'll carry him back, of course."

"Bury him with honor," Gates added. "We'll make a show of it. Good for morale."

Will had remained with Gideon's body and had taken no part in either the pursuit or the looting. His bloodied hands and clothing made him appear to be another casualty, and his friend Pips was relieved to find that he was not. "Some night's work, eh?" said Pips. "But losing our sergeant was a high price to pay for it, 'deed it was."

An hour later, nothing remained of Kecoughtan but piles of still smoldering ashes. Lieutenant Earely was not particularly pleased to learn that he and twenty men were to remain there to build a sconce and secure the fields. The rest reluctantly formed up to return to the boats, most of them carrying souvenirs of one sort or another. Recorder Strachey told anyone who would listen that he had been lucky enough to salvage a dozen silk-grass skirts of the first quality and that he intended to send some back to his sponsors in England. "They're wonderful examples of what heathen savages can do when they try."

Will ordered four guardsmen to save matting and poles from one of the burning houses and to make them into a bier to carry his sergeant back to James Towne. "Here, give me your cloak," he told Strachey.

"How dare you, soldier. I'll do no such thing!" Strachey angrily replied.

Captain Brewster was returning to the gate when he heard Strachey's refusal. "I think it would be well to do as this man asks," he said. Then, stooping to pick up Gideon's sword, he turned and handed it hilt first to Will.

When the returning barges came in sight of James Towne, most of its inhabitants were at the waterside waiting eagerly and anxiously for news. Maggie was horrified when she saw Will step ashore. "You're hurt. Where did the buggers get you? Show me where?" she demanded. It took several minutes of explanation for her to realize that the blood was not his. "Thanks be to God!" she declared.

Will laughed and hugged her, then stepped back. "Do I look any different?" he asked.

"Different?"

"Yes. Do I look any different? Do I look any taller?"

Maggie shook her head in puzzlement.

"Well, I should do," Will replied, "now that I'm Cap'n Brewster's sergeant."

Chapter Eleven

❧

Five days passed at Orapakes with no summons from Powhatan nor even any certainty that he was there. For John Jefferys, the waiting became increasingly nerve wracking. He passed the time exploring the village, an exercise that taught him little. Although children and women smiled and even spoke to him, the men remained warily aloof. Indeed, on the sole occasion when he wandered beyond the houses and started down a well-worn trail, two warriors materialized out of nowhere and signaled to him to stop and turn back. Only later did he learn from Harry Spelman that the path led to the temple where all Powhatan's tribute and loot were stored, and where he met with his council and his priests. No one was allowed there without both an invitation from the Emperor himself and an armed escort.

On the afternoon of the sixth day while John was watching four young men shooting at hide targets, one of them noticed his interest and came to where he was standing. "I talken Glish," he proudly announced. "You use *hawtoppe?*" he asked, pointing to his bow.

John allowed that he did, but he had never handled an Indian bow. He explained that the English long bow was heavier and, he suspected, stronger.

"I am Tanxmoninaw, as you would say, Little Crow." He handed John his bow. "You try," he said.

The bow was lighter, and the stone-pointed arrow less well balanced than John was used to. His first attempt at the target a hundred yards distant missed and drew laughter from Little Crow and his friends, each of whom next took turns, every arrow piercing the target close to the center. When John shook his head in amazement at their skill and his own failure, Little Crow explained that every day before breakfast Indian children were required by their mothers to shoot at targets, and there was no food until they hit it, he added with a laugh. "You learn; you eat," he added.

John asked to be allowed two more shots. The first hit the rim of the target, but the second hit so close to the center that it shivered an arrow already lodged there. The Indians clapped their hands in admiration. One said something that John could not understand. Little Crow translated. "He say, you could be as we."

John replied that he took that as a great compliment, and said that he would like to practice more. But before he could do so, Harry Spelman found him. "There is news," he said. "Come away."

As they walked back to John's lodge, Richard explained that the other English interpreter, Tom Savage, had arrived to report that he had heard that Kecoughtan had been destroyed. "I'll wager Powhatan already knows. He'll take it as a personal affront, Pochin being one of his sons."

Harry went on to explain that Powhatan had a vested interest in Kecoughtan, having destroyed its earlier inhabitants, replacing them with people of his own Pamunkey tribe.

"So what do you think he'll do?" John asked.

Harry shrugged. "Who knows? Powhatan's a patient man. It's my guess that he'll wait to hear your message from the Governor. By the way, what *is* the message?"

Although he had not been ordered not to reveal its contents, John was wise enough to keep it to himself. He said as much, and begged Harry not to take offense. "But I can tell thee this. He won't like it."

A few minutes later John had another visitor. "I'm Tom," he said. "Welcome to the lion's den." Thomas Savage was fifteen and had been Powhatan's principal interpreter for the past two years and had spent more time with him than had Harry Spelman. Tom was tall, black haired and dark skinned, the result both of sun tanning and the constant smokiness of Indian dwellings. Although he still wore English clothing, shell beads around his neck and as a bracelet around his left wrist suggested that were his hair cut in their fashion he could easily pass for an Indian. "Before you ask, I'll tell you that my name really is Tom Savage. But you lives with what you'm born with," then added with a laugh. "'Tis lucky the Indians don't use last names."

With the niceties of introductions behind him, Tom turned to the purpose of his visit. "Before this day is done, Powhatan will be ready to receive his Lordship's message. I'm to tell you that."

"Why not now?" John asked.

"Because he's bringing in some of his *weroances*," Tom went on to explain that the Emperor wants his relatives and allies to hear what Delaware has to say, and more importantly to hear what he has to say in return. "And, yes, he does know about Kecoughtan. So speak your words carefully."

"Carefully?" John retorted. "I must read what is written!"

"Well...try to read it in a...in a servile way."

Left to himself, John opened the leather pouch and read Delaware's message for the first time since that morning at James Towne. Trying to make the words sound conciliatory – though that was one absent from his vocabulary – proved virtually impossible. There was no soft way to make demands which, if not met, would lead to dire consequences. He decided, therefore, to read the words without any kind of emphasis in the hope that by doing so, Powhatan would not see him as making the demands himself. In any case, Delaware's writing was hard to read, and the more he stumbled the less demanding he would sound. Having come to that conclusion, all John Jefferys had to do was wait. And wait he did until late in the afternoon when Tom Savage came to escort him.

"It's now," he said. "They're ready for you."

"They?"

"It's as big a gathering as I've seen since they did their show for Cap'n Smith," Tom told him. "Both his brothers are there, most of the important *weroances*, and the priests and councillors, wives, children, and other people I've never seen before. He means to impress you with the fact that you're not talking to one man but to his whole nation," Tom added. Then, "Don't forget the gifts. I'll carry the sack for you, if you'd like."

John would have forgotten them, so nervous had he become at the thought of speaking in front of such an audience. Tom picked up the sealed bag and hefted it. "Heavy," he said. "I'll wager its a load of those cheap hatchets. If they are, Powhatan knows the difference between iron and steel. You'd better pray they're the good sort."

As soon as John stepped out of his lodge, lines of women and warriors flanking the entrance to Powhatan's palace began shouting, screeching, stamping their feet and waving rattles. The sudden burst of discordant sound was such that it robbed him of every intelligent thought, and he remembered little of his progress to the doorway beyond his desire to clap his hands over his ears. But when he got there, the racket stopped as abruptly as it had begun.

"Here we go," said Tom with a wry smile. "Good luck."

"You mean, you're not coming with me?" John gasped.

Tom assured him that he was, and that he would be translating for the people who had yet to learn English. He had no time to say more before four robed elders hustled John inside. He expected to find a single long hall, but instead he had to weave his way around alternating screen walls that skillfully prevented any enemy from charging from one end of the building to the other. The last two such screens created anterooms where visitors could await their turns to enter the council chamber – at least that was how John interpreted them. In each room there was a small, smoking fire that made his eyes run. Belatedly he realized that although there were roof holes for the smoke to escape, those were the only sources of light. How, he asked himself, was he going to read his Lordship's carefully chosen words in semi-darkness? It turned out, however, that in the Great Chamber mats rolled on cords from the outside opened slits in the roof that allowed pools of light to reach the floor. A fire occupied the chamber's center, and on either side, like choristers in choir stalls, sat ranks of elders flanked by red-painted bowmen. Beyond, on either side of a central dais sat and squatted several young women who John assumed to be Powhatan's wives. Between them, on a bearskin covered throne sat the emperor resplendent in a shell-encrusted deerskin robe that made him appear shrunken inside it. His neck was hung around with strings of beads and pearls. There were several feathers in his gray hair that hung to his shoulders around a face that was still rotund. Several long gray hairs straggled from his chin and a few more grew over his thin-lipped mouth. He would not, John thought, be a particularly impressive person were it not for his fiercely penetrating eyes that stared at John as though to bore into his mind.

On entering the chamber, the *cronoccoes* — Powhatans councillors and priests — waved rattles and chanted, but stopped when he raised his hand. From one side of the dais stepped a tall man of middle age, his hair cut into the familiar side lock, and his lean torso draped in a tasseled robe.

"That's Papaschicher," Tom Savage whispered from behind John's ear.

He proved to be the Emperor's orator, and launched into a speech that grew more impassioned the longer he ranted, not a word of which could John understand. Tom began to translate but soon gave up. "He's saying how great Powhatan is and how puny we are," Tom explained and let it go at that. Eventually Papaschicher came to a halt, seeming more out of exhaustion than from any lack of praise for his king.

More rattling followed the end of the speech, and again halted abruptly as Powhatan rose to his feet. Standing, John realized that he was taller than he had supposed, and every inch a monarch comfortable with his powers of life and death over his subjects. "You are welcome, son of your lord and son of your great King James. You do honor us with your presence, and we, in our turn, honor you."

If, as Tom had said, Powhatan knew about the sacking of Kecoughtan, John could detect nothing but benevolence in the old man's words. "Great Lord Powhatan, in the name of my Lord Delaware, Governor General of Virginia, I return your greeting." John replied.

"You bring me gifts?" Powhatan asked.

"Yes...indeed, yes. They are right here." John assured him.

"And of what nature are they? I would like one of your grinding stones."

"Well, no, not a grindstone."

"Then what are they?" Powhatan's tone had hardened.

John explained that the bag held by Tom Savage had been sealed by his Lordship and that his orders were to break it only in the Emperor's presence. Powhatan nodded and seemed content with the answer. Tom cut the cord and John reached into the sack and brought out a leather bag which he opened and from it poured glass beads into one hand. Powhatan nodded again, but seemed unimpressed. "They're blue, " John declared, having remembered that Powhatan was said to be particularly partial to the color. Again Powhatan nodded, but with no evidence of sudden delight.

"And copper," John added, pulling two six-inch square plates from the sack.

"Good" said Powhatan flatly. "More. Show me more."

"Knives, too. Six of them." John groped in the bag and discovered that only hatchets remained. "And fine new hatchets, " he said, tipping them onto the ground in front of the dais. Papaschicher stooped and picked one up, turned it over, weighed it in his hand, then passed it to Powhatan.

"This is the gift your Lord sends me?" asked Powhatan grimly as he threw the hatchet down at John's feet. "Does he think me so ignorant that I do not know what is good and what is not?"

"No, I'm sure he doesn't...I mean...no, I've heard tell he thinks..." John stammered.

"He thinks what?" Powhatan had stepped down from the dais and stood glowering into John's face. "What does your father think? Tell me."

"Well, he's not really my father, and..."

"And you think I did not know that?" Powhatan demanded. "He

takes me for a fool. You all think my people are less clever than yourselves. If that be true, why are your people starving and dying inside your own trap while we are free to go where ere we will? Answer me that."

John had no answer. Debating face to face with a king was a far cry from arguing with Will over whose turn it was to feed the sow. Not only was he in awe of Powhatan but he was irate that Delaware had sent him so ill prepared. Together, those sensations left him with his heart pounding and virtually speechless.

"If you *tassantasses* are so clever, why do you not learn to live in our *tsenacommacah?*"

"Our country," Tom Savage whispered.

Powhatan did not wait for an answer. He turned away and returned to his throne. "Now, speak the words your Lord has sent me," he ordered.

A murmuring from the assembled nobles made John glance around at the sea of expectant faces staring at him from the shadows beyond the shafts of sunlight. He spotted Machumps among them, but saw nothing but hostility in his face.

"Don't keep him waiting," Tom hissed.

But John could not do otherwise. In extracting the folded papers from the satchel, the second sheet slipped to the floor, and after retrieving it, he still had to position himself in the light to read them. Haltingly he began. "In the name of our sovereign lord King James the First of Great Britain, France, and Ireland, I Thomas West, Lord De La Warr, Governor of Virginia Britannia, send greetings to the emperor Powhatan, and wish..."

"Enough!" rasped Powhatan. "Get you to the words!"

"The words, sire, But these *are* the words..." John stammered.

Tom prodded him the back. "He means get to the point!"

Reluctantly, John passed over the niceties and picked up where his Lordship complained of the harm done to the settlers by the Paspahegh, the bribing away of the Dutchmen, the alleged imprisonment of missing Englishmen, and the stealing of tools and weapons. "It is my firm belief," John read on, "that these outrages hitherto used

157

against my people, not only abroad but at our fort also; have been done without your knowledge, but by your worst and most unruly people. Being a great and wise king, you must give an universal order to your subjects that these mischiefs must be no more."

"Must?" Powhatan rasped.

John swallowed. "Must, sire. The word is so writ. If not," he read on, "the Lord Governor and Captain General will be forced to defend himself and offend the Great King, which he is loath to do."

"Is he, indeed?" Powhatan grunted.

"The Great King well knows," John continued, "that his people have killed four of ours at our blockhouse, and has detained others. Those responsible must be punished, and our people returned to us. We must also have returned to us such arms as you have stolen. Do all this and and we will hold fair quarter and enter friendship with you as a friend to King James and his subjects." The wording went on to remind Powhatan that he had previously vowed friendship and homage and had received from the King a crown and scepter, the symbols of civil state and Christian sovereignty. Having done so, he was obliged to do his duty to his friend King James. To refuse would force the Lord Governor to use whatever means might be necessary to compel compliance.

"That is the sum of your Lord's words to me?" Powhatan asked.

"Well, more or less," John answered. "There's just the...er...the bit about being your Majesty's friend and well-wisher, and greetings again in the name of King James..."

Powhatan had heard enough, and said so. For what seemed to John like an eternity, Powhatan sat with his chin cupped in his hand, stroking the thin strands of his beard. When he spoke, he did so in measured tones very different from his orator's previous ranting. "You will remind your Lord that I, too, am a king and that this is my land. I shall do or not do as I think fit. No *tassantass* tells me what I must do. But I will tell your Lord what *he* must do. He will remain where he is. He will not venture further into our lands or our rivers, and if he does I shall command my people to kill yours. We shall do unto you all the things that you fear of us. Tell him this exactly as I have spoken."

John drew in a deep breath and replied that he would try to do so.

"And tell him also," Powhatan continued, "that I want no more cheap trinkets or axes that break. Nor do I want any more messengers unless they bring me a coach and three horses so that I may ride as do great *weroances* in England."

John did his best not to laugh, but even his half smile did not escape the eyes of Powhatan.

"Now go, young messenger," Powhatan told him. "Let there be no laughter in your voice when you tell my words, for you heard none in mine."

Chapter Twelve

❦

John Jefferys' departure from Orapakes lacked the ceremony that had marked his arrival. Indeed, there was no ceremony at all. Minutes after being precipitously ushered out of Powhatan's presence and escorted back to his lodge, Tom Savage caught up with him. "You're to go now," he said. "And I'm to go with you. The great man wants to know what *our* great man has to say in reply. I wish to heaven Powhatan had stayed at Werowocomoco," he sighed. "'Twas less than half the distance."

The two Indians who had escorted John to Orapakes were waiting to take him back to James Towne. They looked no more friendly than they had before. John had hoped to bid Harry Spelman farewell, but he was nowhere to be seen; nor was there any sign of Machumps.

"Everybody watches everybody else," Tom explained. "Very little happens here that doesn't reach Powhatan's ear. And if he doesn't like what he hears, woe betide you! He's had men beheaded for a chance remark that he considered disrespectful. So it's no surprise that nobody wants to show friendship toward a *tassantass* he's just ordered out of his town."

It was the evening of Monday, July 16, when John and Tom set out on their trek to James Towne. They had gone barely a mile when a lone Indian stepped out of the thicket beside the trail. John was in the act of drawing his sword when he recognized his archery friend. Little Crow said nothing, but with a smile and a nod handed him a bow and a sheaf of arrows and was gone as quickly as he had so suddenly appeared. John had no idea whether these were Little Crow's own, or whether he had traded for them on his behalf. But either way the gesture made a deep impression. "How…how very brotherly of him," John gasped.

Tom Savage was less impressed. "Brother today, foe tomorrow," he replied. "Let's not linger."

At James Towne, all had not been going well. The euphoria of razing Kecoughtan had worn off. Will had been detailed to supervise the coffining of Sergeant Gideon, and was enraged by delays in the burial occasioned by the Governor's insistence on making it another opportunity to be seen and heard. His speech, when he got around to giving it, proved to be more a paean of praise for the Lieutenant Governor's victory than it was for the sergeant's sacrifice.

"There, Will, don't fret," Maggie told him. "What did you expect? Bill Gideon wasn't a gentleman. He was like the rest of us, one of the other sort. The poor soul was lucky they allowed him a coffin. My Peter went with naught but his old shirt and the lice what shared it." Like most of the winter's survivors, she was still bitter that her chance of escape had been snatched away by Lord Delaware's arrival.

Will couldn't blame her, but he winced at her outspoken dislike of the Governor and all his kind. The Jefferys family had been on the Delaware estates for as long as anyone could remember. "They was good masters," Will repeatedly insisted.

"Well, they wasn't mine!" Maggie would reply, and launch into a stream of Billingsgate invective. "The only one of that bunch what was any good, was John Smith. He knowed what's what, did that one. But much good it done him. Twice they tried to kill him and when they failed, they shipped him out." Maggie's litany of the leadership's failures would have been enough to curdle milk. "Take that Ratcliffe feller what was governor before. He tried to have our people build him a bloody palace, but Smith put a stop to that. Then there's Gates; a fine mess he's made of everything, what with him and that John Martin whose not worth a kettle of warm spit!"

Will had heard it all before, and some he knew to be true. But, as he tried to impress on Maggie, without loyalty there would anarchy.

"We'll all be killing each other," he insisted. "We have to have a leader. Somebody has to give the orders and the rest of us have to obey."

Maggie's reply, ever since he had been made a sergeant, was the same. "You'd make as a good a leader as any of them. The men would listen to you because you're one of us, you know they would."

"Hush, woman!" Will told her. "That kind of talk can get us both hanged." But in their bed at night, he wondered whether she might be right. Suppose Delaware should die? Weren't there rumors that he was ailing, and General Wainman too? Hadn't his Lordship's brother, Francis West, taken a ship and escaped? Now Gates was said to be returning to England. Might not others follow him? All these possibilities plagued Will's darkness hours, but he always fell asleep with the same conclusion. His fate was in the hands of God. Whatever role He had in mind for Will Jefferys -- Will Jefferys would play it.

From his relatively comfortable bed in the Governor's House Lord Delaware had similar thoughts. God had brought him to Virginia and God would preserve him and his administration. That his bones ached and his vision seemed less clear than before, were troublesome, but not sufficiently worrying to bother Bohun with them. The doctor had more than enough to do trying to stop the sickness in the camp. Ten had died in the past week and many more were ailing. And then there was poor old Ferdy Wainman. He had been sick off and on ever since they arrived. But, as the old settlers said, if you could get past the first months they called the seasoning time, you'd be fine — providing there was food to feed you.

In his Lordship's mind, everything was going pretty well. The seizure of Pochins' corn fields at Kecoughtan ensured a good crop, providing the savages could be prevented from burning it. Sir George Somers and Samuel Argall should be back any day now. In fact, by the Admiral's estimate they were already overdue. With the hogs from Bermuda to tide them over until the next supply fleet came from England, careful rationing would keep his people lean but not hungry. All his Lordship needed to fill his cup of satisfaction was to bring Powhatan to heel, and that he expected would be accomplished by the clarity of his ultimatum. In retrospect, Delaware told himself, he had been wise to ignore Chaplain Laurie's softening advice. There was only one way to treat savages and heretics. Any other was a formula for disaster.

His Lordship's earlier emphasis on Christian charity and the wooing of the ignorant Indian to the light of Christian doctrine had begun to wear thin. The appalling fate of John Ratcliffe, the bread-stuffed mouths of the dead at Kecoughtan, and casualties resulting from Paspahegh raids on the causeway blockhouse, all brought him to the conclusion that if Powhatan did not kneel, destroying his people and their crops was the only sure path to peace.

On the morning of July 19, a runner from the blockhouse reported that John Jefferys, Tom Savage and two Indians had been sighted on the other side of the causeway waiting for the tide to fall. Delaware ordered the church bells rung, and his guard turned out. Will, now sergeant of the left file, had the honor of commanding the escort that was to bring his brother from the blockhouse. All the officers and gentry scrambled to make themselves parade presentable. Ensigns unfurled the King's standard and the flags of the Governor and his Lieutenant Governor. Delaware's and Gates' trumpeters stood ready, and Tom Dowse, the reluctant hero of Kecoughtan, was there with his drum sticks poised. It was, even to Maggie's critical eye, a brave sight.

When John saw Will at the head of the guardsmen, he immediately went to embrace him.

"Not now, brother," Will hissed. "I'm on duty."

"On duty," John replied with a laugh. "How so? I don't see Gideon to say us nay."

"Sergeant Gideon is dead, brother. Anon, I beg you." Then to his file, "Escort, in two ranks by the left, right turn. To the fort, queeeeck march!" Flanked by the guardsmen, John Jefferys had no opportunity to question Will further, and had to be content to give Tom Savage an amused if puzzled look, to which Tom only shrugged.

John had expected that in the time he had been gone, there would have been noticeable evidence of improved conditions in the camp. But he saw none. On the contrary, the men who bothered to watch him pass looked as sullen and slovenly as before. He could not tell whether there had been any recent rain, but the lanes between the tents and shacks were a quagmire, and no shovelers were in evidence trying to clean it up. The fort palisades, on the other hand, had been greatly strengthened, and the west entrance had a new gate that swung easily on not-yet-rusted iron hinges. Along the parapet platform behind the palisade stood fifteen or twenty waving settlers, Maggie Beale among them. Captains Brewster and Phettiplace were at the gate to greet and lead the returning messenger to the church where the rest of the officers and gentry were waiting – with one notable exception.

"Where's Wainman? Where's Sir Ferdy?" Delaware demanded. "We can't start without him."

Dr. Bohun stepped forward. "My Lord, Sir Ferdinando is sick. He cannot leave his bed."

"That's too bad," Delaware replied. "He's missing a good turnout." With that, he walked the few paces to greet his messenger. "Welcome young master...Jack."

"John, m'Lord."

"Jack, John, 'Tis the same is it not? The savages treated you well, I trust?" Delaware asked, but did not wait for an answer. Instead, he launched into a formal speech of welcome that reminded the gathering of its Christian heritage, its duty to its king as exemplified by the courage of this fine young Englishman, and an assurance that the Lord is its shepherd and His flock would prevail. "And who is this young man?" Delaware asked, pointing to Tom Savage. The question was asked in the benevolent tone of a rich uncle.

"This here be Tom Savage, m'Lord," John replied. "The one Cap'n Newport left with Powhatan."

"Ah, yes. I've heard tell of you," Delaware smiled. "By my order, you are now welcomed back into our Christian world. Rest assured, you are freed of any obligation to the devil's children. Attend me later, and I will talk with you." Then he held out his hand to John. "Come," he said. "Come to my chamber and I'll hear your news." The Governor then dismissed his troops and thanked everyone for attending on what he called "this propitious day."

Will returned his spontoon — the semi-ceremonial weapon of a sergeant — to its rack in the guard house, and went to find Maggie. "How did I look?" he asked her. "Did I look like a sergeant?"

"You did," she assured him. "Every inch."

Meanwhile, the Governor General for Life courteously ushered his returning messenger into his house and sat him down at one end of the long table that occupied much of the council chamber. Joining them were Chaplain Laurie, Dr. Bohun, Sir Thomas Gates, George Percy, John Martin, and George Yeardley. "Where's that Strachey feller?" Delaware demanded. "If he's our recorder, he needs to record!"

While Laurie went in search of him, John sat nervously listening to the optimistic discussions going on at the other end of the table. He was tempted to stand up and shout, "Wait! You don't understand!" but thought better of it. Instead, he waited his turn.

With Strachey found, and his Lordship seated in his velvet-cushioned chair, he and his council were ready to hear Powhatan's response. "The old savage treated you well?" Delaware asked again.

"Aye, my Lord," John replied.

"And you gave him my gifts?"

"I did, my Lord."

"Good. Savages like such trifles. I'm told for a handful of beads, they'll sell you their wives." Delaware looked to his aides for their reaction and got an appreciative laugh in return. "And what is he sending to us? How many bushels?"

"Well, m'Lord," John stammered. "I don't think he is. I mean, he didn't say aught about..."

Delaware stared down the table at his messenger. "But he did like my gifts, did he not?"

There being no way to skirt safely around the truth, John told him, "No, m'Lord, he did not."

"Did not?" Delaware gasped.

"No, m'Lord. He said the hatchets were worthless, and that he thought you...*we* were taking him for a fool."

"Indeed." Delaware's voice hardened. "You read him my message?"

"Aye, my Lord."

"And he will release the prisoners and return our arms as I instructed?"

"Nay, sire, he will not." John realized that he could no longer delay the moment that had weighed on his mind from the moment he left Orapakes. "As best I remember Powhatan's words, m' Lord," John began, "he said that he is a king and that this is his land. He says that no stranger can tell him what he must do."

"Is that so?"

"Aye, my Lord. He said that he wants me to tell you what *you* must do." Delaware's face flushed red, and he pounded a fist on the table, but he said nothing. Dr. Bohun stepped forward, laid a restraining hand on his master's arm, then nodded to John to continue.

"Powhatan told me that he will not come to you. But he will give you leave to remain here at James Towne providing you do not venture further into his lands or onto his rivers. I think those were his words. And if you do so, he will kill us all."

"And that is all he said?" Delaware demanded.

"Not quite my lord," John answered. "He said he would accept no more cheap trinkets or axes that break. And he wants no more messengers, unless they bring him a coach and three horses."

"The devil take him!"

Barked Gates, "Get you gone, young master Jack...John. If you value your hide, you'll repeat not one word of this!" Delaware seemed stunned. It had never occurred to him that the king of naked savages would defy the power of England. But, as Percy later commented, his Lordship had never stood face to face with Powhatan.

An anxious Dr. Bohun saw his master slump back into his chair, his mouth open and pant for breath. "Gentlemen," he pleaded, "help his Lordship to his chamber. 'Tis the heat," he added, "nothing more, I do assure you."

When Yeardley and Percy returned, Gates bade them sit again. "Assuming that the good doctor is right, and that our Governor is in no immediate danger," he told them "I think it best that I do not tarry here until the *Deliverance* and *Patience* return — which may be a week or...who knows? His Lordship, has urgent letters that must go to London and we, here, must have supplies. So it is my intent to prepare the *Blessing* to sail as soon as she is able. How say you all?"

It seemed unnecessary to add that the destruction of Kecoughtan was, for Lieutenant Governor Gates the kind of victory that he knew would impress his superiors back in London. It was immaterial that he had caught the savages sleeping and that most of them had escaped before their fragile town burned. In the minds of Company administrators' a town destroyed and its goods looted would be on a par with the exploits of Sir Francis Drake at Cadiz. This, therefore, was the ideal moment for Gates to return to England — before any other calamity could tarnish his success. "Well, gentlemen, what say you?" he asked again.

Yeardley, Percy, and Strachey agreed. Only John Martin had a better idea. "With great respect, Sir Thomas," he began, "Suppose his Lordship is more ailing than Bohun believes, may it not become your duty to remain to act on his behalf? That being so, would it not be best for me to return to England in your stead?"

"I think not." Gates told him. "Now if there be no other business, I suggest we go about our separate tasks. I'm sure we all have much to think on."

So did John Jefferys. Reunited with Will and Maggie, he began to tell them all that had happened, how he had met Harry Spelman and Tom Savage, and how on arrival he had been feasted by the great Opechancanough and how there had been so much food that after the meal there was still enough to give away to servants.

"Damn 'em all to hell!" Maggie muttered.

"Where did you get the bow?" Will wanted to know.

"'Twas a token of friendship," John replied.

"Friendship?" Maggie snorted. "Friendship between us and them savages!"

He told her that the gift was from one bowman to another, one friend to another, and that it meant no more than that. But Maggie was not impressed. "Well, I don't know. Who'd 'ave thought it, and you a young Christian lad," she scolded.

Will was more interested in learning what had passed between John and Powhatan. But John was reluctant to say anything that might bring trouble on their heads. "I'm told to say naught about it."

"But surely you can tell us whether his Lordship's words were well received?" Will demanded.

John wanted to tell his brother everything that had been said, particularly about Powhatan's request for a coach and horses. But he kept his peace and would say only that he had done his duty by delivering the Governor's message and bringing Powhatan's answer back.

"Then tell us how they treated you." Will asked. "I've heard tell they give a visitor a filly to keep him company of a night. So what about you, little brother? Did they..."

"That be none of your business!" John snapped as his face reddened. When he saw Will grinning, he added "What if they did? No different to what you got scrubbed down for in London."

"I don't believe it." Maggie gasped. "You bedded one of them filthy creatures!"

John explained what had happened, how he had returned to his lodge and found Taropoto already there, and how he would have offended Powhatan had he turned her out. "'Sides, she were a princess."

"A princess?" Will laughed. "She told you that? Did she tell you that her dam was the Queen of Sheba?'

"No," John asnwered. "She didn't tell me who she was, and I didn't ask." He added that it was not until he awoke and found her gone that Harry Spelman told him that Taropoto was a young sister of the queen of the Paspahegh. Will gasped and asked whether he had told this to his Lordship, and breathed a sigh of relief when the answer was *no*.

"I should think not!" snapped Maggie. "You should be ashamed of yourself, beddin' with one o' them!"

"Be you not bedding with Will? " John angrily retorted.

"Never you mind about that!" she snapped in return.

"Whoa, whoa!" Will interjected. "This is us, remember?" There was no point in quarreling, he insisted. His brother had done what he thought had to be done. And, he added, "I'll wager it wasn't the worst of duties." Maggie replied that she had heard enough, and angrily went to the door. "And when I come back, my Will, I'll want to hear how you got scrubbed down in London!"

Across the market place in the Governor's House, Dr. Bohun was telling George Percy that their governor was not a well man, and that any stress could so weaken him that he would be vulnerable to any of the illnesses that were taking their toll in the camp. "And Sir Ferdy," he added, "he's no better, and I'm affeared for his life." Bohun had bled him twice in the past three days, and while that may have drawn off some of the ill humors, the loss of blood had to be weakening. The doctor went on to say that he was about to advise his master that he should quit the Governor's House and return to his cabin aboard the *Delaware*. "He can rule the colony just as well from there where the air is fresh," he insisted.

Percy did not disagree, and ten minutes later Bohun told the Governor what he advised. Somewhat to his surprise, Delaware raised no objection. Instead, he agreed that his quarters aboard the ship were no worse than those on land, and were probably somewhat better. However, he insisted that Bohun make the announcement so that it was he and not Delaware who proposed the move. "It wouldn't sit well, if 'twere thought that I was deserting my command or leaving out of fear," he insisted.

Late that afternoon, Bohun's written statement was posted on the church door, and four or five at a time the settlers who could read shared the news with their friends and neighbors. As Delaware had expected, it received a mixed response. Some reacted as he had predicted they might, but most thought the move made sense and wished that they, too, had ships to live on.

By nightfall his Lordship was back aboard the *Delaware* and calling for a council meeting the next morning.

When Percy, Yeardley, Martin, Strachey, Captain Brewster, and the other council members assembled in the ship's great cabin, Delaware had already made up his mind concerning his response to Powhatan's defiance. "Gentlemen," he began, "we must conclude — reluctantly, I may say — that Powhatan and all his people are our implacable enemies. They will not be brought to righteousness by kindness, nor will they be bribed into compliance. We have no recourse, therefore, but to draw the sword and cut them down root and branch." He went on to say that as the Paspahegh were the closest and most belligerent foes, they should be the first recipients of English vengeance.

Percy thought that a wise decision, but Martin questioned whether it might not be more immediately productive to ship troops up the Pamunkey River and strike directly at Powhatan himself. Delaware thought not. To ship a sufficient force would leave James Towne vulnerable to the Paspahegh, and require both ships, the *Delaware* and *Hercules*, as well as barges and longboats to effect the landing. "If the Dons come calling, we'd have nothing in the river to keep them from destroying our fort," he firmly stated. "No, it'll be the Paspahegh, and the sooner the better."

The Paspahegh's capital village lay on the north bank at the mouth of the Chickahominy River seven miles above James Towne Island. The tribe also occupied a large tract on the south bank extending all the way to the island and beyond. The locations of some of the smaller villages were known and others not, all of them on the creeks running into the Chickahominy, their rears protected by dense forests and almost impossible to surprise by land. Percy's proposal, therefore, was to attack and destroy the larger, north bank village and leave the lesser settlements to be attacked later.

Delaware, replied that he would have to think on that. He had heard that the Paspahegh had a temple on the south bank closer to James Towne and that it was from there that the priests manipulated the policies of Wowinchapunck, their king. "We must kill the priests," Delaware declared. "They are a blasphemy against Our Lord Jesus Christ. As long as they live, He will not be well served."

Percy admitted that he was less interested in theology than in

171

practicality, and insisted that if he could cut off the Devil's right hand, the left would quickly wither and die.

"So be it, then," Delaware agreed. "But make no mistake. I want their king, their queen and all their progeny executed, every last heathen one of them!"

Immediately after the council meeting ended, its members were rowed ashore to begin preparations for the assault. But they were met with bad news. Sir Ferdinando Wainman was dead. Nothing could go forward before the funeral. Though not unexpected, his death cast a pall over James Towne. Although Wainman had played only a subsidiary role in Lord Delaware's aggressive timetable for the resurrection of the town, he had made no enemies and was seen by many as a benign influence on his more hot-headed colleagues.

"He were a good man, right enough," Maggie allowed. "We needs more o' the likes of him than his Lordship and that John Martin."

"Hush, woman!" Will warned. "I've told you before where words like that can get us."

Maggie shrugged, and said it was a fact anyway, and that everybody knew it. For his part, Will had to admit — at least to himself — that while he knew that Delaware's actions were necessary to keep the colony alive, he was beginning to have doubts that it was worth many more deaths. The sickness in the camp was growing, and the loss of Sergeant Gideon was weighing on his mind. If the promised relief fleet should be lost, perhaps Delaware would agree to abandon the colony. He knew it was wrong to hope that its crews would drown, but their loss could be his savior.

Now that he was Sergeant Will Jefferys, a noticeable coolness was developing between himself and his old comrades in the guard. Its two corporals made no secret of their resentment that he had been promoted over them. In turn, the guard corps was living apart from the old colonists and the likes of Maggie Beale, who were beginning to see them as occupying troops who were doing nothing to improve the lot nor the futures of those who had survived the Starving Time. After their first construction tasks were done, they were idling their time away while waiting for new orders, and Will felt himself responsible for their inactivity. But there was nothing he could do about it. With the Governor having retreated to his ship, there was even less chance of appealing to Captain Brewster who now spent much of his time being ferried back and forth. And then there were the layabouts in the camp. In Will's eyes, their captain, Jeremiah Douthitt, was an idiot with no command experience who was doing nothing to drill his men into a disciplined force. Camped with them, Will had discovered, were twenty-five miners from Wales and Cornwall, and six iron smelters from Sussex, none of them part of the army, and answerable only to Delaware and to a rarely seen Swiss mineral man.

On the only occasion in which Will had guard duty patrolling the perimeter of the cleared area beyond the fort, he had to break up a fight between three of the Finsbury lads and two of the iron men. After peace had been restored, one of the Cornishmen said his name was Henry Funnell from Padstow. He wanted to know when he and his fellows were going to get something to do. "We've bin here these many days," he said, "and we've done bugger all. We was told there was mines to be dug, but nobody but that Switzer feller seems to know where they be. I'll tell thee this, Sergeant, lest we gets off of our arses right soon, we'll be thinkin' about seizing a boat and headin' to sea, and doin' a bit o' piratin' maybe. We aint' stayin' 'ere to die o' the fever."

Will told him that he didn't want to hear that kind of talk. It would be treasonous to even joke about it, he said.

"It ain't no joke, I can assure you, Sergeant. But you find us somethin' to be about, and you'll not hear another word out of my lips," Funnell assured him.

Nevertheless, Henry Funnell's threat was another of the worries that Will thought best to keep to himself. For now, however, Captain-General Wainman's funeral preparations were all that mattered.

Chapter Thirteen

The funeral of Sir Ferdinando Wainman was the kind of event that Lord Delaware relished. Everything from the carpentry of the coffin to the placement of the pall was supervised by his Lordship. Eight guardsmen, with Sergeant Jefferys in command, served as bearers carrying the coffin from the dead man's house to the church – not directly from one to the other, but out through the west postern gate, around to the south main gates and back up to the marketplace through an avenue of pikemen. There the cortege was received by a solemn Delaware and his officers. The procession then moved to the church, down the central aisle to the grave dug to the right of the new cedar communion rail. Both chaplains read sermons and the Governor delivered the eulogy. He called Wainman a brave and noble soldier who had died in the service of his king and his God. Delaware also managed to include passing references to the perfidious heathens, to the priests of Baal, and the curse of Catholicism. Upon lowering the coffin into the grave, Captain Holcroft gave the order to fire an artillery salute from each of the three gun platforms. As the cannon boomed out, the two trumpeters standing outside the church blew a somewhat ragged fanfare of farewell. George Yeardley had questioned the wisdom of expending so much gunpowder, but had been overruled by Delaware who considered that the Captain-General of Ordnance deserved nothing less. "Formality," Delaware assured Yeardley, "is the foundation on which our authority stands. To deviate is to die."

The smoke and smell of gunpowder were still drifting across the market place as the mourners straggled out of the church. Delaware took in a deep breath and declared that there was nothing quite as sweet as the smell of spent powder. "Mark me well," he told Captain Brewster, "those damned savages will soon get to know it and fear it, or I'll want to know the reason why!" Unable to think of any useful reply, Brewster settled for a knowing nod. He had been with Yeardley in deploring the waste of powder.

Within hours of Wainman's funeral, Delaware once again aboard the flagship, called on his captains to assemble as a council of war. "With our worthy Gates gone and Sir George Somers not yet returned," he announced, "I appoint Captain George Percy to command our enterprise against the Paspahegh. You, Captain Brewster. will lead two files from my guard. But I want fifty men to be drawn from our army to be commanded by you, Captain Davis, with Captain Douthitt doing whatever he is able to assist you."

"They are not well disciplined, my Lord. Are you sure...?" Davis began.

"That I know full well," Delaware replied. "But it will give them something useful to do. Besides," he added, "loosing an army of rats into a granary can quickly do wondrous damage."

Later that day the renegade Indian, Kemps, returned to the fort claiming that he had valuable information that he would share only with Sir Thomas. When asked which Sir Thomas, he answered that it was Gates he wanted to see. But Percy, remembering that Smith had called Kemps one of the two "most exact villains in all the country," concluded that he already knew that Gates was gone, and came to the fort to spy on preparations for the Paspaheph assault. "The Devil take you, master Kemps!" Percy told him, and promptly put him in irons and lodged him in the cell behind the guard house.

No one had visited the Paspahegh's principal village in more than a year, Wowinchapunck having repeatedly demonstrated that he was no friend of the *tassantasses*. Knowing that from time to time the Indians moved their villages, Percy saw Kemps's return as heaven blessed. He would guide his captors to the village — at gun point if necessary.

As Gates had in planning his attack on Kecoughtan, Percy looked for a black night and a rising tide to carry his boats upstream to the Chickahominy. The dark of the moon fell on August 8, and on the following night, shortly after dusk, he began boarding seventy soldiers onto two barges. Will and John Jefferys found themselves assigned to the lead vessel commanded by Percy, supported by Brewster, and Delaware's nephew, William West, while the Finsbury soldiers boarded the second under Davis and Douthitt. For John this was to be his first encounter with the Indians as an enemy. Will assured him that like the assault on Kecoughtan, the savages would quickly disappear into the forest, and all that he would have to do would be to help destroy the town. But even that was a prospect John could not relish. He had spent more than a week in one of those mat-walled houses and seen many Orapakes families living contentedly in theirs. Although they had been wary of him, he believed that, like Little Crow, in time they would have grown to accept him. Were this to be an attack on Orapakes, John was sure that he would be unable to do what England expected of him. Sitting in the dark with Will on one side of him and Pips Bailey on the other, he wondered what they would say if he were to tell them what was on his mind. One thing was certain: they wouldn't understand. How could they?

Percy and Davis demanded silence aboard each barge, but although Percy's order was obeyed, Davis's was not. His repeated command to stop talking had to be louder than the voices, making nonsense of the call for quiet. Soon, however, Percy's barge pulled away, the silence of its passage broken only by the creaking of oars in rowlocks and the splash of blades dipping into black water.

Knowing that the Paspahegh village would be at the waterside fronting either onto the Great River or onto the Chickahominy, Percy's force rowed a full three miles up the tributary and landed on the west bank intending to advance on the Paspahegh from their rear and drive them into which ever river it proved to be. At first, guide Kemps led the columns inland away from the water. As Percy had planned to stay close to the Chickahominy, he quickly called a halt and had the shackled Kemps brought to him. "Master Kemps," he said, "methinks you lie. And a lying savage is better dead. And so shall you be if you steer us wrong."

The Indian insisted that he had no such intention. "Yonder is the way I know," he pleaded.

"Is it? Be you sure of that?" Percy did not wait for an answer, as he struck him hard about the shoulders and thighs with his walking staff. "Steer us wrong, and I'll have your head off. Lead us true, or it 'll go with us atop my staff!"

The cowering and bruised captive pleaded that if he had taken the wrong route, it was by accident and never intended to mislead. Percy thrust the point of his iron-tipped staff under Kemps's chin, and warned him that he had best make no more mistakes. The stand off had caused the entire column to halt and several of the files to disintegrate as soldiers broke away to urinate or talk among themselves. Getting them back in order took time and much more noise than Percy would have wished. There was every likelihood that Paspahegh scouts knew of the *tassantasses'* approach and even now were alerting the sleeping village. Percy cursed his luck, cursed Kemps, and cursed Douthitt and his unruly charges.

A quarter of a mile from the village, Percy halted his troops and deployed each of his files to attack from the three landward sides. "When they report back to me that they are in position, I shall come up and stand ready to attack," he told his officers. "A pistol shot will be the signal to move in."

Will and John, waiting at the front of Captain Brewster's file, were surprised that there had been no movement from the village. Surely all the noise of stomping and cursing through the underbrush would have awakened somebody? "They're waiting for us, I can feel it," Will whispered.

"How so?" John hissed back.

Before Will could answer Captain West fired his pistol. Somebody yelled "Now!" And amid shouts of "England and Saint George!" Percy's invaders converged on the village from three sides. Will was right. Arrows came at them from defenders amid the houses, but with their targets coming out of the darkness of the forest, few found their mark. Forty Paspehegh warriors armed with bows and clubs were no match for seventy pike- and sword-wielding invaders, and within minutes they were in retreat, trying desperately to roust out their women and children before fleeing into the woods. But no matter in which direction they ran, there were soldiers ready and eager to cut them down.

Once inside the village, the troops broke ranks and scattered in all directions, running in and out of houses, chasing down screaming women and children, and grappling with any warriors who tried to stop them. John saw Twofin Chisman and his friend Smiler pursuing a young woman into one of the houses, but a war club swung at his head instantly diverted his attention. Dodging back to avoid the blow, John thrust his pike into the chest of the Indian who fell forward breaking the shaft. John Jefferys had killed his first savage. In the midst of the confusion and the triumphant shouts of his fellows, John's adrenalin was flowing, but in what direction he knew not. With his sword drawn he ran first in one direction and then another, not wanting to appear reluctant but hoping against hope that he would be spared any further confrontation. Bleeding Indians lay all around, some with limbs hacked off and still alive, others evidently dead. A woman with her head nearly severed lay with a crying infant still in her arms. From the largest of the houses, one at whose entrance withered scalps hung from a pole, ran Captain Davis and three soldiers dragging a naked woman and two children by their hair. John did not see where they went; his attention was attracted by a woman's cries for help — in English.

Running toward the sound, John came around the corner of a house and found a soldier kneeling over a struggling woman, his britches down and his rump bared. Another was kneeling at her head, holding her by the arms and laughing in her face. Without considering the consequences John thrust his sword deep into the anus of the rapist who fell forward, blood spurting over the legs of his victim. The second attacker leapt up and shouted, "Be you mad! He'm one of us!" Only then did John recognize the holder as Twofin Chisman.

"You filthy bastard!" John shouted back, as he lunged at him. But Chisman ran off into the darkness, and rather than pursue him, John stopped to see what he could do to help the woman who still lay with the weight of her bleeding attacker across her chest. John rolled him aside and saw that Smiler had grinned his last.

"John," she gasped. "*Ahkii vwwaap! Ahkii...*"

"Taropoto?"

"Aye," she breathed. "Aye, 'tis..." Her voice faded to a whisper.

John dropped his sword, and bent to pick her up, still unsure how much of the blood was hers. He knew only that he had to get her away from the burning houses and into the woods. Meanwhile, in the center of the village the carnage continued as soldiers drunk with success cut souvenirs from the heads of dead and wounded savages. Eventually, when the sport paled, the soldiery stood aimlessly around too tired, too spent to talk to each other. Percy planted his standard, and ordered a drummer to beat retreat.

Will Jefferys, his heart still pounding, took his place at the head of his bloodied file. Appalled by the scalping and the bestial behavior of the men around him, he wished that he could awaken and find it naught but a nightmare. But the horror was real — and far from over.

John, with Taropoto in his arms, heard the drum as he stumbled ever deeper into the woods. For a moment he hesitated, arrested by its call to duty. He knew that to ignore it made him a deserter and likely to hang if he should be caught. But in his eyes saving Taropoto was the greater duty.

Percy's troops would have to return to their boats, which meant that they would be moving north along the river bank. So, with the first streaks of dawn to direct him, John headed west in the hope of finding a trail. Vines and creepers hanging from the trees did their best to slow him, and by the time he had covered what he hoped was a safe distance, he sank down beside an ancient pine tree exhausted by his load. Now, for the first time, he was able to examine Taropoto's injuries. He had no water to wash away the blood and so did what he could with the palm of his hand. Bleeding abrasions on her back and shoulders were not serious, and the blood on her legs and torso was Smiler's. Only a deep cut across her left forearm needed immediate attention, and with nothing to bind it but his dirty stocking, he did what he could. She was still in shock and sat against the trees, staring and saying nothing. For a few minutes John sat hearing naught but his own heavy breathing. He had not been followed, of that he was certain, and he was equally sure that if Percy's troops were heading in his direction he would hear them long before they reached him. For the time being, at least, he was safe. But then what?

If he could get Taropoto back to a village, could he then not return to the fort claiming that he had lost his way or been knocked unconscious by an Indian's club? But then there was Twofin Chisman. He had seen John kill his friend and had no reason to keep quiet about it. On the contrary, he would be the first to report that Smiler had been murdered by one of Percy's own. Pleading that he had interrupted a rape would avail him naught. Rapine was one of the juicier fruits of victory and had been since the beginning of time. John's future, if future he was to have, would lie with the naturals. He would never see his mother nor England again, and if he should see Will, more than likely it would be on the day of his execution. And he had done it all for this naked, blood-drenched savage. Again and again he asked himself how he could have been that impulsive, that stupid? He had found no answer when he heard twigs crack and saw movement in the underbrush about twenty yards away.

In the Paspahegh village the drummer's call had fallen on many a deaf ear. Soldiers with shell and pearl necklaces hung around their necks and bloodied Indian scalps hanging from their belts, were intent on finding whatever treasure the Paspaheghs might possess. That there was nothing to find but baskets of corn and a little copper, never occurred to them. The woman and children that John had seen dragged out by Captain Davis were squatting beside their house, hands tied, and shivering with fear. The four guardsmen standing watch over them had dragged up an old man and thrown him down beside the captives. He sat silently staring about him, without any sign of comprehension. He may have been blind.

After a brief conversation with Davis, Percy signaled for the captives to be brought into the village center. The still-manacled Kemps identified the woman as the senior wife of Wowinchepunck and Queen of the Paspahegh. The children aged five or six, were her daughters.

"And the old man, who is he?" Percy demanded. But Kemps did not know. "If she's the queen, where's the king? Ask her that." Percy could not understand what passed between them, but was not pleased by the answer: Wowinchepunck and most of the other great *weroances* were away conferring with Powhatan. "Then we'll play the queen to draw the king. We'll keep he – and her pups," he ordered.

"And the old man?" Davis asked.

"He's seen too much. Cut off his head."

"He may be blind," Davis demurred.

"Blind or not. Cut off his head!" And as Percy watched, Davis did so.

A few moments later, a corporal reported that he had found a dead soldier. He had been killed, said the corporal, in an unusual kind of way. But Percy was too busy to do more than ask the soldier's name. "See to it that he's buried before the buzzards get him," he ordered. Then to Captains Davis and West, "Now fire anything that isn't burning, and cut down their corn. And get your corporals to turn this mob into harvesters."

Smoke from the burning houses was already high in the air as John Jefferys, his back against a tree, drew his sword and prepared to defend himself. He had seen Machumps stare down a bear, but he suspected that bears were more comfortable with naked Indians than with *tassantasses* in strange attire. But the point was moot even as it formed. Out of the thicket staggered a wounded Paspahegh warrior. He was as surprised to see John as John was to see him. The Indian was unarmed, bleeding from a gashed shoulder, and posed no threat. Drawing on his small Algonquin vocabulary, John held up his left hand and told him, "*Netab, Netapewh.*"

"Friend," gasped the Indian as he sank to the ground beside

Taropoto.

John sheathed his sword and used his other stocking to try to staunch the blood still flowing from the Indian's shoulder.

Over the burning town turkey buzzards were already circling, gliding back and forth around the edges of the smoke, now and again swooping down only to retreat when they saw that the dead were not yet alone. Percy's men were piling the still unripe corn onto matts from the houses and cutting poles to help cradle the loot. Captain Douthitt and two files of his Finsbury soldiers were already on their way back to the boats with orders to bring them down river to land alongside the village. By the time all was done, the boats beached, the corn loaded, and the rest of Percy's force ready to embark, it was mid morning. The sun was high and the humidity rising, just another sweat-drenched, mosquito slapping day in Virginia Britannica. The men were exhausted and snarling at each other over every imagined sleight or ill-chosen word. The orderly files that had gone up the night before were now forgotten or ignored, everyone scrambling onto the boats jockeying for a place on the thwarts. Guardsmen and common soldiers were indiscriminately mixed together and jeering at each other. Will was one of the last to board Percy's boat, having hung back in the hope of finding his brother. No other guardsman was missing, and the squad he had sent to scour the perimeter reported Smiler as the only English dead. So, with Percy and Brewster demanding that he get aboard, Will could search no more.

Brewster made a space for him at the stern beside a dejected Captain Davis who told him in a voice barely above a whisper, "Will, lad, 'twas a filthy business we did this day. May God forgive us."

"Amen to that," Will sighed.

The queen and her children were bundled onto the bilge planks between the thwarts at the feet of those seated there. Kicks and taunts drew naught but silence from the queen, and when one soldier grabbed her by her nipples, her stoic stare shamed him into letting go. Nor did she react to the tears and wailing of her terrified daughters. "Enough of this catawalling," rasped one of the soldiers.

"I says, we knock 'em over the head and be done with 'em."

"Captain Percy, sir," said another. "Wasn't we supposed to kill 'em all?"

"Who we kill and who we keep is my decision, soldier," Percy replied.

"But we've heard tell it was his Lordship's decision to lop every last one of 'em," insisted Chisman's friend Arty. The murmur of agreement hinted at trouble that everyone would regret.

"Heave 'em over, I says!" shouted Twofin as he stood up. "What say you, lads? Do we ditch 'em?"

"Sit down!" Will ordered.

"And who are you to tell us, you and your murderin' brother?" Chisman shouted back.

Neither Will nor anyone else knew what he meant. The officers may not even have heard, so intent were they on avoiding a mutiny that could threaten the survival of the colony. The oarsmen had stopped rowing and it was clear that they did not intend to continue until the fate of the prisoners was resolved.

Reluctantly Percy stood up at the bow and told the dissidents that while he would not submit to killing the queen, if it was the will of all, the children could be sacrificed. His admission brought a cheer from amidships and shouts of, "Over the side with the little bitches!" and "Shoot their heathen 'eads off!" It was *not* the will of all, but those like Will Jefferys who wanted no more bloodshed, remained silent as the two screaming children were hoisted over the side and dropped into the river. Those soldiers with still-loaded muskets aimed and emptied them at the struggling and sinking targets. The crimson smear that quickly washed away in the current brought another cheer from the boat.

The fun over, the soldiers turned their attention to the queen who sat motionless, apparently unmoved or oblivious to all that had happened. "Now it be your turn, you pretty thing!" someone shouted.

Another voice demanded, "Now what about her?" and yet another shouted, "See if the bitch can swim!"

"Hold, I say!" Percy shouted. "The woman is to live. Anyone

who touches her will hang."

Without waiting to see if his order would be obeyed, he offered an alternative opportunity for his men to vent their spleen. With the Paspaheghs living on both banks of the Chickahominy, there were more villages to loot and burn. Percy knew, too, that somewhere in the woods the Paspahegh's priests had their holiest temple. To destroy that would be a major victory and add fresh laurels for himself. Calling on Captain West, commander of the second barge, Percy ordered him to beach on a sandy shore two miles down river from the mouth of the Chickahominy. The new assault was to be led by Captain Davis, Percy claiming to be too tired to lead another attack. He would remain behind with a handful of guardsmen to protect the queen.

This time there was to be no surprise. Indians had been watching the barges' passage down river and kept pace with them from the safety of the shore-lining trees. Consequently, the first men ashore were met with a shower of arrows, most of them fired from such long range that they were spent by the time they reached their targets. Instead, they had poked a stick in a hornets' nest of shouting soldiery that charged into the woods in pursuit of the retreating Indians. Will Jefferys was still Sergeant of the First File, but with his men split between both barges, he had few if any to command, and so charged pell-mell into the woods along with the rest. Soon the charge wore itself out as first one soldier and then another realized that the enemy had vanished. Each stopped, looked around, and saw nothing but forest on every side. Uncertain in which direction to go or even how to get back to the boats, Captain Davis' rabble was ready to take orders. "Form up, and spread out," he barked. "Follow me, in line abreast!"

The sweep took the troops an exhausting fourteen miles through the forest, and netted two small villages of no more than a dozen houses. But Percy had been right about the big prize.

The long, mat-framed temple stood alone, facing east, in a small clearing, surrounded by wooden posts, their tops carved into animal and semi-human heads. Will was the first to enter and found himself in a surprisingly clean ante-room hung with animal pelts. In the middle lay the ashes of a still-smoldering fire whose smoke drifted up into the sunlight through a hole in the arched roof. Beyond the ante-room he found another larger room whose only light came from the doorway. He could see post-supported biers on either side upon which rested long, mat-wrapped bundles that he took to be the remains of deceased *weroances*. He was about to penetrate further when he smelled burning and heard the crackle of flame-engulfing mats. Other less curious invaders had seen fit to ignite the walls without bothering to venture inside, and only Will's hasty retreat prevented him from being trapped behind burning matting falling from the roof. Within minutes the entire building was ablaze from end to end. As it disintegrated, a massive devilish figure appeared to rise out of the flames. It's head looked more like that of a wolf than a man, a phoenix rising out of the fire and seemingly alive. Several soldiers turned and ran back into the woods. Others, like Will Jefferys, stood stunned by the sight of this rapidly blackening creature. It had to be the Paspehegh's *okeus*, the god that only the priests were allowed to see.

For a moment Will thought he was in a supernatural presence that was about to rise up Christ-like and vanish into the clouds, but, instead, it burst open turning its straw-packed interior into an orange ball of fire onto which the head slowly sagged and then fell off. Will's sigh of relief was heard by Captain Davis who had arrived in time to witness the demise of the *okeus*.

"Surprised you, did it?" Davis asked with a laugh. "Crossed your mind did it, that their god might be as real as ours?"

Will vehemently denied having any such blasphemous thought, but in his heart he knew that something like it had flashed in and out of his mind.

"Any priests here?" Davis wanted to know. Will replied that he had seen no one, but added that when he arrived the ante-room fire was still alight. "They'll not have gone far," he added.

However, Davis concluded that burning the temple was victory enough. "Get your men back to the boats," he told Will. "We mustn't be caught in the forest after nightfall."

The problem, Will reminded himself, was that though chasing savages for miles through the woods was tremendous sport, trudging back was no fun at all. Eventually, however, everyone was accounted for and aboard the boats. To the now rested Percy, the looks of them suggested that no more mutinous thoughts were left in their heads. And he was right. The remaining five miles down river to James Towne was traversed with scarcely a word from anyone, and no one felt constrained to kick or taunt the luckless queen. Had they a mind to notice such details, they would have seen that tears had coursed like streaks of varnish down her tawny cheeks.

On arrival, while the soldiers and guardsmen returned to their separate billets, the officers transferred the queen to a long boat and boarded it themselves to be ferried out to report to his Lordship on the *Delaware*. They left the woman with her hands roped behind her and lashed to one of the thwarts. "Guard her well," Percy ordered the rowers as he clambered up the rope ladder to the flagship's deck. He had expected to be warmly greeted by his Governor the moment he set foot on it. Instead, only Strachey and Dr. Bohun were there to receive him.

"My master is again ill disposed," Bohun explained. "I have ordered him to rest – though the Lord knows, 'tis like asking the tide not to turn."

"Then will he not see us?"

"Of course, he will," Strachey interjected. "We are all agog to hear your news. Tell me, how was it? Was it...?"

Percy cut him short. "Enough, sir! Know you not that I report first to our Governor?"

Strachey winced, began to reply, then thought better of it. Nothing more was said as Bohun ushered the visitors into the Great Cabin. They found Delaware sitting at his table beside his crumpled bed, dressed in a silk robe over a lawn nightshirt. The mixture of candlelight and fading daylight made him appear frail and yellow skinned. But his voice was as commanding as ever.

"Welcome, gentlemen. Thrice welcome," he declared half rising from his chair and then settling back into it. "Tell me all."

So Percy did – along with contributions from both Captains Brewster and Davis.

"Kill them all, did you? Every last one of them, eh? Wish I could have been there," Delaware added. "'Deed I do. And what of our losses?"

Brewster reported one man killed and another missing.

"Missing?" Delaware demanded. "How so?"

"We don't know, m'Lord," Brewster confessed. He went on to explain that the soldier was a guardsman from his Lordship's own estate. "He's John Jefferys m'Lord, the lad you sent with your message to Powhatan."

"Not a deserter then?"

"Hardly, my Lord."

"A prisoner then?"

"Very probably," Brewster agreed.

"Then, by God, we must do everything we can to get him back. He's done us some service, that one," Delaware added. "We owe him that."

"And about the queen?" Percy asked. "What would you have us do with her?"

"Do with her? Do what with her? She's dead, isn't she?" Delaware demanded.

Percy replied that he had thought that having failed to kill the king, it would be wise to keep her alive. Answering his Governor's further question, he rather lamely replied that she was alongside tied to the boat.

Delaware pulled himself to his feet, and with hands pressing down on the table he glared across it. "Did you not hear my order, sirrah? Did I not make myself plain? When I said all, I meant every godless one of them. So kill her!" Turning to Davis he said through scarcely parted lips, "Take her and burn her, and do it now!"

"But, my Lord..."

"The hag's a witch, and we burn witches," Delaware insisted. "So be about it, Captain! Be about it!"

188

A shaken Davis left the cabin, followed by Percy who seized him by the arm. "Stay, my friend," said Percy, "having seen so much bloodshed this day, in my cold blood I wish to see no more. We know not that she is a witch, and 'tis not fitting to burn a queen. I pray you, let it be by shot or sword."

Returning to the fort aboard the longboat, the three officers, Percy, Brewster, and Davis, sat in silence staring at the naked queen who, by the light of the night sky seemed smaller now and little more than a girl. To take her life seemed pointless and un-Christian. But his Lordship had spoken, and there was no more to be said.

Will Jefferys was still at the waterside when the officers stepped ashore. He saw the longboat pole out and head up river toward the mainland forests. Four oarsmen made slow progress against the falling tide, and between two of his fellow guardsman sat the Queen of the Paspahegh, her dark skin appearing strangely pale in the thin sliver of a new moon. Then a cloud passed in front of it – and she was gone.

Chapter Fourteen

"My name Tatacaumexan," the wounded Indian told John in halting English. "I am of the Paspahegh and the great *weroance* Wowinchepunck my father is." John was unsure whether the man really was the son of the Indian king or whether paternity went no further than being his subject. But it mattered not. Here was someone to help him get Taropoto to safety. Remembering that his archery friend's name translated into more easily pronounceable English, John put the question to Tatacaumexan. After determining that it meant a kind of bird, he rightly or wrongly concluded that it was a sparrowhawk. "Then I'll call you Sparrow," he said.

Sparrow allowed that when he first saw John bending over Taropoto, he thought that he had taken her hostage. "I would have kill you, had I good arms," he admitted. "But with only one and no weapon..."

"Just as well," John told him. He also told him what had happened and how he came to be where Sparrow found him. In return, the Indian said that he had been asleep in the village with his wife and girl child when the *Tassantasses* burst into it.

"And they are safe?"

Sparrow shook his head. "Dead," he answered flatly. He admitted to feeling ashamed that he had not stayed to fight to his own death. But wounded, with his family already dead, and the village overrun, he had escaped. "I should have stayed," he repeated over and over.

"But you will heal and live to be avenged," John assured him. He realized as he spoke the words that he, Englishman John Jefferys, had turned on his own people and saw the massacre of the Paspahegh as a crime so despicable that he, too, wanted to avenge their deaths.

At home with Maggie at James Towne, Will Jefferys was experiencing similar feelings of disgust at the wanton slaughter of women and children, but he did not blame himself or his officers. The savages had brought retribution on themselves and should have known better than to leave their families in its path. Maggie, of course, was quick to agree with him, but her concern was for the fate of his brother. "When did you last see him?" she wanted to know.

Will couldn't remember. John had been close behind him when they entered the village, that much he could recall. But after that when everyone was charging about in the dark, it was impossible to see who was where. "If you saw someone in uniform, he was one of us, and if he was naked, he wasn't. That's about all there was to it," he replied with a wry laugh. He added that he guessed that most of the savages had run off, as their strength had been estimated at about forty warriors and only sixteen dead had been counted. "If we're lucky, the ones who got away took John with them."

"Lucky?" Maggie retorted. "The poor lad 'll be better off dead."

The next morning, Saturday, August 11, Lord Delaware was back at his house in James Towne conferring with his officers, reviewing all that had happened in the past two days, and debating what should be the next step in breaking the will of the savages. But also on the docket was a complaint being brought by one of the Finsbury soldiers. "It would be of small account," explained Captain Brewster, "were it not related to the missing John Jefferys. The soldier demands to be heard," he added.

"Demands," Delaware huffed. "Demands do not sit well. But if the wretch has something useful to say, we should hear him out." Delaware then told William Strachey to seek someone who would instruct Captain Douthitt to find the man and bring him to the house. With that determined, the Governor returned to the broader picture. He applauded Percy for the success of his raid, expressed satisfaction that Captain Davis had executed the queen, and offered no opinion about the manner of her children's death. Many more such lessons might have to be taught, he said; and the more graphic they were the fewer would be needed. "Mark me well," he declared, "Ere long, Powhatan will be on his knees to us begging for quarter."

"If we don't all starve first," muttered the ever-complaining John Martin. Delaware heard the remark, and allowed that the food situation was growing rapidly worse. The corn brought back from Paspahegh had been cut too soon; the quantity brought from Kecoughtan had not been nearly enough, and the fishing continued dismal at best. Although the secret sale of supplies to the Indians by the ships' crews had ceased after Delaware returned to his flagship, the damage was already done. "We must continue to place our faith in Sir George and worthy Captain Argall," he declared, and then admitted to his growing concern that they had been gone so long. "Two weeks there and two weeks back, give or take, should have had them here at the latest by the last of July."

"And here we are half way through August," added Yeardley. "Something must have happened to..."

Delaware cut him short. "I'll hear no talk of that! Our very survival depends on the holds of the *Patience* and *Discovery*. I pray God for their safe return – and so must you."

A rap on the door heralded the arrival of Captain Douthitt and Lieutenant Bartram with the complaining soldier who gave his name as Henry Chisman. "Though me friends calls me 'Twofin' seein' as 'cos I lost all but these two on me left and, see?" he explained.

"Your complaint, man!" Delaware snapped. "State your business and be done."

Twofin took his cap off and scratched his head. "Its like this, me Lord. 'Twasn't the savages what killed my friend. 'Twas one of yourn, see."

Delaware looked first to Percy and then at Brewster and demanded to know what the man was talking about. But it fell to Douthitt to explain that the dead man was Thomas Bracket.

"That's him. That's old Smiler," Twofin agreed.

Douthitt went on to say that rumors were circulating in the camp that one of his Lordship's guardsmen had killed him, and that

Chisman claimed to have seen who did it, but that nobody here in the fort will admit it.

"Indeed," said Delaware. "Then suppose he tells us in his own words what happened."

"Well, sir, me Lord. 'Twas when we was in them savages' town and was told to kill every one of them, which we done our best to do, just like we was ordered, see."

"Yes, yes. Get to the point," Delaware snapped.

"Yus, well, sir, you've hit it on the 'ead, sir. The point *is* the point, if you see my meaning," he said with a sly grin. "'Twas the point of your man's sword what done it."

"Done...did what?"

"Shoved it right up poor old Smiler's arse, 'e did, and that's the truth, so 'elp me God."

A puzzled Delaware looked again to Percy and Brewster whose gestures indicated that they knew nothing about the incident. His irritation growing, he ordered Chisman to make himself plain.

"That I will, me Lord, yus indeed." He paused to scratch his ear. "'Ow should I put it? Let's say me and Smiler was 'avin' a bit of fun with one of them wenches, if you gets my drift. It bein' his turn, I was just holdin' 'er arms, see. Smiler was down on 'er when round the corner comes this mad sod. He don't say nothin', at least I don't think 'e done, and straight ways, wham! Up it goes. Just like that! Then 'e comes at me, and I does me best to defend meself, but 'e 'ad a sword and I didn't. So I scarpered. But not before I got a good look at 'is face."

"In the dark, you saw his face?" Brewster demanded.

"It weren't that dark. The hut hard by was afire. You saw that yourself, sir."

Brewster allowed that houses were burning. When Twofin demanded two weeks extra rations in exchange for identifying the attacker, Delaware threatened to hang him by his toes until the name fell out of him. That prospect was enough to reveal the name of John Jefferys. It took his listeners little time to conclude that having killed the rapist John considered himself a fugitive and had run off into the woods.

"His brother," Brewster volunteered, "is Sergeant Will Jefferys, as good a man as we've got. And I'll wager his brother is no less."

"But he killed a man," Delaware icily replied.

'Aye, my Lord, but the circumstances were..."

"Immaterial, Captain. He must be brought back and tried. Then I'll decide what is material and what is not." Delaware was about to call the matter closed when Chisman announced that he had more to tell.

"You talks about that sergeant. Well, sirs, I can tell ye a thing or two about 'im. There's a click of people, miners they are, who is talkin' about takin' a ship and goin' a pirating. And who do you suppose they's talkin' with? Sergeant bloody Jefferys, that's who!"

"And how know you this?" Brewster demanded.

"'Cos I seen 'im."

Delaware decided that he had heard enough, and ordered Douthitt to take Chisman back to his tent and to make sure he kept his mouth shut. As soon as they were gone, he asked whether there was truth in the tale. Brewster told him that the flight of John was almost certainly correct, though he had not inspected the body of Bracket to determine how he died. For all he knew, the man had been killed by the savages. As for the talk of mutiny, he reminded his Governor that although such talk was commonplace in any army, it rarely came to anything. That Sergeant Will would become involved in any such plot was unthinkable, of this he was sure.

Delaware said he was glad to hear it, but added that Jefferys should be watched and that any further contact between him and the miners should immediately be reported. Having had his attention drawn to the miners, his Lordship went on to discuss his half formed plans to send an expedition beyond the falls in search of mines. He reminded his colleagues that a Swiss citizen, a minor Company investor named William Hendrick Faldoe, had come to the colony aboard the *Hercules*. He claimed to know the location of a silver mine some fourteen miles above the Falls into Monacan territory, but would not divulge how he knew it until his Lordship set him up there with troops to protect him. He had declined to draw a map of the mine's location, and being under the Company's protection, Delaware could not force him to do so. "The devil, take the fellow," he huffed, then added, "But I do have the map I got from Dias that shows pin pricks beyond the Falls that he says are silver mines."

'Yes, but Dias is a Portugal," Yeardley argued. "They're no more to be trusted than the damned Spaniards! With great respect, my Lord, anyone can stick pins in a map and claim that they mean treasures. Who's to say that he's not a spy trying to lead us away from James Towne and into the claws of the Monacans?"

Delaware had no answer, but hoped that in time he would have a force healthy enough and strong enough to drive the Monacans back into the mountains. "Sooner or later, we'll do it," he insisted. "London expects nothing less."

Most of these inner council meetings ended with the same admonition from the Governor. No distant adventures will be possible until Sir George and Sam Argall return. But when they do...

Percy and the rest knew the speech by heart. Meanwhile the corn barrels in the store were close to empty, and despite Dr. Bohun's efforts, every day more soldiers were dying – eighteen of them since June, and the hot summer was not yet over. Privately, the councilors were speculating that the *Patience* and *Discovery* had been lost, and that reliance would have to be placed on Sir Thomas Gates' safe passage to England and his return with fresh supplies. But that could take four or even more months.

It took John and Sparrowhawk a week to get Taropoto to Orapakes, two days of it spent resting in villages along the way. But by the time they got there she was recovered enough to walk without help and even to smile. News of their coming had been passed ahead of them at each stage of the journey, and John was astonished to find a very different reception than had greeted him on his previous formal visit. There were no priests or councilors to deliver speeches or shouting dancers to wave rattles. Instead, there were twenty or thirty silent but evidently friendly women holding up their hands in welcome. Five or six of them quickly hurried Taropoto away, leaving

John and his new friend in the center of the village not knowing what to do or say. Sparrow confessed that he was in awe of the Great King and had never before visited Orapakes. He was also in awe of the now-chattering women who crowded admiringly around him.

Suddenly the gaggle of women parted as Machumps emerged from the King's house and hurried to John, a broad smile on his face and a hand extended. "The Great Powhatan bids you welcome, Master John. He wishes to speak with you as soon as you are rested. So come," he added pointing the house where John had previously lodged. "That is *your* house."

Resting did not come easily. First a woman came to light the fire, then another used it to light two mosquito-repelling tapers. A third brought food, and a fourth came to check that the first three had done their jobs. Shortly thereafter Tom Savage came to the door to welcome John back and to say that he and Harry Spelman were thinking about escaping from Orapakes and going to live with the Patomacks.

"Why so?" John asked.

Tom's explanation was simple. They would be safer with the Patomacks than with the Pamunkey at Orapakes. Sooner or later, Powhatan would engage the English and they would be compelled to take one side or the other. The Patomacks were independent of Powhatan and would stay out of the conflict. "Neither of us wants to go back and starve at James Towne," he added. "Besides, the Lord governor might take into his head to hang us as traitors."

"But you were both sent to live with these people."

"Yes, but that was in Cap'n Smith's time, and soon forgotten," Tom answered. "And what of you?"

"Me?" John replied that he had no choice. He had killed a soldier and abandoned his comrades. That, in Delaware's eyes, was treachery and punished with death. "The only thing what ain't certain, is how quick a death it'd be," John added. "No, good friend. I be here to stay."

Tom knew him to be right, but told him that he would be welcome to join with Spelman and himself when the time came for their escape.

John thanked him and said he would think about it, but at this moment he could only think about today and his audience with the Great King.

The call came late in the afternoon. Only Machumps was to be his escort, no warrior guards nor any stomping attendants. The absence of the known made the unknown the more unnerving. Once in the outer chamber, Machumps said that he was no longer needed. "Powhatan will speak in your tongue," he said before leaving John to continue through the several rooms leading to the royal chamber. Small smokey fires were still burning, but no one was there to attend them. He wasn't sure whether to wait to be summoned or to go forward unheralded. After waiting several minutes in the semi darkness he was able to see the doorway into the great chamber and beyond it heard the low murmur of voices.

Had there been a door to knock on, he would have done so. Instead, he settled for the next best thing. "Ahem!" he said loudly as he stepped through the entrance. Beyond the central fire he could see two seated men smoking, one passing the pipe to the other. Remembering that Powhatan was said to be deaf, he tried again. "Ahem!" he repeated even louder. When the first man heard him and stood up, John recognized him as the Great King. But the other taller man he hadn't seen before.

Powhatan peered at John, tipping his head first on one side and then the other. "So you are the young *tassantass* who brought us back our Taropoto," he said, followed by several grunts that John took to be a chuckle. "How strange it is that it should be you."

"Aye, is it not?" John lamely replied.

"We owe you much," Powhatan added with a sweep of his hand in a gesture that evidently included his companion. The man's head was shaved on the right side with the left grown a yard long and plaited with feathers woven into it. His skin was stained or painted almost black and his only clothing was a leather loincloth in several layers, each edged with animal teeth that glowed yellow in the firelight. On his head he was wearing a circlet of copper set with a short pair of stag horns.

"I Wowinchapunck, king of Paspahegh," he intoned. He went on to claim that when the *tassantasses* first arrived, he had allowed them land on which to build their fort, and had given them grain, turkeys, deer, and much else in friendship. But in return, they burned his boats, destroyed his villages, and killed his people. What choice did he have, he wanted to know, but to be avenged and make war in return? Had not, Captain Smith, whom the Great King had made his son, had he not attacked Wowinchapunck in person and taken him chained into their fort, and made him humble before the English?

Some of this John understood, but a lot more he did not. The *weroance's* English was not as clear as Powhatan's and included much shouting and hand waving. "Now you have taken *Wironausqua* and my *Nechauns*, and I fear for their safety." Powhatan translated the words as his queen and his children.

John knew that Percy's order had been to kill everyone in the village, but he could honestly reply that he knew nothing about the fate of Wowinchapunck's family. It was pointless, however, to offer any assurance that they would be treated as the queen and children of a king, having just been told that Smith had taken him prisoner to the fort in chains. Consequently, John's immediate expectation was to be imprisoned himself and held hostage for the queen's safety. If so, he had every reason to expect that if she was already dead, he would very shortly share John Ratcliffe's grisly fate.

"But," said Powhatan, "though you came first to us with arrogant words, they were not your own. Now you come again to us with a gift precious to us all. My people, all our people, know you to be our friend." He went on to say what John already knew. He could not go back to James Towne, and for that reason he would be welcome to remain under Pamunkey protection as long as he should live. "I cannot make you my son," Powhatan went on, "because I have made sons before and they have betrayed me. But you shall have a captain's place at my table. And my brother, the great *Weroance* of Paspahegh gives you his Taropoto for wife."

John gulped. "The great Wowinchapunck does...um...does me much honor, but I..."

"It is done," Powhatan told him. "It is agreed."

John looked to Wowinchapunck and saw his unsmiling nod, but was unsure whether it was in unreserved agreement or only in acquiescence. But it made no difference. Powhatan had spoken and John Jefferys had a bride. He had also become wealthy. He was to receive space for a small field of tobacco and of corn. He would be furnished with whatever Taropoto might need to establish his household, and some time soon Powhatan would take him to his great temple and treasure storehouse there to receive a gift worthy of an honored captain.

That night, back in his lodge, John began to say a prayer of thanks for his salvation, but got no further than "Our Father who are in heaven..." before realizing that in forsaking his homeland he was also abandoning his Christian faith. He remembered his conversations with Chaplain Laurie and how his questions had been answered by, "Have faith, my boy," and how unsatisfying that response had been. Now he asked himself yet again whether the Christian God was the only true God or was there a universal God who watched over all religions? Might not the Indians' *Okeus* be the same in another guise? Clinging to that comforting thought, John fell asleep. When he awoke the next morning he found a still-sleeping Taropoto on the floor beside his bed.

Three days later, John Jefferys was formally married. Standing outside his house, his Paspahegh friend Sparrow served as the bride's father, joining the couple's hands and breaking a string of shell beads over their heads. As the beads scattered on the ground around them a chorus of shouting, stomping, and rattling Pamunkey launched into an anthem of congratulation — or so Taropoto later explained. Then followed a feast presided over by Powhatan himself at which he spoke in both Algonquian and English, publically confirming John's status in the Great King's extended family.

Shortly after the feasting ended, a Paspahegh runner arrived to tell Powhatan that the queen and her children had been murdered. That night the gods wept and rain fell on Orapakes.

Chapter Fifteen

It did not rain that night at James Towne nor would it for another eighteen sweltering days. The death toll continued to rise, mostly among soldiers in the camp; one hundred and fifty dead before August was out. Among the few lost from within the fort was Faldoe, the Swiss mineral man who went to his grave taking his alleged knowledge of the silver mines with him. In the first months of the colony's existence and again during the past winter's Starving Time, some of the dead were interred in empty spaces inside the defenses, but since Lord Delaware's arrival and his restoration of the church, only people of distinction were interred there. Although a minor share holder in the London Company, William Hendrick Faldoe was classed as a "stranger," and treated accordingly. Consequently, his Lordship decreed that his interment be in the "other sorts'" burial ground beyond the military camp. But being a foreigner of consequence his funeral would be conducted with dignity – which meant that Sergeant Jefferys would command a small honor guard to accompany pall bearers drawn from the corps of miners.

At the close of the simple ceremony at which the Reverend Buck said a prayer, the cortege broke ranks, and the guardsmen chatted amicably with the miners.

"Well, 'Allo again," said a voice Will recognized. He turned and found the Cornish miner, Henry Funnell, standing behind him. "Be you givin' any more thought to what we was talkin' about a few weeks back?" he asked.

"And what was that?" Will cautiously replied.

"About takin' a ship an' all," Funnell reminded him. "We're figurin' you might be of a mind to 'elp us, see?"

"I don't know where you got that idea," Will assured him. "I told you clear enough..."

"Oy 'eard you, Sergeant. But it was the *way* you said it, what caught my notice," Funnell explained with a conspiratorial tap to the side of his nose.

Will looked around to see who might be listening. "I'll hear no more o' this..."

Funnell took him by the sleeve. "Walk with me, Sergeant. I 'ave a proposition, all legal like."

Will waved to his men to head back to the fort, while he lingered to hear what the miner had to say.

"'Ere it is then," Funnell told him. "There be eight, maybe ten of us, what's 'ad enough. So we wants old Delaware to give us a boat, a shallop will do."

"You're jesting?" Will laughed.

"No Sergeant, we's dead serious."

"But what makes you think the Governor would give you a boat?" Will asked incredulously.

"Because I've got somethin' 'e wants, don't you see?" Funnell went on to tell how the ailing Faldoe had shared his knowledge of the silver mines with him, and had shown him a plan that depicted the falls and the southern part of the Monacan territory. "He said 'e knew it by 'eart, and told me to do the like. And I did. Then 'e burnt it. So now nobody knows about it, 'cept what's in 'ere," he added, tapping his forehead. Funnell's proposal was simple. He would redraw the map from memory in exchange for the boat and safe passage out of Virginia, and he expected Will to take the proposition to Delaware.

Will answered that he would think on it.

"A man's memory don't last but so long," Funnell added with a grin. "If you sees what I mean."

As Will walked quickly back to the fort, Twofin Chisman stood watching him from between two tents, a broad grin on his face.

Pounding his right fist into his left hand, he muttered "Now I've gotcher."

His funerary duty done, Will returned to his house still very uncertain about whether or not to pass Funnell's proposal up the command to the Governor. As usual, he shared his concerns with Maggie. "You can't trust nobody, you know that," she told him. "But if them miners is plannin' somethin', then you'd better tell it afore somebody thinks you'm part of it."

That was precisely what Will had been thinking, and he said so.

"But I wouldn't just tell Cap'n Brewster, good man though he be. There's no tellin' how the tale can get twisted afore it gets to 'is Lordship," Maggie told him. "You'd best go to the Governor yourself," she added.

For two days Will vacillated. Should he or shouldn't he? What if the Governor decided he was a trouble maker? What if Funnell changed his mind and denied the whole plan? Where would that leave Will? Maybe if he kept silent, the miners would find someone else to voice their proposal? But then, if in presenting it, they should say that they had first asked Will to speak for them and he had done nothing about it, where would that leave him? In the end he decided to take Maggie's advice and apply to see the Governor.

"I'm sure he'll see you," Captain Brewster told him. "Perhaps you'd like to tell me what this is about?"

Will was afraid he'd ask that, but replied that it was a matter that he did not feel he should tell anyone but his Lordship. Brewster gave him a quizzical look, but said only "So be it, then." He might have probed further had not a boat arrived from Fort Algernon with a message that a sail had been sighted off Point Comfort. She appeared to be a small, square-rigged pinnace, the messenger reported, adding that he had no more information than that. Nevertheless, the news generated great excitement in the fort, and Will's request to see the Governor was quickly set aside.

"A lone ship?" Delaware asked. "Not two ships, then?"

George Yeardley, who had received the message, told Delaware that he had asked the same question and been assured that only one had been sighted. "But there could be more over the horizon by now," he added.

But that turned out not to be so. On August 28, seventy-three days after leaving James Towne, Samuel Argall and the *Discovery* returned. "But where..." the astonished Delaware stammered, "where is Sir George?"

Argall replied that he, too, would like to know. He told how month-long contrary winds had prevented the two ships from heading straight to Bermuda as originally planned. Instead, on Sir George Somers' order they sailed north to the New England fishing grounds. On the evening of June 26, as the two ships became enshrouded in dense fog, Somers instructed Argall to rendez-vous at the mouth of the Sagadahoc River. "Though I waited there for six days," he explained, "no sign did I see of Sir George, nor did I as we made our way back down the coast. I fear the *Patience* is lost," he ended.

The news was distressing, but not wholly bad. The *Discovery* came laden with fish which, carefully leavened with the fort's remaining supplies, would keep it going for several weeks. But what then?

"I've been a sailor all me life," Argall told Delaware, "but there's times when stretching one's legs on land can be mightily improving. Methinks a visit to the Warrascoyacks might be just what I need. By now their corn should be in and ready for us to bring home," he added with a laugh.

Delaware already had such a raid in mind, and would have led it himself had his ague not grown worse. Now with Sam Argall back and eager for action, there was no reason for further delay. Besides, it would give the soldiery something useful to do. Morale, according to George Percy, had appreciably improved since the Paspahegh attack, and so another such adventure would further discourage the men from squabbling amongst themselves. "This time," Delaware told Percy, "Sam will command," then hastily added, "not that I imply any criticism of your leadership, you understand."

Percy gritted his teeth, but said nothing. He was still smarting over Delaware's reaction to his having saved the Paspahegh queen.

And he was no better pleased when told that Captain Brewster would be second in command. That decision also meant that the Governor's guardsmen would again be at the forefront. For most this was the best of news, and it would have been for Will Jefferys had not memories of the Paspahegh slaughter remained so vividly in his mind.

"War be one thing," he told Maggie, "but spearing little children in their ma's arms just don't seem right. I ain't a God fearin' man; but I won't be surprised if, when the last trump sounds, we all be called to account."

"I know, love," Maggie assured him. "But if killin' the little 'uns be the only way to rid us of the varmints, somebody's got to do it. It ain't your fault."

He expected no other answer. But he wondered whether, if Maggie had been with him on that night in the Paspahegh village, she would still be so ready for more killing.

Preparations for the assault proceeded at such a pace that Will had no opportunity to secure an audience with the Governor. Instead, he was kept busy in the guard house helping the armorer loading musket charges and supervising the distribution and fitting of the guardsmen's armor. This time there was to be no nocturnal surprise attack, and so need for stealth. On the contrary, this was to be a bold frontal assault in which armor not only protected the attackers but also would put the fear of God into the naked enemy. At least, that was the theory.

The Warrascoyack capital lay on the winding Pagan River which, like most small Virginia rivers, was flanked by creeks and marshes, and three miles overland from the King's River behind a high bluff. The only militarily sensible approach, therefore, was up the Pagan River. "All the more reason, therefore," said Argall, "for the men to be armored. Without it our people would be easy marks for bowmen hidden on the banks. And they know from experience that arrows are wasted on steel." Nevertheless, sitting encased in armor during a fifteen-mile ride down river on a late summer's day would have been no one's choice; and Will was not alone in envying the sailors who hauled sails and manned oars wearing naught but their britches.

His Lordship had graciously, albeit reluctantly, been persuaded to allow Argall to borrow his telescope which he now used to scan the shore for any sight of savages as the flotilla made its way down river. But he saw no one. "But they're there, and they've seen us, I'll stake my beard on that!" he shouted to Brewster in the following shallop. And he was right.

News of the *tassantasses'* approach reached Tackonekintaco, the Warraskoyacks' *weroance,* before it was even certain that the Pagan River was their destination. Earlier dealings with the aged king in which he had promised to sell the English 500 bushels of wheat when his August crop came in, had proved an empty promise. Now, therefore, Argall intended to take it, and Tackonekintaco was equally certain that he would not.

By the time Argall's boats nosed into the bay at the mouth of the Pagan River, the Warrascoyacks' two principal towns were being evacuated and their grain stores stripped. Even when the river narrowed to where the attackers were in easy bow shot from either bank, no arrows thudded into the hulls or zipped into the water. Only birds in the trees remained to break the silence. "God's blood!" Argall swore as he stepped ashore into the first deserted settlement.

Will led one file in a house-to-house search for grain baskets only to return shaking his head and confessing that he had found nothing and nobody. No English trade goods or stolen tools and weapons remained — nothing but mats, wooden dishes and earthen pots.

"Burn it all! Burn everything!" Argall ordered. While the first village was still blazing, the victors reboarded and continued up river to the second, larger village. Both he and Brewster were too seasoned old soldiers to be lulled into supposing that the next settlement would be as deserted as the last. "The bastards are just as likely to have emptied the first to ambush us in the second," Brewster advised. But he was wrong. The second town was undefended, as empty as the first, and burned as quickly.

Will looked around him at his sweating guardsmen whose armor looked red hot in the reflected flames of the burning buildings, and heaved a sign of relief that they had found no women and children to murder. For Argall, however, the expedition had achieved nothing beyond further alienating the savages. Angrily he kicked at the ashes with his boot, and cursed Tackonekintaco and his heathen soul to eternal damnation. "Everybody back on the boats!" he ordered.

As the invaders pulled away down river, Indians watched from the forests and laughed. They knew that in a very few days their villages would be rebuilt and the harvest safely back in their granaries.

It was on the somber voyage back to James Towne that Will had an opportunity to repeat his request to speak with the Governor. Again Brewster asked the reason, and again Will answered as he had before. The next morning while on duty in the guard house, Captain Brewster informed him that his Lordship was ready to hear what he had to say. "But be careful," Brewster warned, "his ague wracks him and his temper is tinder dry."

This was not the best moment to be carrying what amounted to an ultimatum, and Will knew it. But having asked for the meeting he could hardly say that he had thought better of it. Furthermore, it was not reassuring to see Captain Douthitt leaving the Governor's House as he approached it.

The door was opened by Ensign Scot who announced him: "Sergeant William Jefferys, my Lord."

Will was surprised to find that this was not, as he had hoped and requested, a private meeting. In attendance were Argall, George Yeardley, John Martin, and George Percy, all seated at the long table and staring intently at him. A grim-faced Delaware barked, "Well man, speak your piece."

Haltingly, Will told what he knew about the proposed desertion and the offer that the conspirators had asked him to propose. When he finished, Will looked from face to face expecting some kind of reaction, surprise, anger, disbelief, anything, but got nothing. All four heads turned toward Delaware waiting for him to answer. Finally, he did.

"Sergeant Jefferys, tell us this. How long have you known about this conspiracy?"

Will replied that it had to have been about a month, but quickly added that he thought it was no more than common soldiers' talk.

"Did it not occur to you that you had been promoted to sergeant and so you are no longer a *common* soldier – the word is yours – and that as a sergeant it was your duty to report what you say you heard?"

Will repeated that he thought it mere gossip. "I would have done so had I believed elsewise," he insisted.

"But now you believe that there is a conspiracy. Am I right, Sergeant?"

"Aye, my Lord."

"And yet you waited two days without reporting it."

"Two days, my Lord?" Will blurted. "I did not say two..."

"Would it surprise you to know that we have known about this ever since you met with those miners?" Delaware asked coldly. "You have been watched ever since. Would it also surprise you to know that it was at my instruction you were assigned to the burial of the Faldoe fellow? If you value your skin, sirrah, you will now tell me the names of your fellow conspirators."

"But my Lord..." Will began, "I am no con..."

"The names, man! The names!" Delaware shouted.

" I swear, my Lord," Will pleaded, "I only spoke with one..."

"His name then!"

"I'm not sure I remember," Will answered. It was, it could have been, I think Harry, Henry.."

"Henry Funnell, is it not?

"Aye, my Lord. I think.."

"I *know*," Delaware told him. "I also know that as you stand here Captain Douthitt is arresting Master Funnell, and unless I am very much mistaken, before the week is out, he'll hang. And so may you, young man, after he is put to the question."

"But, Sir," Will gasped, "if I were one of them, why would I come to you?"

"Because, sirrah, you mistakenly believed that Faldoe's ace trumped the rest of the pack."

Will was still protesting as Ensign Scot hurried him out into the arms of two guardsmen who seemed to take pleasure in delivering him to the guard house jail. A Finsbury soldier already held there on a charge of hitting a corporal told Will, "Think yourself lucky you ain't in the hole." He pointed to a trap door in the wooden floor, and explained that when captive savages were brought in, they were kept in the wood-lined pit John Smith had called the dungeon. "If you're thinkin' of escaping down that way," Will's voluble companion assured him, "you'll be wasting your time. There's no way out but up, and there naut down there but dirty great jumpin' bugs."

Later in the day Maggie was allowed to bring Will a lump of bread and a bowl of soup which he shared with his companion. But apart from that visit, no one came near him. His cell mate said his name was Jack, and that he had been there for two days without any food. There being no chamber pot or any other furnishings in the cell, Will asked him what he should do when natural necessity called, to which Jack answered by pointing to the trap door.

The man was perhaps forty years old, Irish, and had been a mercenary soldier all his adult life. "Made a fair do of it, 'til oy was fool enough to sign on for this lark," he explained bitterly. "They told us there'd be gold here for the takin, and what' did we get, eh? What did we get? I'll tell ye what we get. 'Tis naught but sickness and shit!"

Will tried to explain that although he, too, had been promised riches, it was duty to his Lordship and to his family that brought him to Virginia.

"Duty!" Jack spat into a corner. "Let me tell you, boyo. Duty ain't no different to slavery. A man's duty is to hisself and nobody else. You does what you think is best for you."

"Aye," Will replied. "And look where it's gotten you."

Jack laughed. "Ah, well..." he said, and let it go at that.

As night fell, Will and Jack sat in opposite corners to try to sleep. Both were thinking about freedom, Jack trying to devise a means to escape, and Will hoping to be reprieved. They were awakened some time later by loud voices and much clatter from the guardroom. Then they heard their cell door being unlocked and by the light from a candle in the guardroom, they saw the silhouette of a limp figure being dragged in. A guard opened the trap door and two of them dumped their prisoner feet first through the hole before slamming the door shut. "Don't neither of you touch that trap, if you know what's good for you," ordered one of the guards as he departed, plunging them again into darkness. Several minutes passed before Will heard groans coming from below.

"We ought to do somethin'," Will whispered.

"Like what?" Jack replied.

"Well, the least we can do is to find out who he is," Will insisted, as he groped for the baton securing the trapdoor. With the door opened, he hissed "What's your name?"

Back came a gasping, pain-wracked reply. "Henry...Funnell."

Jack was right. There was nothing they could do but whisper baseless encouragement. It would take a rope or a ladder to get Funnell out of the dungeon. He had been severely beaten, a thumb-screw had burst both of them, and he feared that his right arm had been broken. "But I didn't tell them nothin'," he gasped, "narry a bleedin' word."

Early the next morning, Captain Brewster came to the cell. "Well, young Will," he said, "You've gotten yourself into a fine pickle, and no mistake."

"Aye, that I have," Will ruefully replied. Before he could voice any defense, Brewster told him that his Lordship had questioned the miner Funnell who had said nothing to involve Will in the conspiracy. He was, therefore, released to resume his duties.

"And what about Funnell?" Will asked. "The poor fellow be in..."

"He hangs tomorrow," Brewster replied. "Now get you gone, and think yourself lucky!"

Home with Maggie, Will was relieved, angry, tired, and in no mood to be lectured. She knew all about stable doors, and so kept her peace. It was enough that he was safe and suffering no more than a sore back from sleeping on the cell floor. That she could massage. His mind would have to take care of itself.

The next morning, back as Sergeant of the First File, Will Jefferys once again found himself in the unenviable role as leader of the execution squad that was to march the prisoner out of the fort to the hanging tree on Smithfield Green. But Henry Funnell was in no condition to march. Instead, he had to be carried by guardsmen supporting each of his arms so that his feet barely touched the ground. Those of the Finsbury troops still well enough to stand were on parade with the corps of miners conspicuously at their front to await the arrival of Lord Delaware and his officers who walked grim-faced to the field escorted by the remaining files of his guards.

His Lordship's speech was shorter than usual and his diction halting. He reminded his listeners that they were about to witness English justice as proscribed by law. Conspiracy to commit treason against the state had no other penalty than death. In seeing it carried out, every man should know that the same fate awaited any others who might conspire to quit the colony. In closing, Delaware, assigned the soul of Henry Funnell to be judged by a merciful God. "Executioners, do your duty!" he ordered.

The condemned man had been hauled up a ladder propped against the tree, with the noose around his neck and run through the pulley attached to the projecting limb. His left arm hung limply at his side; his thumbs were black with dried blood, and his head sagged onto his chest. To Will who remembered Funnell as a sturdy and robust Cornishman, this still weighty but sorry travesty of a man could as well be already dead. But just before the ladder was jerked away he lifted his head and with his jaw sagging, mumbled, "I swear to God, I never told on nobody."

For several moments he swung back and forth, his legs kicking and twitching as his face turned a purplish red. Then the rope broke.

Henry Funnell lay on the ground, the noose still around his neck, but, as Will had to report to Delaware, he was still breathing. Dr. Bohun ran out to attend him as did the Reverend Buck, one to minister to his life and the other to his soul. Both agreed that he might survive.

A voice from among the troops shouted, "Let him live!" Another called, "You told the good Lord to judge him, and he has! So let him be!" The supportive murmuring from the troops convinced Delaware that to do otherwise would transform a useful lesson into the seed of rebellion, and so he wisely elected to pardon Funnell and placed him in what he described as the "healing hands of our good doctor."

While returning to the fort as grim-faced as he had emerged, his Lordship was heard to demand, "Have we no better rope than that?"

The Funnell debacle was to generate much caustic amusement at the Governor's expense, and even the sycophantic William Strachey was moved to record it as an "execution proving strange and unheard of." For Will there was relief that the foolish man was to live and even more profound relief that his death would not be on his conscience.

"'Twas God's will, and no mistake," Maggie concluded. "And God's will, too, the poor wretch didn't name you. I doubt there'd 'ave bin two rotten ropes in one morning," she added.

In mid afternoon Captain Brewster ordered Will to report to the Governor's House, a prospect that promptly rekindled waning fears. "What for? Why?" Will wanted to know. But Brewster walked quickly ahead of him without replying.

This time Will found Delaware alone save for his doctor who was about to leave, a bleeding bowl in his hands. Ashen-faced and fumbling with a sleeve button, Delaware turned to Brewster and begged him to, "Help me with this damn thing, there's a good fellow." Then, with the button fastened and his coat adjusted, he looked hard at Will. "Sergeant Jefferys," he said, "you and your brother have caused your liege lord a deal of anguish. How say you to that?"

"My Lord, I never..."

"Never mind." Delaware cut him short. "I'm persuaded that you spoke true. I am also persuaded that if your brother be alive, Powhatan holds him prisoner. And I'm sure you want him back, do you not?"

"With all my heart, my Lord," Will replied. Surprised by the question, he was nervously wondering where this was leading — when Delaware told him.

"I am ordering you to bring him back. You may take four of your file with you, and that tame savage Kemps as your interpreter. But you will find your brother. If he be a prisoner you will free him, and if he be not, then you will make him yours. Do I make myself clear?"

"Aye, my Lord," Will assured him.

"Then go, and God be with you," Delaware intoned as he waved him away.

No sooner had the door closed, than the Governor leant across the table to Brewster and asked, "Do you think he really does understand?"

"I'm sure he does, Sir," Brewster answered. "Will Jefferys is a good..."

"Yes, yes, I know all that," Delaware snapped. "I mean, does he realize that if he brings his brother back as a deserter, I'll hang him?"

Brewster let out a long sigh before replying, "Let's hope he never has to find out."

Chapter Sixteen

Two guardsmen ordered by Captain Brewster to find Kemps and bring him to the guard house failed to do so. As best anyone could remember, the Indian had left the fort one or maybe two days earlier. According to the cook he was hunting game for the common kettle, but in Ensign Scot's recollection he had gone on a private mission to Ottahotin, *weroance* of the Kiskiaks. Scot remembered Kemps saying something about building a bridge of understanding. "But you know how these savages are," he explained to Brewster. "They mix their words up with ours and you're never quite sure what they're saying."

Mathew Brewster did not like Kemps as a man, and did not trust him as an ally. Were he in command he would have him shot. He was convinced that the savage had tried to guide Percy away from the Paspahegh village; but for reasons he couldn't fathom, Delaware had taken a liking to him. On the only occasion that Brewster had expressed his doubts, Delaware brushed them aside saying that a loose cannon was better than no cannon at all. "But with great respect, my Lord..." Brewster began to reply.

"God's life, man," Delaware snorted, "he's the only savage who comes to church on Sundays. Kemps is our savage, not theirs!"

That, as far as Brewster was concerned, had to be the end of it. Nevertheless, as his Lordship had earlier, it worried him that the man was allowed to come and go as he chose. Now he was gone and no one seemed to know when he'd be back. Consequently, Will Jefferys' mission would have to wait. To go without an Indian translator and guide would almost certainly see him dead before he got half way across Paspahegh territory.

As soon as the Governor dismissed him, Will returned to Maggie to tell her the good news. "His Lordship's sendin' me to find John! He really is! What think you of that?"

"What does I think o' that?" she answered, not looking up from pounding their corn ration. "I think you'm a complete fool, that's what I thinks!"

"Why so?" Will went on to tell her that he could pick four guardsmen to protect him and a savage to guide him to Orapakes.

"What savage?" Maggie asked.

"'Tis that Kemps; the one who lives here and is a Christian."

"A Christian, my eye!" Maggie snapped. "I've seen him; he's a slimey bugger who says what serves his purpose. More fool Delaware for being taken in by him, that's what I says."

But Will was convinced that he had been given the opportunity of his life. Nothing could be more important or more gratifying than to be able to save one's own brother. Maggie stopped her pounding and sat down to hear him out. But when he was done, she shook her head, and sighed.

"Will, my love, think on it," she told him. "We don't know what happened. We don't even know if the lad's alive. If he were captured, how are you goin' to free him? Five of you against all them savages?"

Will confessed that he didn't know, but he would find a way, of that he was sure.

"But suppose he ain't a prisoner? Suppose he ran off and joined 'em, what then?"

"He'd never do that!"

"Suppose he 'ad no choice?"

"Then he'll want the chance to come back," Will angrily replied, mopping his brow with his sleeve. "I don't know why you always look on the dark side!"

"Because, love, I've seen it all too often," Maggie replied. "Let me ask ye this. What if he's joined all them other runaways what fled to Powhatan in the winter? What if he don't want to come back? The Governor says you're to bring him back a prisoner. Do ye know what'll happen to him if you do? They'll hang him, that's what."

"Give over, woman," Will snapped as he sat down heavily on the bed and buried his head in his hands. "Jesu, 'tis hot today," he muttered.

"'Tis cooler than it was," Maggie answered.

A few minutes later Pips Bailey came knockng at the open door. "Hey Sarg," he said. "The Cap'n wants to see you in the guard house. Is it true you're goin' lookin' for your bro'?"

Will agreed that it was so, and before he could say more, Pips was demanding that he be chosen to go with him. "'Tis time we 'ad a bit o' fun away from the bleedin' officers," he added.

Maggie watched the two men cross the market place toward the guard house and was amused that Pips was prancing along clearly excited by the prospect of an adventure. But then she looked at Will's back and saw it less straight and commanding than it had become since he was made sergeant. Had she said too much? Had she destroyed his confidence? Surely, not? He never listened to her advice anyway. "You're just a crockety, old woman," he'd tell her with a laugh.

"What me, old?" she'd reply. "Not when you're around, m' lad!" She watched him enter the guard house, and went back about her chores. Inside, Brewster was waiting to explain that Will's departure would have to wait until Kemps returned. It irritated him more than a little, that he was unable say when that would be. "Could be tonight, tomorrow, next week," he confessed. Then he added, "But you're to be ready as soon as he gets here. You understand his Lordship's instruction, do you not?"

"Aye, Cap'n," Will replied.

"No questions, then?"

Will took in a deep breath, "Not that I can think of, sir. No, sir, none that..."

Brewster looked hard at him. "Are you all right, lad?" he asked. "You're sweating like a hog."

"'Tis hot today, sir."

"I'll tell you what, Sergeant. You go back to your quarters and I'll get the doctor to come and take a look at you." Will assured Brewster that he was fine, but when ordered did as he was told. He was still on his way when Dr. Bohun returned from visiting the camp sick and met the Captain in the market place. Brewster pointed to the departing Will and explained his concern, adding that he had spent the night in the windowless jail cell.

"Not in the dungeon?" Bohun asked.

Brewster told him no. But added that the stench coming up through the floor was enough to make anyone sick. "If he's got to walk to Powhatan and back, we need him fit."

But Will Jefferys was not fit, and by nightfall the fever was upon him. Dr. Bohun's advice to Maggie was to keep his head cool and his body covered. "He must sweat it out," he said.

"But is there no physic you can give him?" Maggie implored.

Bohun shook his head. "Alas, woman, I have none," he confessed. He did not add to Maggie's dismay by admitting that even if he had a sea chest of fresh medications, he wouldn't know what was best to give him. The diseases that were killing so many seemed to vary from victim to victim, and he said as much a few minutes later when he visited his next patient. "How does, my Lord?" he asked.

"Neither worse nor better than I was when you asked me this morning," Delaware mumbled. "But the gout burns something fierce," he added.

"At least that's one I know how to treat, " Bohun told him. "But out in the camp I'm still finding strange fluxes and agues, malaria, scurvy, and the Lord knows what. There are swellings and sores, all of them different. If we had some fruits from the Indies, I could control the scurvy, but without..."

"For the sake of heaven, good doctor, don't plague me with other men's ailments!" Delaware snapped. "They're all in the camp, are they not?"

Bohun shook his head. "No, m'Lord, there's a new one in the fort this afternoon."

"Someone we know?"

"Sergeant Jefferys m' Lord."

"Oh," Delaware grunted. "He's the one I was sending out to find his brother. So now we lose both of them. Brewster tells me they were good lads, and from home, too."

Bohun replied that Will might recover. It was much too soon to tell. However, it gave him an opportunity to repeat yet again the warning that he had been voicing ever since he set foot at James Towne. The island is an unhealthy place by reason of the rotten and stinking mists rising out of the marshes. Drinking the brackish river water, mosquitoes in the ditches, and the lack of personal hygiene, are all contributing factors, he insisted. "'Tis well known that in camps many loathsome and stinking venomous vapors are engendered, all of which corrupt airs enter the body and vent in one fashion or another. My Lord, unless the camp be cleansed, and the men be sleeping up off the ground, we may lose all."

Delaware testily replied that he had already given directives to that effect.

"Then they are not enforced," Bohun replied. "When Sir Ferdinando was alive the camp was better kept than it is today."

Delaware sighed. "You are a very tiresome fellow, to be sure. But you are right," he allowed. There the discussion ended. Bohun had said what needed to be said, and his master might or might not remember it tomorrow. His own health being of such concern to him, it was highly likely that beyond reprimanding the useless Captain Douthitt, nothing would be done.

It rained hard in the night, a reminder to Dr. Bohun of the warning from last year's survivors that September was a rainy month in Virginia, and that when the weather breaks new sicknesses follow. But as Maggie listened to the water dripping down her chimney, only one sickness was on her mind. Will's fever was mounting, and no matter how often she soaked her cooling rag in river water, the sweat beaded on his brown, his hands shook and his breath came in chest-heaving gasps. Her neighbor, Sara Fielding, came by shortly after sun up and gave her unrequested clinical opinion that

Will Jefferys was as good dead.

At the same time in far-away Orapakes, his brother was rising to another day that seemed as close to Eden as he could imagine. Taropoto had gone with him to the river to bathe, had prepared his breakfast, and now he was ready hunt with his friends, Sparrowhawk and Little Crow. His only regret was that he didn't have a good English bow to bend. The Indians' hazel bows just didn't feel right, though he congratulated himself that even with those, his aim, if not his distance was improving.

"Made up your mind, 'ave you?" The question came from Harry Spelman who was leaning against a corner post of John's lodge.

"About what?" John countered.

Spelman laughed. "What else? Why about throwin' in your lot with these heathens."

"Heathens, Christians, what be the difference?"

"Well, if you don't know, all I can say is that our clerics haven't taught you much." With that, Spelman shook his head and walked away.

That evening after John returned from an unproductive hunting trip — two arrows lost and nothing downed — he began to question Taropoto about her religion. Spelman's barb had hit its mark. What were the differences between her beliefs and his? "Tell me about the *Okeus*," he asked her. "Have you ever seen him?"

Taropoto laughed at the idea. "Of course not," she assured him. She explained that only the priests ever see him, but that he comes down out of the air into the temple and tells them what to do, and then rises again into the sky. In response to John's further questions she told him that the *Okeus* was a great god but that there were other *kwiokosuk*, lesser gods of fire, water, of wild game and the like.

John then asked whether the *Okeus* was the god who created heaven and earth. "No," she replied, "the god of creation is *Ahone*; he is the sun, and the moon and stars answer to him. That is why we pray to him in the morning when we bathe," she explained.

"But *Ahone* is a different god to the *Okeus*?" John persisted

"Some say so, and some say not," Tarapoto replied.

"And you?"

"I do not question. It is enough to believe," she answered. "Is it not enough for you to believe in your god and to accept him without question?"

John nodded, knowing it to be true.

"Other people see our gods in their own ways." She went on, "the Potomacks see their first god as coming down in the form of a great hare who created men and women and kept them in a bag at his housing in the rising sun. But when the gods of the four winds came visiting and wanted to eat the men and women, Ahone sent them away. Then he took the men and women and set them down one pair to each country, and thus the human race began."

"Like Adam and Eve," John told her.

Taropoto shrugged. "Perhaps. Why not?" She added that although the old stories of the gods differed from one tribe to another, no community claimed its god to be better than any other. "We do not fight as you do to make your god better than ours. This we do not understand."

She went on to ask him why the Christian god might not be Ahone in another guise. "We all look to the sun for life, do we not? We all see the same sun, so why cannot there be one god for us all?"

John replied that he was sure Chaplain Laurie would have an answer, but confessed that he did not. "We believe what we are taught to believe," he told her lamely.

Taropoto smiled. "So are we all."

John had never really questioned his own beliefs, but through the next several days he became increasingly uncertain. Believing that men and women were put on the earth by a great hare was unbelievable to be sure. But what about Adam and Eve and the Garden of Eden? Wasn't that an equally unlikely story? And had he first heard it not in church but from a drunkard in a tavern, would he accept it as the truth? Although, day by day, John became no more ready to accept the Great Hare, he did become less and less convinced that Dr. Laurie's Genesis stories made sense.

About two weeks after John's arrival at Orapakes — he was already losing track of days — Machumps told him that he had been instructed to escort him to the Great King. "He will speak with you." That was all Machumps would say in answer to John's questions. He expected to be taken to the same long house where he had been received by Powhatan twice before; instead Machumps led him into the woods along the path on which he had been halted in his first explorations of the town's perimeter. But this time no guards barred the way.

"You be not much of a talker," John told Machumps.

"Only a fool talks when he has nothing to say," came the reply.

They had traveled about a mile into the forest when they came to a clearing in the middle of which stood another large house. It looked to be about thirty yards wide and maybe fifty or more long. It was by any standard a very large building. Outside, near the single entrance, were four posts carved in the shapes of a dragon, a bear, a giant man, and another animal that John couldn't name. Four warrior guards were posted, two at the door and the others patrolling around the building.

"Now I leave you," said Machumps, pointing to the entrance. "You go alone." But John was not alone. As soon as he stooped to step through the doorway he was met by two shaven- headed priests who mutely escorted him through two ante-chambers before they, too, left him.

Light came through three openings in the roof creating shafts in an out of which flying insects shimmered in the sunlight. In the gloom beyond the brightness, John could see shelves lined with baskets, rolled mats, and skin bags containing he knew not what. To his amazement, stacked against the walls were as many muskets as he had seen in the corps-de-garde at James Towne. There were pikes, shovels, pickaxes, a pit saw, and swords. Skin-covered earthen jars of several sizes occupied another shelf, and yet another was piled with innumerable bear skins. As John became used to the semi-darkness, he could see more and more, and there being no one there he began to wander around peering into jars and boxes filled with beads, pearls, and cowry shells, some on strings but many more that were not. An English sea chest with its lid open was filled with plates and scraps of copper, some green with age but others glittering in the sunlight. But to John, most eye-catching of all were the stacks of bows and arrow-filled baskets hung on the walls, and to one side an English long bow and a leather quiver of red-fletched arrows. As he reached out to examine one of the arrows, a voice from somewhere behind him said "Fear not, take one."

Startled, John spun around but saw nothing but the insects dancing in the sunlight.

"Asqweowan. That shall we call you. Your name will be Asqweowan." As he repeated the name, Powhatan stepped out of the shadows. Wearing neither a cloak nor any strings of beads, he appeared much smaller and older than John remembered. "You are welcome in my house," Powhatan told him. "You are no longer a *tassantass* or you would not be here. Few of my people ever expect such a privilege." Then stepping past him, Powhatan picked up the long bow and the sheaf of arrows, and handed them to John. "They are yours," he said. "I believe you have wished for such a bow."

"But.." John gasped. "How could you know?"

"I know everything," Powhatan replied gravely. "It is necessary that I do."

Powhatan took John by the arm in a grip that surprised him. "This bow you will promise to draw only for me, never against me." The words where spoken as a statement that should brook no argument. And there was none.

"That I swear to you," John told him.

Powhatan nodded and smiled. "I would have you sit by me," he said as he steered John to a stool beyond the sunlight. "The other young men who speak our language, Savage and Spelman, they came not freely and cannot be trusted. You I believe I can trust.

John assured him that he had made his own decision and would honor it.

Powhatan nodded. "I would have you teach me to talk in a book, as you do. Can you do this for me?"

"Get me paper, and I can try," John replied.

Powhatan nodded, and abruptly changed the subject. "There is this you must know. If a rattlesnake stays under its stone, we do not disturb it. But if it ventures into our village with its fangs bared, we must kill it. So it is with the *Tassantasses*. That is why I sent you to your fort with that message. If they come out from their rock and threaten our rivers and forests, then we have no choice but to sever their heads. And this I must do — and so must you."

Living amongst the Indians as one of them was a decision that had already been forced upon him. John was resigned to that, even happy to make his life with Taropoto, but the prospect of killing his own kind was something he had pushed to the back of his mind in the hope that it would never become an issue. But now Powhatan had brought it to the forefront, and John hesitated to reply. To his relief, however, Powhatan appeared not to expect an answer. Instead, he saw in John a young and receptive listener. "I will tell you what is in my heart," he said. "Never since the *tassantasses* came into my land have I been free to say words that are not spoken as a king or said to deceive. But to you I will speak truth."

"But why me?" John asked. "Why not to Harry Spelman or Tom Savage? They've been here with you for years."

"Ah," Powhatan smiled. "But they are your people still. They were sent to me, exchanged with me. They are not my people and not to be trusted." He went on to explain that when the first English settlers arrived, learning to speak their language and for them to understand his was necessary to both sides. But once interpreters were no longer needed, the boys were useful only as messengers. Although they could be relied upon to accurately bring English messages to Orapakes, Powhatan had no confidence that those he sent to James Towne were delivered in the way he intended. "The only use those boys are to me," Powhatan went on, "is to send them out with words that serve our purpose or to feed them lies that hide our intentions." He turned and stared at John as though expecting a response, and when he got none, he went on. "They are spies in our village, but as long as they do not realize that we know them to be so, they can be useful. But once they are not," he added, "we may kill them. What say you to that?"

John was no more ready with an answer to this question than he had been to the others. "I would hope..." he replied. "I would hope that you will remember the service they have done you... and be merciful."

Powhatan patted his arm. "A good answer. I shall remember it when the time comes." Telling John that he might order the execution of Spelman and Savage, was no unconsidered admission. Indeed, very little that Powhatan said was ever unconsidered. He was testing John's loyalty to one side or the other. If he warned the boys of their danger, John's own commitment to the Indian cause would be proved specious, but if he did not, then his allegiance to Lord Delaware and to England would be forever compromised. But sitting in the semi-darkness beside the Great King, young John Jefferys had no time, nor perhaps the ability, to analyze the implications of what he was being told.

"I have many questions," Powhatan told him, "and we shall talk more another day. But now I ask you this: Machumps tells me that the *tassantasses* talk much of the word 'civilize.' They say that it is something they have but we do not. Is it some kind of weapon that we have not yet seen?"

John would have laughed had not the question been so seriously asked. He also knew that he had no easy answer. "No, not a weapon," he replied. "To be civilized, I suppose, means God-fearing."

Powhatan thought for a moment before replying. "We fear the *okeus*. How different is that?"

"Well, no, I mean I suppose..." John stammered. "It also means obeying the King's laws."

"My people obey my laws."

"Aye, to be sure. But it also means having the things we need to make... well, to make life pleasurable... being happy...and possible."

"But we are happy," Powhatan assured him gravely. "So what are the things that make a man civilized?"

John wished he could find a way to tell Powhatan that these were questions he had never before heard asked, and that he was a simple English country lad with no more schooling than the Bible lessons he had learned from Chaplain Laurie. Instead, he did the best he could. "Well, like tools for us farmers."

"We have tools."

"But not like ours."

Powhatan smiled, and again patted John's arm. "That be true," he allowed. "Yet we live well enough with our own. So what else makes a man civilized?"

"We have guns," John told him.

Again Powhatan smiled. "So do we; not enough, but we have them. Does that then make me civilized?" he demanded.

John shook his head. "Not in God's eyes. Not in English eyes."

"So your god and the English are one."

"Aye, I suppose it be so," John allowed.

Powhatan grunted and sat silently considering John's answer. Then he asked, "We call you *tassantasses,* strangers, and you call us...?"

Reluctantly John answered, "Savages."

"Savages, I know. Then tell me this," Powhatan continued, "You have one of my people, the traitor Kemps, who has accepted your God. Is he now civilized, no longer savage?"

John replied that he didn't know, but in his heart he felt sure that no matter how fervently Kemps embraced Christianity or how often he attended Chaplain Laurie's sermons, he was still an Indian, still a savage.

"It would seem," Powhatan went on, "that we are as fire and water. You people from across the ocean are pale of skin and we are not, and no washing can make us otherwise." His questions were becoming more rhetorical – a word that would have been beyond John's vocabulary. He only knew that he should not try to answer. Instead, he sat wondering how Will would have replied.

The old king went on to remind John of the Indians' attempts to live peacefully alongside the strangers; how he had sent food when they were starving, and how his people had shown them how to hunt and fish, and which berries to eat and which to avoid. But in return the English had burned his villages, desecrated the temples, raped his women, plundered his goods, and brought diseases that his medicine men could not cure. "If we are to survive," Powhatan explained, "we must live apart from the *tassantasses* and keep them from us." He added that the message he had sent by John to Lord Delaware was not spoken in anger. It was the result of careful consideration. He added that his brother, Opechancanough, advised otherwise, demanding that the English be destroyed now before they become too many and too strong. But his other brother, Opitchapam who would succeed him as *mamanatowic*, was for waiting in the hope that through English stupidity and lack of survival skills, the settlers would starve to death. The priests, Powhatan explained, agreed with Opitchapam whose opinion carried more weight than did the bellicose ranting of Opachancanough. "I am an old man, Asqwewoan," and I wish there to be peace in my time. So I shall let them stay on their island, but we shall not truck with them."

"But Sire," John replied, "they will not stay. We...*they* are here to take your land and all that lies beyond it, and to make your people their slaves. They will succeed or die in the trying."

Powhatan stood up. "Then Opechancanough will be right," he said sadly. "Now go. We shall talk more another day. And be you good to Taropoto."

John assured him that he had vowed to do so, then stumbled out through the darkened ante-chambers into the evening sunlight. He had forgotten to take the coveted long bow.

At James Towne, Lord Delaware's health was deteriorating as Will Jefferys' improved. Maggie had done her job well, and as Dr. Bohun had predicted, time and a caring nurse often overcame the lesser fevers. But not so in the camp where the death toll again began to climb after three weeks of recession.

"When will Sergeant Jefferys be well enough to march?" was Captain Brewster's daily question. And each time Maggie gave him the same answer.

"He'll be ready when I says 'e be!"

However, Brewster thought it unwise to give that answer when the Governor repeatedly asked the same question. In truth, Brewster wondered why Delaware made such an issue over the fate of one young man. If John Jefferys was dead, there was no point risking more lives just to be sure. If he was a prisoner he had the wit to escape, and if he had chosen to stay he was best left to do so. But Mathew Brewster was a practical man more skilled with the sword than as a reader of his "better's" mind. To Delaware, an order once given had to be obeyed. Will had escaped the fate of a conspirator and instead had been sentenced to find his brother, and find him he would. Then, too, there was the perceived affront of the Governor General for Life losing his own voice in the person of his envoy. Indeed, in a moment of confession to his chaplain he admitted to hoping that Will would find his brother alive and would be compelled to bring him back as a deserter. The prospect of one delinquent brother hanging another would be justice at its most elemental. Chaplain Laurie said only that he hoped the outcome might be otherwise.

Later in the day John received a visit from Machumps. "The Great King bade me bring you these," he said.

"*Hawtoppe* and..er...*usquion*," John replied. And Taropoto clapped her hands. Mechamps smiled and nodded as he handed John the English bow and its sheaf of red-fletched arrows.

The following morning's counsel meeting aboard the *Delaware* found his Lordship in a more temperate mood than usual. He had slept well, woken refreshed and certain of his destiny. Remaining within the James Towne palisades was not an option. To do so, he insisted, would be to concede to Powhatan's demand, emboldening him as never before. The encamped troops would soon be in open revolt if for no other reason than to end the boredom of waiting. "We must strike at every village large or small, the way you did at Paspahegh, Master Percy. We must show them who is master of Virginia!"

"When and where, my Lord?" Argall asked.

" Everywhere, Captain! Leave no hut unburned and no savage spared. If we take or destroy their corn before winter is upon us, we'll starve the bastards just as they would us."

George Yeardley was next to risk voicing an opinion. "Sir, we would do well to remember that there are tribes still friendly toward us. They're resentful of Powhatan's authority and will welcome his downfall."

"Like who?" Delaware demanded.

"Well, like the Patawomecks. Smith had good relations with them."

"Too far away," Delaware grunted. "Who else?"

"'Tis hard to say, my Lord. But there are several smaller tribes only loosely allied to Powhatan," Yeardley persisted.

George Percy agreed. "There is a queen with a very long name who has a village on the south side of the river at Appomattox. She, too, was friendly to Smith," he added. "Her brother is Coquonasum, *weroance* of the whole tribe, and can field about a hundred warriors."

"And the queen with the very long name?" Delaware asked. "How many there?"

"Maybe twenty," Percy replied.

"Her name is Opossunoquonuske," volunteered the always eager to help Secretary Strachey.

"Really?" Delaware replied coldly. Then to Argall, "How many in all can Powhatan send against us?"

Captain Argall confessed that no one was sure, adding that much of the information gathered since the first colonists arrived in 1607 was old and unreliable. With no continuing trading with the Indians, current intelligence was wanting. "Many of the savages have become diseased," Argall explained. He did not think it pertinent to add that the diseases were those brought by the settlers. "Then, too," he went on, "several large tribes have broken up into smaller units as the result of fraternal disputes. And at least one tribe has been slaughtered and replaced by Powhatan's own people. But putting all the numbers together, two to three thousand seems likely."

"Good Captain," Delaware grumped, "there's a world of difference between two and three thousand when we can barely field two hundred."

"My Lord, two hundred well drilled men in armor trained with pikes and pieces are a match for three, even six thousand naked savages," Argall answered.

"Perhaps," Delaware allowed. He added that it was time to outrank the incompetent Captain Douthitt and transform his rabble into a disciplined fighting force. "Samuel, this is your charge," he told Argall. "Yours and Mathew Brewster's." Delaware went on to outline a bold plan to pull all Captain Holcroft's and Lieutenant Earely's men from the forts at Kecoughtan and on the adjacent Southampton River, and to leave only a skeleton garrison at James Fort. "As soon as the leaves are off the trees and the devils less able to hide, we shall reestablish our fort at the Falls, make contact with the Monachans, and in the spring attack Powhatan from the west. You nephew," he said to William West, "you were there with John Smith. 'Tis true is't not, that the Powhatans are ever at war with the Monachans?"

"No, sir, 'Twas not I but my uncle Francis who was at the Falls with Captain Smith."

Delaware could be relied on to bridle at any mention of his brother whom most 1609 survivors believed to have deserted the colony and fled to England. He turned red in the face and was about to reply when Percy interrupted.

"My Lord, you are entirely right. The Powhatans and Monachans do hate each other. They're like the highland and lowland Scots. But there's no surety that the Monachans will side with us."

Delaware answered with another of his increasingly frequent grunts and dismissed his councillors with a curt, "Gentlemen, be about your business." His previous ebullience had abated in the face of his staff's questions and doubts. There was nothing his Lordship hated more than to have his plans questioned by underlings, except, perhaps, being questioned by people he thought might be right. Furthermore, he was disgusted with himself for having confused his nephew with his brother.

Later in the day a sentry at the blockhouse reported sighting Indians invading the island from the Back River. Blaring trumpets and Tom Dowse beating the call to arms brought Will Jefferys from his sickbed. The second and third files of guardsmen manned the palisades; the camp troops milled about, and on Captain Brewster's order Will led the first file out through the eastern gate to confront the attackers. But they found none. However, he did come upon the long-dead and rotting remains of a soldier from the camp. Will concluded that he had been a sick man who had wandered away into the woods, but as animals had been there first there was no recognizing him. Will was still deciding whether to drag the corpse back to the fort or to send out a squad from the camp to bury him, when a shout from the blockhouse heralded the capture of two Indians caught trying to escape across the causeway.

Two of Lieutenant Puttock's sentries followed by a gaggle of Finsbury soldiers, dragged the Indians into the fort and threw them down at the feet of the Governor and his hurriedly assembled officers. Delaware's first response was to chide Puttock for leaving his post in the face of the enemy. But when told that there was no other enemy, he offered no apology. "If these savages were alone, they have to be spies," he declared. "Get Kemps to question them. We know what we do with spies?" he asked with a short laugh. " Well, don't we?"

When nobody answered, Yeardley suggested that it would be prudent to wait for Kemps's report before deciding anything. "We don't want to make more enemies than we already have," he added.

By this time Will Jefferys' guardsmen were back empty handed, some relieved that they had faced no danger and others disappointed by the missed opportunity to "get at them savages." Will's friend Pips Bailey was among the latter.

"They've got to let us do somethin'. Sittin' around watchin' men die ain't no way to live." Pips insisted. They tell us we're here for love of England and the King. But I tell thee, Will, most of us don't give a farmer's fart for England or our Scotch king. We came to get rich like we was promised."

Will begged him to keep his voice down, and warned that he was talking treason.

In the market place, with Delaware and his aides gathered around him, Kemps quizzed the captive Indians. In a voice that shifted from shouting to cajolery and back again he extracted a few sullen responses that meant nothing to most of the listeners. "They say they were but hunters and meant no harm," he concluded.

"Do they not?" Delaware grunted. "Whence came they?"

"They are Chickahominies, m' Lord."

His Lordship looked around at his officers, and with a grim smile said, "Chickahominy, eh? But was not this island the Paspahegh's hunting ground? Perhaps these fine fellows lost their way?"

Kemps failed to understand Delaware's cynical question or the polite laughter that followed it. "Lord, I do not..."

"Enough!" Delaware rasped. "Hunters, they say. Ask them whether they are good bowmen."

The puzzled Kemps asked the question and reported that both men were skilled with the bow.

"Ask them which of them is the best."

Responding to Kemps's question, the surprised captives looked at each other and laughed nervously, each nodding at the other.

"They are equally able," Kemps reported.

"I say that they are not." Delaware declared, " I say that he is the best," pointing to the prisoner on the right. Yeardley and Percy exchanged questioning glances. Had their Governor gone mad?

"A good bowman is a nonpareil among men," he went on. "But a bowman who cannot draw the string is no better than a woman. Captain Brewster, have our butcher cut off his right hand. Let Dr. Bohun attend him." With that, Delaware turned away and walked unsteadily toward his house. For a long moment no one moved to follow him. Then with a sigh, Argall broke the silence. "See to it, Captain," he said, then quickly followed his Governor.

When told what was expected of him, the normally mild-mannered Dr. Bohun put protocol aside and strode into his Lordship's chamber, kicking the door shut behind him. "My Lord, I do most fervently protest! I am a physician not a surgeon," he insisted. "But no surgeon amputates with a butcher's cleaver. The skin must carefully prepared around the bone so that it can be folded over. The veins and arteries must be skillfully stitched to stem the bleeding. A famous French Maitre Gulemuw has written..."

"A pox on your French surgeon!" Delaware rasped. "We are not assaying to save an arm but to lop a hand. Tell them to cauterize it with a blackmsith's iron. Now go, good doctor, I pray you."

When Will and his file paraded the next morning, the job had been done. In the night the two Indians had been driven from the fort after being told by Kemps that the Lord Governor General sent them as a warning that any other savage venturing unheralded onto the island would leave both his hands behind. In requiring Kemps to deliver that threat, his Lordship either did not, or chose not to consider the painful position in which he had placed his interpreter. Sending the marked man, Kemps, as guide and interpreter for Will Jefferys concerned Delaware not at all. In his eyes a savage was a savage, expendable even when he was *our* savage.

On the morning of Tuesday, September 18, the Governor received his council aboard the *Delaware*, and immediately Captain Argall questioned the wisdom of sending Will Jefferys in search of his brother, and urged that the plan be abandoned.

"Why ever so?" Delaware replied in apparent surprise.

"With respect, my Lord, sending back a savage with his hand severed was, I admit, a bold and emphatic statement."

"As 'twas intended."

"Aye, sir. But what of Will Jefferys? By all accounts he's one of our best men. Do you want to see him sent back unable to aim a piece or wield a sword?"

Delaware leaned across his Great Cabin table and glared at Argall. "They wouldn't dare. Come now, gentlemen. What else do we have to discuss this fine September morning?"

Chapter Seventeen

❧❧

In the days since his meeting with Powhatan, John Jefferys had received more schooling than ever he had at Withyham. Machumps had been ordered to instruct him in the lore of the Powhatan Alliance and to tell him as much as he knew about the make-up of the separate tribes and their entangled lineages. A *Quiyoughquisock*, a priest named Oreih, had been assigned to him by Powhatan to explain the fundamentals of his religion and the role of the priesthood in the lives of his people. As Oreih's English was sparse and much of what he said had to be translated by Taropoto, those lessons were hard. Much more to John's liking was the instruction he got from his friends Little Crow and Sparrow, teaching him the rudiments of tracking, showing him how to judge the weight of a bear by the size and depths of its footprints, how to gauge the freshness of deer tracks, and much else that seemed obvious once his eyes were opened. Taropoto's language lessons were informal and progressed through the daily need to communicate, but from them John Jefferys and his Indian bride grew ever closer. Nevertheless, words that came bubbling like spring water from her lips turned to rocks in her husband's mouth. He was grappling with the word *mummmacushenepaw*, meaning 'I have been asleep,' when a commotion erupted at the edge of the village.

A formidable deputation of Chickahominies was arriving, numbering twenty warriors led by their feather-caped, and horn-headed general, Kissanacomen, and three elders, all demanding to speak with Powhatan. Not until they reached the open center of the village could John see that among them were two unarmed Indians, one of them lacking his right hand. The Chickahominies were an independent tribe whose association with Powhatan was businesslike but never cordial. Consequently, their visits normally involved prior planning and a ritual of courtesies from both sides. An unheralded arrival, therefore, was unusual, and at the outset unwelcome. Powhatan declined to greet the delegation and referred it Opechancanough. But on hearing what had happened at James Towne, he relented and received Kissanacomen and the priests privately in his lodge. John never heard what passed between them, but on the day following their departure, Powhatan called a meeting of all his priests and chief warriors, and included him among them. But as nothing was said in English and as each speaker found it necessary to make his point amid a flood of ranting and shouting, John grasped very little. Nevertheless, he came away with the impression that the affair of the amputated Indian turned the key on a door that was already shut. Powhatan's empire was now at war with the English in general and their governor in particular. It was no longer sufficient for Delaware to live in peace within the confines of his island.

As Will, Kemps, Pip, and the three other assigned guardsmen set out from the fort, none knew that word of the Governor's treatment of the alleged spy had been carried from the Chickahominy to Powhatan at Orapakes, or that the mutilation of one man was having so great an impact in the region. Kemps must have guessed, but he said nothing about it, probably because he was deeply ashamed of his role in condemning the luckless victim who, for all he knew, may have been exactly what he claimed to be – an innocent hunter.

Kemps led the little platoon along a trail that kept to the eastern bank of the Chickahominy River thereby avoiding the principal Paspahegh settlements. But they had to pass through two villages of the Mattaponi, as well as Ozenick, the first of the Chickahominy villages. In none of them did they find any men of warrior age. No women came out to greet the visitors, and those that came close did so only to snatch their children away. Nevertheless, Kemps assured John that they were being watched. "They see us," he said, "and I doubt not that the news is already at Orapakes."

At each place where women did not deliberately shun them, Will instructed Kemps to ask whether anyone had seen a fair-haired young Englishman who might have been wounded or taken prisoner. Although nobody admitted to having seen him, the question explained his mission and preceded Will from village to village all the way to Orapakes. When they heard the news, John and Taropoto were sitting outside their lodge, she cross-legged on the ground and he seated on a wooden box seared with the VC brand of the Virginia Company. Squatting or sitting Indian fashion on the ground were contortions that came no more easily than did the word *otassotagwopur* that described what they were doing – sitting close together. It was Machumps who came to tell John that his brother was on his way and that Powhatan had given instructions down the line that he was not to be opposed. "No doubt he comes to take you back," Machumps guessed. He will not be here until late in the day, so you have time to make up your mind to stay or to go. The Great King will not hold you," Machumps added.

John assured him that he would not waver. His mind was already made up. "I gave the Great King my word, and I shall keep it. Besides, I be wed."

Machumps smiled. "Tied by love and tied by honor. Those be strong bonds."

"Aye," John allowed. "But I think it well that I test them not here at Orapakes. I'll go out and meet my brother on the trail."

"We shall send warriors to protect you."

John laughed at the idea. "What, protect me from my own brother? Never!"

Machumps shrugged. But Taropoto insisted that she should go with John. "I am of your brother's family now. So I must know him, must I not?"

With Will reportedly still an hour or more distant, John had time to ponder his decisions yet again. Accepting a rural life with the Indians rather than an existence within the social and physical confines of urban James Towne, was easily made. But to hone that choice down to family proportions was not so simple, and facing Will to put it into words was a prospect he did not relish. But it had to be done.

With Taropoto by his side, John waited for his brother at the south end of a vine creeper bridge that crossed a stream about a mile from Orapakes. Although his mind was not tuned to symbolism, John sensed that the brook defined the division between his old life and his new, and that crossing it or not crossing it became his private river of no return.

The sound of Pips whistling preceded Will's arrival and prompted John to go forward to meet him, leaving Taropoto at the bridge. For a moment the brothers stood smiling at each other. Then they embraced, Will whole heartedly and with relief, but John tensely and with unspoken reservations.

Will pushed John back to arms' length and looked him up and down. "You be not hurt, then?"

"Not a scratch."

"So the savages freed you? They must have known we were coming for you. Mayhap his Lordship has taught them a lesson. But no matter. You are free, and we are here to take you back Had I been a godly fellow, I would have bin prayin' for this day, I surely would."

"But brother..." John began.

"So let's away. We can put several miles behind us ere nightfall."

"Wait. I would speak apart with you." John nodded in the direction of Pips and the others.

Will gave him a quizzical look and motioned his guard to drop back. "So what's to be said that cannot be..."

"I be not comin', and that's an end on't," John blurted.

Will's jaw dropped. "But why...The savages allowed you parole, is that it?"

John shook his head and answered that no such bonds held him. Beginning with the attack on the Paspahegh he told Will everything that had happened. Then he motioned to Taropoto to come forward. "This is my wife." He paused before adding, "I would have you greet her as a sister."

"Not in this life!" Will retorted. "Those devils have fed you some potion that poisoned your mind. Married, you say? How could you be wed without bans, without a parson?"

"But..."

"Listen to your brother. No matter what they have done to you, in God's eyes you are not wed. So come away. Let's not linger!"

When John refused, Will told him that if necessary he was to take him by force, but John stood his ground. "I'll not run from you, brother," he answered. "But nor will I leave my wife. There be six of you and two of us. So take us both if you must."

As Will signaled to his men to seize them, the odds changed abruptly. A dozen of Powhatan's Pamunkey bowmen appeared astride the north end of the bridge and others emerged from the forest on both sides of the trail. Will and his companions were now outnumbered three or more to one. He shook his head and sighed in resignation. "So be it. Stand alone if you must. But in the eyes of God and man you are disgraced, as be your dam, and I too; we are all disgraced."

John held out his hand. "Think it not so, I beg you," he pleaded.

As Powhatan's men retreated into the woods, the brothers embraced and wished each other well, neither expecting to see the other again. Taropoto took John's hand, "*Uskepiih yohacan wiowah*" come quickly home husband," she urged. By the time they crossed the bridge and turned to look back, Will and his men had already disappeared beyond the trail's first bend.

On October 1 when Will reached James Towne he found the camp cleaned up and the troops drilling with some proficiency on the strand beside the river. Captain Brewster was the first to greet him. "Welcome, sergeant, but where...?"

"He would not come," Will answered grimly. Throughout the journey he had pondered how to answer that question. His first inclination had been to say that his brother was dead, but if he should later be discovered alive, he, Will, could be tried for treason.

If, on the other hand, he reported that he could not find John, there was the danger that one of his guardsmen might reveal the truth. It wouldn't be Pips, of that he was sure. But he had picked the others at random and did not know them well. In the end he concluded that the truth was the only viable answer.

"Would not? You mean *could* not?"

"Alas no, Captain. He means to stay." Will hesitated to reveal the rest, but did so in the hope that it would help explain John's decision.

"Wedded to a savage! In the name of Christ Jesu, does he not know that he is damned in the face of God?"

"He may not think so, " Will replied.

"Maybe not," Brewster snapped. " But his Lordship certainly will. 'Deed I hardly know how to tell him. But stand down your men at the guard house, then go you home. I'm sure his Lordship will send for you anon."

Maggie's nosy neighbor had been the first to tell her that Will was back, and so she was at her door to greet him. She stood there with arms folded, not as a scold but as a buttress to control the pounding of her heart. Her smile of relief faded as she looked past him and saw that he was alone. "So John be dead?" she asked. Will shook his head and told her that he might as well be so. When he told her about the savage woman, whose name he couldn't remember, Maggie burst forth with her familiar tirade against the evil and filthy savages. "In the name of Jesus, how could he do such a thing?" she demanded, "pox-ridden pieces of shit that they are!"

Will had no answer. "He be but young," he offered lamely.

"Young, fiddlesticks!" Maggie retorted. "Bed her if he must, but wed her...?" She stopped in mid sentence. "You mustn't tell his Lordship. He'll have your hide on a hurdle if he finds out you saw John and let him go." Will replied that it was too late. Captain Brewster would have already told him.

"Then the saints preserve you," Maggie muttered as she sat down heavily onto the side of their bed, her head in her hands. Suddenly she looked up, and with a wry smile told Will, "Lose a brother but mayhap get a son."

"What mean you by that?"

"I think I be with child," she told him. There was neither pleasure nor dismay in her voice. She was merely stating a fact.

Will's response was no different. "'Tis no place to bear a child," he said.

"Blame yourself." Maggie gave him a reassuring pat on his arm. "'Tis a woman's luck to pay the price. But who knows, it may turn out for the best. There's naught more to be said."

His Lordship, however, had much to say, and most of it could be heard in the marketplace. "God's blood!" he ranted. "The brother should have shot him!"

"That was not your instruction, my Lord," Brewster replied. "You may remember you wanted him brought back either freed or prisoner."

"But if he could do neither...And wed to a savage, you say? God's death! Dares this bumpkin make a mockery of us all!" Suddenly Delaware stopped, paused, and coldly concluded. "The boy is dead. We shall put it about that he died bravely. Sore wounded, he lay in the woods until the savages found him. He defended himself to his last gasp. He died in defense of our civilization, honoring England and the King."

Brewster replied that too many already knew the truth.

"Then let it be known that the man who brings me his head shall go home on the next ship with ten gold angels in his pocket," Delaware snapped.

"And Sergeant Jefferys, what of him?" Brewster wanted to know. "Does your Lordship want to see him?"

Through barely parted lips, Delaware hissed "'Tis better that I do not."

After Brewster withdrew, George Yeardley, who had been present throughout, risked offering a suggestion. "My Lord, I have an interesting notion. This Jefferys lad is said to have wed a natural in some kind of devilish ceremony. Suppose we bring the boy and his wife back and marry them properly."

"This is no time for joking, Master Yeardley."

"And I do not, sir. Brewster says that she's the sister of the Paspahegh queen. She would be a royal bridge between their religion and ours."

"Nonsense!" snapped Delaware. "A sister of the wretched Paspahegh witch is nothing.

"But suppose it was not this boy and that woman, but someone else, a gentleman, we could persuade to wed one of Powhatan's many daughters?"

"No gentleman would do that," Delaware assured him.

Yeardley scratched his neck. "Well then, suppose we find someone from the camp and make him a gentleman. We send him to Powhatan just as Newport and Smith sent him boys they called their sons. We tell Powhatan that we can forge an alliance by such a marriage, and by letting that happen we would break the power of their damned priests."

Delaware stared hard at Yeardley. "I think you should let Dr. Bohun look at you," he said, thereby ending the discussion.

Two days after John's meeting with his brother, Harry Spelman came to him and said that he and Tom Savage needed to talk with him. John assured him that they could come to his house whenever they liked. To that, Harry tipped his head in the direction of Taropoto, and whispered, "Privily," then beckoned to John to follow him.

In a shaded space beneath a forest canopy two young men were waiting, Tom Savage and a German somewhat older who identified himself as Samuel. Spelman explained that they were fearful that when Powhatan would begin open warfare with the colonists, all three would be in danger of execution. Remembering Powhatan's reservations about the reliability of the two English youths, John was reluctant to offer an opinion.

"We think we are watched," said Spelman.

"We are all watched," John replied.

"Aye, but more closely than before." Harry recalled how in a recent visit from Essenetaugh *weroance* of the Patawomekes, he had shown a liking for the young men and had said that he would welcome them. "We are of a mind to go to him," he said. "What about you? Will'st thou come with us?"

But John told them that he had a wife and an obligation to remain.

"Der be more of us in uder villages," Samuel explained. "De, too, must run."

"I wish you all good luck," John told him. "But for me, I believe Powhatan did tell me true, and so I stay."

"As you will." Harry Spelman held out his hand. "Go you then. We shall not talk on this again. When the hour is right we'll be gone, and you'll not know it."

John shook hands with all three, and hurried back to the village. Aware that Powhatan was indeed watching the young Englishmen, he could not blame them for planning to escape. At the same time, he wondered how far they would get before being caught and what their fate might be when they were brought back. Later that day he saw both Tom and Harry joining young Indian men in a game of football and giving no hint of their intentions. It was while watching the game that he saw a young Indian woman standing alone and apart from all the other chattering wives and daughters. "Who be that?" he asked Taropoto.

"She is not a good one," she replied. "She is the wife of Kocoum one of the Great King's captains."

John was curious to know why she was standing so obviously alone. Taropoto explained that her name was Matoaka and that she had been too friendly with the English. "The Great King still thinks much of her, but we know better," Taropoto told him with unexpected vehemence. "She is too free with her *muttusk* is that *usqwausum.*"

The word was new to John, but before he could ask for a translation he was distracted by shouts from the ball players. One had scored a goal by kicking the straw-filled leather ball between two trees, an achievement that drew yelling and stomping from the spectators.

Winning was also on the mind of Lord Delaware, as was the enigma of handling the Indians once victory was achieved. On the morning of Friday, October 5, he called a meeting aboard his ship to seek the advice of his officers. "Gentlemen, God willing, we may defeat and cow the savages, but that is no more than a beginning. So I would hear your views on how best to control and rule these heathens after our swords are sheathed?" He looked from face to face. "Well? Has no one any sage advice?"

Percy was the first to respond. "My Lord, the simplest solution would be to kill them all. But as that is not possible, herding them like sheep into pens of a few hundred subsistence acres would be my choice."

"And what say you, Master Yeardley?"

"Well, sir, I'd say that George's idea has merit. But where do we find the sheep dogs?"

Argall's proposal was more practical. "The priests and wizards control every aspect of their lives. Remove those, and they are a rudderless ship. I say that we destroy their beliefs and replace it with the Trilogy. Christianized, the savages will be on the road to civilization. It'll take time, my Lord, but 'tis the only way."

Delaware nodded. "But first we must win." He went on to redefine his plan to establish a new fort at the Falls, adding that the Company was anxious to have him move his primary settlement away from the unhealthy James Towne. He was sure, he said, that a better location could be found once he had control of the head waters. "You have two weeks to make ready."

When Will Jefferys heard the news his first responses were of elation that something important was about to be accomplished and relief that the campaign was not to be directed toward Orapakes and so should not involve his brother. But as the days passed, his memories of the horrors of the Paspahegh slaughter remained in the forefront of his mind. Lying awake at night he remembered the faces of the queen and her daughters, and the empty gaze of the old blind savage in the moment before his head was severed. How much more of this was there to be? he asked himself. Then he remembered something that Sergeant Gideon had told him: One must play the monster to slay a monster. It had made sense in the days before the assault on Kecoughtan, but now Will feared that playing and being were becoming inextricably entwined.

"Too much thinkin'll get you to be like your brother!" Maggie told him. "And look where he's gotten himself!"

Chapter Eighteen

꩜

A s Harry Spelman had predicted, John Jefferys knew nothing of
the escape until it was over, and then only from Taropoto who
had heard it from the wife of one of the warriors sent out to bring
the young men back. Tom Savage, she said, had betrayed his friends
and returned to warn Powhatan of their escape. The German had
been felled with an axe, but Spelman had not been found.

That Tom Savage would do such a thing was hard for John to
believe, yet on the few occasions that he saw him, Tom deliberately
avoided him. But with Powhatan making ready for war, there was
no time to ponder Tom's motive. Every day *weroances* from vassal
tribes were arriving with their principal captains, all expecting to be
formally greeted, feasted, and entertained. On the outskirts of the
village phalanxes of bowmen practiced their archery and took sides
to practice combat with axes, cudgels, and wooden swords. Nearby
half a dozen of Powhatan's elite clumsily loaded and fired muskets
stolen from the fort.

When word arrived that the English were boarding their boats
and moving out from James Towne the activity at Orapakes dra-
matically increased. Priests draped under the skins of bears with
their faces half hidden by fancifully created monstrous head-dresses,
chanted and rattled to whip the young warriors into a frenzy of
shouting and dancing excitement. Drums made from water-filled
pots with skins stretched taut over them produced subtly differing
tones, but amid all the rattling and chanting they added only to the
din. The women, too, joined in the dancing and stomping, their

skins turning from brown to gray by stirred dust and the ashes from fires tossed into the air by the priests and their acolytes.

John was watching all this with Taropoto at his side when out of the dust and smoke came Machumps to tell him that as soon as the Great King talked with the last of his allies, he would speak with him. For what seemed like hours, John sat on the floor of the first antechamber as priests and dignitaries hustled in and out, some emerging alone and sober faced, others coming out in groups talking excitedly together. John was able to understand a word here and there, but he supposed that the *weroances* had been given specific orders, some of which pleased them and others that did not.

When it came John's turn to enter the council chamber he found Powhatan seated on his throne as he had been when John first brought him Lord Delaware's demands. On either side sat the brothers, Opitchapam and Opechancanough, and beyond them four priests and several councillors partially hidden in the shadows.

"Asqweowan, my young friend," Powhatan intoned, "I am resolved that this is to be your time of trial. You will take the bow and the arrows I have given you, and lead twenty of my men who know you. When you have proved yourself and the last of the *tassantasses* are gone, you shall be made a *weroance* and have people of your own." Powhatan signaled to him to go, then changed his mind. "There is a word the *tassantasses* use that means mercy for the vanquished, is there not?".

"I think Sire, that the word is 'quarter.'"

"You will allow no quarter."

John pursed his lips, then nodded. "*Kennebautows*," he replied.

"Go now, and prepare yourself," Powhatan told him.

As John crossed the crowded village center he saw women busily painting their menfolk with red stain, and with white and black colors turning pleasant faces into devilish masks. The bare torsos they painted with a multitude of streaks and swirls that Taropoto told him had mystic meanings and protected them from harm. Dressed still in his English leather britches and jerkin and his once-white woollen shirt, John Jefferys felt conspicuously out of place. But not for long. Taropoto stripped him to the waist and took up her bowl of red pigment in one hand and a turkey-feather brush in the other. "Stand still," she ordered.

At James Towne, Sergeant Will awaited orders to take his men aboard the *Delaware*. The Governor had already made it known that he intended to command the expedition from its deck. But to Will's dismay, his own orders were different. "You are to command his Lordship's miners," Captain Brewster informed him.

"Miners? Bloody miners?" Will gasped.

Brewster explained that the skilled miners were essential to the success not only of the expedition but of the colony's future. As Will had some association with them, they knew him and would be more likely to accept his orders than they would other officers'. That was his Lordship's rationale. 'Tis an important role," Brewster assured him. He added that Will would have a single-masted ketch at his command. Tom Dowse, the taborer, would be his steersman, and he could take a guardsman of his choice, as well as one sailor from the recently arrived *Dainty*, a small vessel that had brought twelve men, one woman, and a couple of horses destined for the common stew pot.

"Why Dowse?" Will wanted to know.

Brewster laughed. "He can keep you amused. Besides, if the wind fails and the tide's against you he can beat the cadence as the miners try to man the oars. He'll be useful, never fear. A word of advice," he added. "Keep toward the south shore. The Quiyoughcohanoks and Appomattocs are less likely to resent you."

His Lordship's health, it turned out, delayed the *Delaware*'s departure. Instead, it fell to Captains Brewster and Yeardley to lead the way up river in separate barges with Will and his miners following in their ketch. It was the morning of Sunday, October 28.

The Great River, first known as the Powhatan, but by now the King James, was as smooth as polished silver, not a ripple to furrow its surface. The haze that had obscured its banks throughout the summer was gone, and the trees stood clean and clear. It was, in almost everyone's eyes, a splendid day to be on the water. The exceptions were Will Jefferys' miners who, in the absence of a sail-filling breeze, had to bend to their oars against the stream. Unused to that form of exertion they were soon complaining and threatening to jump overboard and join the savages. Tom Dowse had surrendered his place at the helm to guardsman Pips while he tapped out the cadence for the oars' strokes, all the while attempting to entertain by telling jokes of the kind that had amused the Delaware children.

"Who's heard the tale of the fair ship and the maid?" Tom called out.

"Not I," laughed the cheerful Pips. "Go on, tell it! Never mind them grumping miners."

"Here's a good one for ye, then. There was this fair ship of two hundred tuns," Dowse began. "She was lying by the Tower Wharf when this country lass come along, see. She asked how old the ship did be? And they told her she was a year old, just one year old, mind. Ye have to listen close to this. The lass says 'God bless me, if she be so big grown in *one* year, what a greatness will she be when she comes to my age?' That's the wit in it. When she comes to my age?"

Only Pip chuckled. The miners continued to scowl as they leaned back and forth over their oars.

"God damn the lot of you then!" Dowse muttered. " I've 'ad lords and princes laugh at that one."

"That's your trouble right there," Pips told him. "I'll wager, there ain't a lord or a prince among this lot. So sing us a song, why don't you?"

"How about this one?" Dowse suggested. "*Come Lasses and Lads.* Everybody knows the words."

"Come lasses and lads.
Take leave of your dads
And away to the Maypole hey,
For every he
Has got him a she
With a..."

Sergeant Will had had enough. "That'll do, thank thee Master Dowse. Attend to your drumming!"

The thump, thump, thump of the cadence and the more or less synchronized splashes of the oars were the only sounds to disturb the silence of the morning. A heron standing imperiously on a log chose to ignore the passing boat, but a family of mud turtles craned their necks in its direction before sliding off into the water.

"Them would make good soup," said Pips. "I could do with a nice bowl of turtle soup."

"Shut your mouth!" muttered the closest sweating oarsman.

After three hours of arduous rowing the ketch picked up a breeze as it rounded a marsh- flanked bend in the river where a lone Indian in a canoe was spear fishing in the south shore shallows. He looked up and gave several cheerful waves as the sail filled and the boat sped by. Will waved back and shouted "Good day to ye, friend!"

Will Jefferys, however, was not alone in responding to the wave. On higher ground beyond the marsh a second Indian saw it and ran back into the forest.

The boat continued to make good way behind a freshening breeze, and although the miners no longer had to row, they continued to grumble amongst themselves. To Will, their Cornish dialect was as foreign-sounding as the Indians', and his inability to understand what they were saying, made him uneasy.

Another hour under sail brought the ketch around a sharp point to the mouth of the Appomattocs River where several Indian women were waving and shouting. "Steer toward the shore," Will ordered. "We'll see what they want."

As the boat eased inshore Will realized that the women held bowls and were offering food. Some even made gestures suggesting eating and drinking. The miners also recognized their meaning and made it clear that some intended to go overboard and wade ashore. "Wait!" Will ordered. "If anyone goes ashore, we all go together."

The savages were obviously friendly, and Captain Brewster had said that the Appomattocs were considered to be peace loving. Letting the miners stretch their legs would make them more tractable.

Besides, spurning the women's invitation could damage the existing good relations with the tribe. All of this passed through Will's mind as the ketch inched inshore and its bow slid to rest in the mud. This was the miners first sight of near naked Indian women, and in their haste to scramble over the side two fell into the water thereby generating much laughter and squealing among the waiting girls. Will and Pips were the last to leave the boat having lingered long enough to ignite the long fuses of their muskets. "We can't be too careful," Will said as he blew on the glowing yard-long match.

But as soon as he stepped ashore three men came from behind the women, one obviously a person of some importance. He smiled and nodded in greeting."*Netapaugh, netapaugh.*"

Will had no idea what the words meant, but as they were said with a smile and friendly gestures, he smiled back and used the only sentence he had been taught, the one that every soldier had to learn to avoid unintended trouble. "*Mataguenatoxoth,*" he said. "I do not understand."

The Appomattoc village lay back from the river but was visible about two hundred yards distant into the woods. Before Will and Pips were even out of the boat chattering girls were escorting miners toward it. However, it was Tom Dowse in his colorful attire who quickly became the center of attraction, a role he enjoyed to the fullest as he skipped and jumped his way toward the village. Will made to follow, but his greeter held up his hand to stop him. Then the Indian pointed at the muskets and vigorously shook his head. Going unarmed into the village was not to Will's liking, but with his miners already there he really had no choice. Consequently, he ordered Pips to put the guns back in the boat, and then followed his hosts to join the rest of his men who were being seated in a large circle around a smoking fire. It turned out, however, that he was the guest not of an Appomattocs *weroance*, but of a *weroansqua*, Queen Opossunoquonuske who, attended by several waiting women, emerged from her house to greet him. Unlike the shapely queen of the Paspahegh, this was a fat, masculine appearing woman whose cold eyes belied her brief smile. She wore a copper crown on her head and more copper in strips around her arms. Her long black hair hung to her waist partly concealing her large breasts, and a deer-skin apron reached to her knees leaving her buttocks bare. However, her nakedness that seemed so disconcerting to Will, in no way detracted from her imperious behavior toward both the women and the men of her domain. With snaps of her fingers she ordered servants to refill the bowls and gourd drinking vessels of her guests, and when the eating and drinking was done she called for a pipe and made a ceremony of lighting it and passing it to Will. When he choked on the smoke she snatched it back, took a deep draw and slowly expelled the smoke through her nostrils.

That was the moment when Will first sensed that Opossunoquonuske's welcome was less than it had appeared and that he should order his men back to the boat. However, several of the miners had already left the circle to enjoy the favors of Appomattox maidens. Consequently, a swift yet courteous withdrawal was no longer an option.

Once the queen realized that none of her guests understood her language she could speak freely with her people, and did so throughout the feasting. If the scenario had not been planned in advance, its elements were in place by the time the last empty bowl was carried away. Complacent and well-fed miners lounged back on their elbows while others sat belching into their boots. None noticed that their Indian companions had become less attentive or that they repeatedly glanced in the direction of their queen. When she stopped smiling and shouted *Tsaepaih matcherew!* only her guests failed to react. In the nearby huts unsuspecting miners were clubbed to death while their britches were still around their ankles. Pips took an arrow in his chest as Will leapt to his feet. But other miners, less wary or agile were slow to stand up. And four never did. Tom Dowse managed to dodge behind two of the women as they fled from the circle, but the sailor was less fortunate. Two men clubbed him to the ground and beat his head in as he lay there.

Only Dowse reached the boat. It was now afloat on the rising tide enabling him to cast off and clamber aboard. He was still trying to pole it off with an oar when the first arrows hit the hull and lodged in its lowered sail. Others followed as more Indians lined the shore to shoot at him. With remarkable presence of mind Tom pulled up the rudder and used it as a shield as first one and then several more arrows thudded into it. Helped by the tide, the ketch drifted off into deeper water. Out of arrow range, he reseated the rudder in its gudgeons and only then had time to take stock of his situation. He had no idea how to sail a boat. It was too broad in the beam to be rowed by one man. All he could do was drift and hope that one of the other boats would find him. However, he was not as alone as he thought and feared. Invisible from the stern, Will Jefferys was clinging to the trailing mooring line.

Instead of following Dowse toward the boat, Will had escaped east into the woods. Only once did he turn back in the hope that some of the miners might be following him. Instead, he could see the *weroansqua* still sitting impassively on her stool as her guests lay dead or dying in front of her. Both women and men danced gleefully around, but none followed him as he skirted the target shooters along the shore and dove into the river to grab the boat's trailing mooring line.

With Dowse's help Will clambered over the bow, and between them they were able to set the sail. But whether to follow Brewster's and Yeardley's boats up river or to drop back toward James Towne were decisions that had to be promptly made. Will's orders had been to carry the miners to the Falls, but with them all dead or captive he had no choice but to sail down river and face the wrath of his Governor.

At Orapakes John Jeffery's course was as clearly set. He had to lead his twenty warriors into battle with his own countrymen. Taropoto knew how difficult this was to do and did her best to reassure him. Her people fought amid the trees where English guns could not find them, she told him. "Is that not so?" And John agreed that it was. "If they come with their swords, you must run away. They must not catch you," she added. "Never let them do that."

He was all too aware that should he be taken he could expect as unpleasant a death as his Lordship could devise. Nevertheless, running away from anything was not in his nature. Besides his bow and his red-fletched English arrows, he still had his sword and he expected to use it to whatever end the *Okeus* or his mother's God had in store for him.

"Yesterday," Taropoto told him, "I went to speak with Uttamatomakkin who is a very wise priest who can see much that we cannot. He looked into my hands and told me that you shall become a great *weroance*, and that our son shall..."

"Our son, you say?"

"Aye, *wioah*, our son. He will follow and become a great man who will do much to bring our people together in friendship."

"And what else did he say?"

"Nothing that can be true."

"But if nothing else can be true," John asked with a laugh, "how can it be that we have a son?"

"That it can," Taropoto replied quietly. "You ask what else he said. I'll tell you. He said that I shall be a friend to that *usquausum* Matoaka and that one day I may cross the great sea. A friend to that *cucheneppo*, never!"

Before John could question her further, Sparrow was at their door to tell him that his men were waiting and that he was first called to a war council being held by Nemattanew, Powhatan's most flamboyant captain. With turkey feathers glued to his body from head to foot and swan's wings attached to his shoulders, Nemattanew looked capable of flight. Although he did not number that among his many attributes, he did claim that he was impervious to English bullets. Nevertheless, for all his boasting, the man was a charismatic orator and leader able to convince his men that they, too, were invincible. This was John's first encounter with him, and after getting over the surprise of his commander's comical dress, John soon fell under his spell.

For an hour or more John sat listening as Powhatan's general gave orders to the various vassal *weroances* and lesser officers, telling which side of the Great River they were to defend and where to do so. Although John did not understand most of what was being said, Nemattanew outlined his strategy with a stick in the sandy dirt, and watching intently John realized that the Indian knew every hill and brook along the river. When his turn came to receive his instructions he was surprised to hear Nemattanew give them to him in English. He began, however, by saying "The Great King named you Asqweowan, but I shall call you Red Arrow." Then he went on to instruct John to take his men up to the Falls, there to cross the river and move down past John Smith's abandoned fort and be ready to oppose any landing by the English. But John would not be alone. Powhatan's son Parahunt was *weroance* of the country that bore his father's name and had fifty seasoned warriors already in position. More would follow from among the Chickahominy on the north bank and from the Appomattocs on the south. John left the meeting certain that the settlers were about to face their most formidable challenge.

Taropoto was waiting for him with his sword, his English bow and his arrows. She handed them to him, and while he stood with his hands full she put her arms around his neck and kissed him. "My Johnny," she whispered, *cummomais, cummomais.*"

There was to be no love in the reception that his brother would receive when he boarded the *Delaware* to report to his Governor General.

"God's death, man!" Delaware roared. "You'd have best died with them! My miners were at the very core of our endeavor. Without them we achieve nothing. I'll have you broken on the wheel for this, you miserable..."

George Percy stopped him in mid sentence. "Prudence, my Lord, I beg you. Be not hasty. This good fellow had the courage to come to you. His judgment may have been poor, but naught else."

"Judgement? Poor?" Delaware huffed. "We are undone, Master Percy, and you say..."

"I say that the miners can be replaced," Percy retorted. "But now is the time for them to be avenged, and this young sergeant may be the fellow to lead us to them."

Delaware's fire slowly subsided. "You may be right. Yea, by God, I believe you *are* right," he grudgingly allowed.

With Brewster and most of the other officers already gone up river, and with Percy and Argall to stay and defend James Towne, there was only John Martin left to command the attack – a prospect that evidently failed to excite anyone. Delaware, therefore, decided that he would direct the attack from shipboard and that Will would take as many healthy guardsmen as could be mustered to destroy the Appomattocs' village.

On the morning tide of October 31, the flagship towing two pinnaces and a jolly-boat left James Towne on the rising tide and headed toward the mouth of the Appomattocs River. Will had sought leave to go ashore to see Maggie before they left, but Delaware would have none of it. Whether he feared that his sergeant might desert rather than massacre the savages was never known. In reality, Will was enraged by having been duped, and nothing trumped his desire to get even. He told himself that he'd see a dozen savages burning in hell before they would atone for the death of his friend Pips.

Leaning on the taff-rail Will watched for any innocently fishing Indian who might give warning of the *Delaware's* approach. But no canoes were to be seen, nor were there any savages along the shore. At Will's suggestion, the much more amiable Delaware ordered anchors dropped before rounding the point about two nautical miles below the estuary. Using one of the pinnaces Will took two corporals and twenty-six guardsmen ashore, an operation impossible to perform in total silence. He was surprised, therefore, that he was able to cover the distance through the woods without any evidence of having been spotted, But knowing the savages' reputation for stealth and surprise, he advanced with matchlocks primed. He had loaded his own with both ball and swan shot in the belief that he could do more painful damage with it than with the single ball, and he had ordered eight others to do the same. Only four of his men wore armor and were armed with pikes, their role being to hold off the enemy while the rest were reloading. Will had learned from his experiences at Kecoughtan and Paspahegh that men in armor might escape arrows but they were useless in chasing down the fleet-footed savages.

The smell of smoke was the first indication that the village was only a short distance away, but having previously approached it only from the river Will had no idea what to expect. He, therefore, sent Corporal Mark Fletcher ahead to scout for any obstructions that might hinder a direct assault. But Fletcher returned saying that he could see none. There were people in the village. He thought them to be mostly women. There was also a temple, he said, lying back from the houses, but there seemed to be no one there.

Will promptly detailed four men to fire the temple while the rest would invade the village shouting at the top of their lungs to make it appear that there were many more of them than there were. He expected to be received by volleys of arrows, but none were fired, all the young men having been ordered away by the queen's brother, Coquonasum, to augment the Algonquin army assembling near the Falls. Consequently, Will's shouting invasion served only to send frightened women and children running in all directions. He was the first to reach Opossunoquonuske's house and was appalled to see nine fresh scalps hanging from a pole outside it. As he burst through the doorway, he saw her leaving through the back and raised his musket to fire. But he knew that she would be out of his sights by the time the match lit the primer, and so he lowered the gun and ran after her.

 Being used to be carried from village to village on a litter, Opossunoquonuske was no runner. At any other time the sight of her naked, elephantine posterior lumbering into the forest would have been laughable. But run she did as best she could, still clutching her copper crown. Will raised his musket again, and fired. At a range of thirty yards the swan shot lacerated her back, but it was the ball that killed her. Without a sound she fell forward onto her face, her crown rolling away into the underbrush. The sound of gunfire and the screaming of the terrified savages behind him, prevented Will from savoring his moment of revenge, and he ran back into the village without waiting to reload. Within maybe three or four minutes the shouting and screaming stopped to be replaced by the crackle and rush of flaming buildings, and that, too, was over in a very few minutes. Piles of smoking ashes and still-burning posts were all that remained of Opossunoquonuske's village. The only thing left standing was the pole at her door with its scalps singed and smoldering. Will ordered them cut down and thrown into the embers. Victory was complete.

With the excitement over, Will found his men standing or wandering sheepishly around at a loss to know what to do next. A few were stripping bead and shell necklaces from the dead, and one ripped the deerskin cloth from around the waist of a young woman and waved it in the air. But for the most part the guardsmen were sobered by what they saw and embarrassed by what they had done. Will had expected his anger to have turned to gleeful satisfaction. Instead, he felt numb. The smell of burning flesh from those who had died in their homes sickened him, and the faces of the dead women and children were a reproach he feared he would never forget.

"Corporal Fletcher, signal to the boats to come up," he ordered. "We be done here."

Chapter Nineteen

John Jeffery's twenty warriors reached the raceway of the Falls shortly after dawn on the same day that his brother destroyed the Appomattocs village. The passage over and between the water-worn rocks was easily accomplished. It was a hopping, jumping bridge that had served the tribes of both sides for thousands of years, but was still dangerously slippery when the river above it was wind blown. John's removal of his English boots after the first slip, was cause for much merriment. "Red Arrow still has much to learn," said Sparrow. And John was all too aware that he was right.

Numerous files of Indians had already crossed, and John estimated that they might number three or even four hundred, all fiercely painted, their faces appearing grim even when they laughed. He was surprised to find everyone as relaxed and eager as they would be if they were preparing for nothing more dangerous than a deer hunt. Not until a Powhatan village priest arrived to harangue them did they revert to the stomping fervor that John had seen during the war preparations at Orapakes. The chanting grew louder and louder as the warriors kept cadence by pounding their leather shields with their ball-ended clubs, and before long John, too, was swept up in the ecstacy of excitement. Then the pounding stopped as suddenly as it had started. The arrival of the feather-bedecked Nemattanew brought instant silence.

John and his men were assembled too far away to hear what the general the English called "Jack of the Feather" was saying to his assembled troops, and he would not have understood had he been closer. But it was evident from the occasional whoops and shouts that Jack's words were being rapturously received. At the end Nemattanew waved his swan-winged arms toward the rising sun, and one by one the columns moved east onto the forest trails.

Lord Delaware's boats had reassembled around their mother ship at the mouth of the Appomattocs River taking advantage of the fact that it was here that the James River changed from brackish to fresh water. The barrels of potable water in such short supply at James Towne were now full and ready for use when the new settlement would be set up at the Falls. Will's report of his destruction of the Appomattocs village and the execution of its queen had caused his Lordship to clap his hands in satisfaction and to tell him that he was a most excellent fellow and should be rewarded. But he neglected to say how.

Once past the Appomatocs estuary, the river rapidly narrowed, becoming dangerously shallow in places and beset with sweeping S-bends that kept the helmsmen of sailing ships continuously challenged. Captains Brewster and Yeardley had wisely elected to heave to until their governor caught up with them, which he did about five miles further up stream. The advice he received from his captains was not to his liking.

"If your Lordship is to lead this campaign," Yeardley told him, "we'd best leave the *Delaware* here and continue in the smaller and more maneuverable boats."

"Our proposal, sir, is this," Brewster explained. "We take turns in sending men ashore to march parallel to our passage. When they tire we take them back aboard and replace them with others. In this way the soldiers will be able to stretch their legs and have something to do other than gripe."

"Soldiers, Captain, are soldiers. We have no need to coddle them They'll do as they're ordered," Delaware snapped.

"True, m' Lord, but only to a point," Brewster replied. "We must remember that most of these men aren't regulars. We scraped them out of the gutters of London."

"Cannon fodder, my Lord," Yeardley agreed.

That brought a wry laugh from Delaware. "We must count ourselves fortunate that the savages have no cannon," he said. He added that his officers' proposal made sense, and although it meant leaving his comfortable quarters, he would join them in the boats. Dr. Bohun later advised against it, saying that his patient's health would be jeopardized. But Delaware insisted that as Governor General it was his duty to lead his army.

For two days the boats made their way up the ever narrowing river, off-loading and reloading troops as they went. The land progress accelerated after the first cautious sorties met with no resistence, indeed, without so much as sighting a savage. But on the morning of the third day as Lieutenant Earely's lead column was making noisy and ill-disciplined progress along an old Indian trail, it ran into an ambush that left one man dead and five wounded. Muskets were fired in all directions wasting powder and shot blowing leaves off trees, but to no avail. The enemy was gone as quickly and silently as he struck.

Thereafter, Brewster's sobered and nervous troops continued their advance with a deal more caution. Scouts trudging through the underbrush guarded their flanks, and two reluctant volunteers went ahead by a hundred yards to test the way and draw the Indians' fire. Meanwhile Lord Delaware sat in the stern of the *Virginia* pinnace scanning the shoreline with his telescope. He could see nothing, the river-flanking trails lying about a hundred yards into the woods.

"'Tis a damnable thing, not knowing what's afoot," he concluded. "Tomorrow, we'll cease this skulking. The troops will march like soldiers, drums beating and colors flying. Then we'll know where our men are and it'll scare the savages to death." Both Brewster and Yeardley questioned the wisdom of this order, and argued that the enemy was not that easily intimidated, but Delaware was adamant. "If necessary, I'll lead them meself!"

As was customary in European military campaigning, at the end of each day, the soldiery was ordered to dig a ditch and throw up an earthwork around their camp and to top it with brushwood. The shovels and axes were hauled in a cart behind the column to be handed out to the tired and complaining soldiers. The distribution was in progress on the evening of the fourth day when the soldier issuing the tools was hit by a lone arrow that pierced his heart. It hit with such force that the steel-pointed shaft projected from his back and only its' red feathers were left sprouting from his chest.

How the man died was of no concern, but the fact that he had been felled at the rear of the column was cause for general alarm. How could the scouts have failed to see that there were savages close enough to shoot? That was the question. Not until a member of the burial detail noticed that the arrow was European and mentioned it to his corporal that the word reached Brewster. His first thought was that a Spanish force had landed to ally with the savages in ousting the English, but he soon settled for a less worrisome explanation. The savages were equipped with arrows sold to Powhatan by Captain Newport or stolen by defecters from the fort.

On the Friday morning the Governor General decided go ashore to make his presence felt. Along with him went the core of his guards with Will Jefferys' back in favor and in command. From the safety of the forest's edge his brother watched the boats glide in, his bow gripped and his arrow nocked. As the *Virginia* pinnace drove into the shallows a gust of wind caused it to veer and send it broadside toward the shore. For an instant Delaware was in his aim. But John hesitated too long, and the boat again swung bow in. Simultaneously Brewster's large barge hit the muddy beach and began decanting its troops who were greeted with a shower of arrows that fell as thick as teeth on a louse comb. Soldier Twofin Chisman cursed his Lordship, his captain, his God, and his luck, as he stumbled up the beach dropping his musket rest on the way. As he stooped to retrieve it an arrow passed over his head and hit the man behind him in the throat. Brewster's shouted commands were ignored as his musketeers fell over each other in their haste to get clear of the open shore. Several more were wounded before the Indians withdrew deeper into the woods leaving the hull of the *Virginia* bristling with spent arrows. Muskets and rests littered the shore where their owners had dropped them as they ran for cover. Now they came sheepishly back to collect them and to clean the sandy mud out of their guns' muzzles and pans. Delaware watched in disgust, realizing, perhaps for the first time, just how little use heavy and inaccurate firearms were against the elusive savages. He remembered, too, that he had only recently read Sir John Smythe's *Certain Discourses* making that very point. A victory over the Irish Earls or the Spaniards in the Netherlands depended on who could stay on the field and withstand the attrition the longest, but here there was no field nor any sword-wielding enemy to fight. The Governor for Life began to have disquieting reservations about his ability to use force to bring the savages to their knees. Slow starvation might yet be the only answer.

Lumbering through the woods three soldiers led by Twofin Chisman found themselves in a clearing and in the midst of it a single long-house which, from the carved monsters at its entrance, appeared to be another temple or perhaps the home of a medicine man. Inside, wolf and bear skins hung from the walls and rafters. Rows of pointed-ended earthenware jars stood upright in the sandy ground, some containing corn but others dried animal entrails and a dark brown substance that looked like molasses. Much more inviting were the contents of an English iron cauldron that hung on a tripod over the embers of a fire. Resting in the soup-like brew was an equally inviting gourd ladle.

"Will ye look at that!" Twofin laughed. "Dinner! He must've knowd we was comin'. Who wants first swig? How about you, Snotsy?" he asked the nearest of his companions.

"Hey, you in there! Come you out!" The reedy voice was Captain Douthitt's.

"I'd best see what the stupid bugger wants," Twofin grunted as he handed the ladle to his friend.

"You, Chisman, what do you think thou't doing?" Douthitt demanded. "Nobody goes in anywhere without my order. Get back where you belong!"

Twofin shrugged and ambled away into the woods. He had no idea where Doughitt thought he belonged, but as sure as buggery he wasn't going to stay to find out. His captain was still standing in the clearing shouting orders when the first of Twofin's friends emerged. One minute he was laughing and wiping his beard with his sleeve the next he was clutching first at his stomach, then at his throat before collapsing writhing on the ground. Moments later his two companions left the house and tripped over him as they, too, fell to the ground.

"Get up, you men!" Douthitt shouted. "This is no time to play the fool!" It took him slightly longer to realize that they were dead.

With Lord Delaware's troops having abandoned their marching in file in favor of advancing on a front about a quarter of a mile wide, the Indians fell back, sometimes making whooping noises or shouting *wingapo, chamah!*, and other words of welcome to keep the English on edge. John Jefferys and his warriors regrouped on the north bank of a stream that snaked its way through the pine tree forest. Though only six feet wide and scarcely a foot deep, it was flanked by several yards of marshland. John knew that Delaware's men would be forced to tread warily, and being unable to aim their heavy muskets as they crossed, they would be easy targets. He was right.

Half a dozen of the Finsbury soldiers and three guardsmen reached the stream simultaneously. For a moment they hesitated, but hearing no sound but the gurgle of the stream and the chattering of a squirrel overhead, they left their cover and stepped gingerly down into the mud. The flight of the arrows scarcely broke the silence as they hit their marks, dropping four of the soldiers face down amid the marsh grass. John focused on the three guardsmen, but had to step out into the open to be sure of his shots. He hit one of the three before the man could raise his gun, but a second fired and missed by a yard before John's arrow felled him. Only the third guardsman remained. As he turned to reach into his quiver for another arrow a familiar voice called "How now, brother?"

Once again the Jefferys brothers faced each other across a stream, a rivulet separating the old culture from the new – the past from the future – John with his ancient longbow and Will with his firearm.

"Brother," shouted Will, "I scarce knew you, but your britches and your fair hair make you neither one thing nor t'other. Who's to fire first?"

John lowered his bow. "Not I," he said. "Shoot if you must, but I'll not run from you."

"'Tis my duty, brother."

"Then do it."

The sound of the shot sent birds fluttering up from the trees, and as the smoke from it drifted slowly away John Jefferys dropped his bow and slumped to the ground.

"Got 'im, sarg!" came a shout from Will's left. Twofin Chisman was already reloading.

Dropping his unfired musket, Will waded through the mud to reach his stricken brother. The ball had smashed his chest and pierced his lung, and the blood welling from the wound spoke for itself. "So brother, you did your duty," John muttered. "I'll not blame you."

"But 'twas not..." Will began.

John cut him short. "I beg thee, go to my wife. Tell her that I did love her beyond living. Do that for me."

"That I will. Somehow, some day."

John's voice was barely above a choking whisper. "Go home, brother. This is no place for you. Go ye home to our dam. Go home to England ."

But Will never did.

Epilogue

❦❧

A s Lord Delaware had feared, he was unable to sustain his advance to the Falls. He abandoned the fort in February, 1611, and after his nephew, William West, was killed there, the Governor-General for Life, accompanied by Dr. Bohun and Captain Brewster, retired to England to recover his health. He would die on his way back to Virginia in 1616. Sir George Somers never returned from Bermuda and died there on November 9, 1610. His heart was buried on the island and his body taken to England for burial at Whitchurch in Dorset. Somers' whereabouts after he parted from Captain Argall on July 26 until his arrival at Bermuda three months later is one of history's enduring mysteries. Sir Thomas Gates went again to Virginia as governor, remaining for three years before returning to England. He died in the Netherlands in 1621. George Percy was appointed interim governor after Delaware's departure, but left Virginia in April, 1612. Thirteen years later, he lost a finger fighting Spaniards in the Low Countries, and died unmarried in 1632. Captain Christopher Newport fell out with the Virginia Company, became an admiral for the English East India Company and died on the island of Java in 1617. George Yeardley was knighted and appointed Governor of Virginia in 1618. He died there in 1627 and was buried in the church at James Towne. The never popular John Martin remained in the colony and established the plantation on the James River now known as Martin's Brandon. Captain Samuel Argall returned to England with Lord Delaware. He was knighted in 1622, and commanded the English flagship in an attack on Cadiz in 1625 and died shortly thereafter. William Strachey returned to London in 1611 where he wrote valuable reports on conditions in Virginia, but failed to win the acclaim he so ardently sought. He died in poverty on June 21, 1621. Lieutenant Puttock, commander of the block-house, was killed by Paspahegh Indians in February, 1611. Thomas Dowse, the reluctant hero, married, was living in Elizabeth City in 1623, and was granted 400 acres in Charles City in 1626. Henry Spelman also remained in the colony, rising to the level of Captain, only to be killed by the Anacostan Indians in March, 1623. Thomas Savage settled on the Eastern Shore of Virginia, married, and was alive a year later.

Of the Indians, Powhatan died of old age in 1618. Opitchapam succeeded him but was dead by 1622. His brother, Opechancanough, would launch only partially successful attacks on the settlements in 1622, and again in 1644 when he was captured and murdered while confined in a cage at James Towne. Wowinchapunck, *weorance* of the Paspahegh, was killed in an attack on the blockhouse on Febru-ary 9, 1611. In the same year Kemps died of scurvy in his home at James Towne. Nemattanew, alias 'Jack of the Feather,' also known as Munetute, who claimed to be impervious to bullets, died from a pistol shot after being captured in 1622. Machumps continued as a go-between for Powhatan and was welcomed at the governor's table at James Towne in 1612. Like so many others among the players, both Indian and colonist, his subsequent history is unknown.

And what of Will and Maggie Jefferys? Being figures of fiction, your guess is as good as any.